THE LAND REMEMBERS

THE LAND REMEMBERS

*The Story of a Farm
and Its People*

BEN LOGAN

The University of Wisconsin Press

The University of Wisconsin Press
1930 Monroe Street, 3rd Floor
Madison, Wisconsin 53711-2059
uwpress.wisc.edu

3 Henrietta Street, Covent Garden
London WC2E 8LU, United Kingdom
eurospanbookstore.com

The Land Remembers was first published in a hardcover edition by Viking Press, Inc., and a
large print edition by Hall in 1975; in a mass market paperback edition by Avon Books in
1976; in 1985 by Stanton & Lee; in 1986 by NorthWord Press; in 1992 a collector's edition by
NorthWord Press; in 2000 a 25th anniversary edition by NorthWord Press, an imprint of
Creative Publishing International; and in 2006, with a new afterword, by Itchy Cat Press, an
imprint of Flying Fish Graphics.

Printed in the United States of America

This book may be available in a digital edition.

Library of Congress Cataloging-in-Publication Data

Names: Logan, Ben, 1920– author. | Meine, Curt, writer of introduction.
Title: The land remembers: the story of a farm and its people / Ben Logan.
Description: Madison, Wisconsin: The University of Wisconsin Press, [2017]
| Introduction by Curt Meine. | "Copyright ©1975 by Ben T. Logan;
afterword ©2006 by Ben T. Logan; introduction ©2017 by
the Board of Regents of the University of Wisconsin System"—Title page verso.
| "The Land Remembers was first published in a hardcover edition by Viking Press, Inc.,
and a large print edition by Hall in 1975; in a mass market paperback edition by Avon Books
in 1976; in 1985 by Stanton & Lee; in 1986 by NorthWord Press; in 1992 a collector's edition
by NorthWord Press; in 2000 a 25th anniversary edition by NorthWord Press, an imprint
of Creative Publishing International; and in 2006, with a new afterword, by Itchy Cat Press,
an imprint of Flying Fish Graphics."—Title page verso.
Identifiers: LCCN 2016058732 | ISBN 9780299309046 (pbk.: alk. paper)
Subjects: LCSH: Logan, Ben, 1920– —Childhood and youth.
| Authors, American—20th century—Biography.
| Farm life—Wisconsin. | Wisconsin—Social life and customs.
Classification: LCC PS3562.O444 Z469 2017 | DDC 9775/7 [B]—dc23
LC record available at https://lccn.loc.gov/2016058732

Laurance, Lee, and Lyle, the only ones left who shared that hilltop world with me, told me when we met that I didn't get all my facts straight. We argued some about that, but mostly I just reminded them of what a neighbor used to say—"When you're trying to tell somebody who ain't been there just how hot it is in a hayfield with the temperature at a hundred degrees in the shade, it's not lying if you make it a hundred and ten."

Now only my brother Lee and I are left.

Contents

Contents

"He Walked Through Open Doors"

An Introduction to *The Land Remembers*

CURT MEINE

A friend asked Ben Logan, then eighty-nine years old, what he considered the most important quality in his outlook on life. "Having curiosity," he responded. "I still have a tremendous curiosity about things. I still have an irresistible urge to push open the door of an old deserted farmhouse to see if those who once lived there left fragments of their life story. We need to stay tuned into things, keep our minds open." His friend then asked him what he wanted his epitaph to be. Ben answered: "He walked through open doors!"[1]

Which brings to mind the opening lines of the rambunctious chapter "A Day of Our Own" in *The Land Remembers*:

> In spite of long days in the fields, something in the summer brought the four of us boys together. A day when we did not have to work was very special. It was ours. We were free. We could vanish into the child-hiding green of hundreds of acres of countryside and make a world out of a single day. (150)[2]

In a book rich with details of the daily responsibilities on an early twentieth-century midwestern farm, the passage provides an uncharacteristic departure. And it hints at the reason behind the book's broad and enduring appeal. Logan walked through open doors in both directions: inward to gather the fragments of his own life story and outward to connect his story to the life of the land that held and nurtured it. At that threshold of his inner and outer lives, Ben Logan made a world.

It is a world that hundreds of thousands of readers have come to know and feel that they too somehow belong to. First published in 1975, *The Land Remembers* appears here in its ninth edition. It remains one of the most popular books ever to come out of Wisconsin. Readers from far beyond Wisconsin discovered the book and found in it something of their own story. Later, after Ben returned to Seldom Seen Farm, "pilgrims" (as he called them) began to show up at his door. Logan understood that they were looking for something in the world that he recollected. "Perhaps more than anything else their quest is for solid values and a sense of community" (292). *The Land Remembers* brings its readers to the thresholds of family and place, innocence and experience, memory and longing.

⚜

Part of the broad and lasting appeal of *The Land Remembers* lies in its seeming timelessness and placelessness. Its stories deal with universals: childhood, parents, siblings, neighbors, seasons, weather, farming, foods, plants and animals, education, holidays, quiet mysteries, and, of course, the land. Such shared themes have allowed the book to reach, as Logan would cheerfully note, not only childhood acquaintances and fellow midwesterners but anonymous New York City subway riders and sophisticated urban book reviewers—all of whom felt he was somehow describing their own experience. (Now, he could also include Amazon.com commentators. "This book is so-o-o good it made me feel as if I had lived on that farm and in that family. Ben's words transcend farm life. Even city-folks can relate.")

Yet *The Land Remembers* is profoundly the story of a specific time and place: the western edge of Wisconsin's Kickapoo River valley, in the unglaciated Driftless Area, in the mid-1920s to mid-1930s. Ben Logan was born in the rural Town of Seneca in Crawford County, Wisconsin, on September 9, 1920. His book collapses into a single round of seasons an array of memories from his early boyhood years up until the age of sixteen. Occasionally his generalized narrative yields to explicit dates: the advent of tractors in the neighborhood around 1929; the "never-ending cloud" of dust storms from the Great Plains that occurred with increasing frequency after 1931; the adoption of soil conservation practices in the mid-1930s.

These dates allow us to appreciate the particular circumstances of Logan's early life. The farmscape of his boyhood was in fact undergoing rapid social and environmental change. Readers encounter, as he did, the emerging forces of rural economic development—the advent of telephones and "filling stations," new lamps and hybrid corn—and then the wrenching reality of economic depression. The mechanization that the Logans' old neighbor Abe found so unsettling ("Seems to me a tractor gets a man up in the air too high") was transforming midwestern farming. With its several scenes of mingled draft animals and internal combustion engines, *The Land Remembers* sits along the ridgeline divide between rural America's agrarian history and its increasingly industrialized future.

It sits, too, within a landscape that was highly vulnerable to, and in many places devastated by, extensive soil erosion. Seldom Seen Farm lay at the heart of the Upper Mississippi River's unglaciated Driftless Area. In the years of Logan's childhood, the region was in the throes of a crisis. The watersheds of the "hill country" were deteriorating, their erodible soils sloughing away after decades of ill-suited farming practices. In an exchange between his mother and father at the end of his "Drouth" chapter, Logan distills the conservation lessons learned:

> "I guess we can't be expected to know everything in advance," Mother said gently.

"That's right. But we can damn well go slow when we start changing things. We can admit that we're playing around with something that's a lot bigger than we are." (113)

"An age of innocence had ended," Logan concludes.

In a book that is sweet with innocence, there are more than a few such sober endings. The most abrupt, and the date that grounds the book heartrendingly in its time, jolts the reader at the opening of the final chapter: "Mother died the winter I was sixteen. There was no warning" (300). Cecil Estelle Logan (she was called Stella) died on February 10, 1937. And that is the point at which the story *in* the book begins to blend into the story of Logan's life *and* the book.

Ben Logan left us fragments of his life story. In other writings, in interviews and public talks, and in afterwords included in later editions of *The Land Remembers* (including this one), Logan gradually revealed more of the biographical context of his writing. Collecting and connecting these fragments, we see how his life and his book grew together.

The tight family "circle of life" that Logan described in *The Land Remembers* unraveled soon after the point at which his book ends. After his mother died, Ben remained on the farm until the following year, when he enrolled at the Wisconsin State College in Platteville (now the University of Wisconsin–Platteville). After two years at Platteville he transferred to the University of Wisconsin campus in Madison in 1940. Ben's brother Sam died in 1941 at twenty-five, a consequence of his earlier battle with scarlet fever. As World War II came on, his brothers Lee and Laurance joined the U.S. Navy—inspired perhaps by their father's Norwegian seafaring youth?

Logan spent two years at the university in Madison. Throughout his educational career Logan had grown through his interactions with key teachers: a Platteville geologist who encouraged Ben's interest in natural history; an English professor, Rachel Salisbury, who "dared me to be emotional in my writing, to put more substance in my stories"; Helen C. White, the prominent literary scholar and doyenne of the English Department in Madison; William Sumner of the UW Department of Agricultural Journalism, who pushed Ben to take courses that would broaden his thinking. "The trouble is," Sumner complained, "most journalism students write pretty well, but they don't have a damn thing to write about!"[3]

It may have been through Sumner's influence that Logan enrolled, in the spring of 1941, in Aldo Leopold's undergraduate class in wildlife management.[4] Not yet widely known as an iconic figure in environmental thought, Leopold had been teaching at the university since 1933. Though the class focused on wildlife, Leopold's aim was broader: to develop in his students the capacity to "read the landscape"—to appreciate the dynamic and interwoven stories of human and natural history available in any and all places. That fall Logan also took Leopold's course in wildlife management techniques.

For Logan, as for so many other students, Leopold's understanding of land, ecology, and history came as a revelation. Logan later wrote, "[H]umans are not separated from all the other living parts and places and mysteries of what Aldo Leopold called THE LAND—all things on, over, and in the earth. When I first heard him say that in a University of Wisconsin classroom, it was a moment of great discovery. His definition of land included me, made a place for me in the immense mosaic of life" (275).

Less clearly, Leopold may also have influenced the aim and tone of young Logan's writing. Leopold was by now accustomed to teaching the sons and daughters of Wisconsin's farms. He had become adept at walking a fine line, encouraging his students to see land critically, through the eyes of an ecologist, but also to appreciate how our "land relations" (as he sometimes termed it) reflect deep and sometimes problematic cultural forces. Leopold had just recently begun to compose the essays that would eventually be published as *A Sand County Almanac*. He was himself striving to negotiate the tension between science and literature.

Logan recalled later in life that Leopold "bristled against [Logan's] emotional attachment to the land." Leopold understood the power of these attachments, and his student might have influenced Leopold's own tone in the *Almanac* essays. In their stories of the land, both the professor and the aspiring writer would, in their different ways, acknowledge such emotional bonds while being wary of sentimentality. In their writing both would give voice to an abiding land ethic—Leopold overtly, Logan implicitly.

Logan graduated from the University of Wisconsin with a degree in agricultural journalism in the spring of 1942. His aim was to complete his degree before joining the war effort, so that he would qualify to become an officer. Ben followed his brothers by enlisting in the Navy and received officer training through the end of 1942 at the U.S. Naval Reserve Midshipmen School on the campus of Northwestern University. In Evanston he spent his first Christmas away from Seldom Seen Farm. "I went for a walk on Christmas Eve and it was snowing. When it snows . . . soft . . . no wind, it softens everything, even the sound is softened. It's as if it put innocence back into the city."[5]

Logan deployed to the Mediterranean in 1943. He recalled, "I was the officer on a LCT, a Landing Craft Tank, or Little Crappy Tub as some people called it. It was 110 feet long and had a crew of 15–20 men. We'd go into the beach loaded with men or equipment. We'd stay at the beachhead ferrying men and equipment from ship to shore for weeks at a time. We'd work 24 hours a day. We lived on the LCT and even slept on it."[6] He entered combat for the first time when the Allied invasion of Sicily began on July 9, 1943. His LCT was among two thousand craft joining in the chaotic but ultimately successful assault. The operation ended on August 17.

The naval forces then moved to mainland Italy at Salerno in early September, and then on toward Naples. At that point Logan contracted infectious hepatitis, the result of a compromised batch of yellow fever inoculations. In the early editions of *The Land Remembers* Logan does not mention the episode. He first did so in a later (2006) expanded afterword.

> I had left my landing craft in a half-destroyed port south of Naples and gone to a U.S. Army clinic. There I was told I had jaundice, which explained my yellowing eyes and terrible feeling of melancholy, and was sent to the hospital. Two fellow officers took my place on my LCT and that same evening the LCT hit a floating mine. Everyone aboard, seventeen enlisted men and two officers, was killed.
>
> It was more than the death of nineteen men. It was the death of all innocence about war. (294)

Logan heard the explosion from his hospital bed.[7] Overcome by grief and guilt, he struggled to make sense of the senseless. He was twenty-three years old. In the days that followed, as Logan recovered, he made a personal commitment. "[T]he feeling of guilt changed to a feeling of obligation. I had a debt I must pay to those men by how I live my life. Life became a precious gift that had been given to me. I must live both for myself and for those who died." Yet only with time would he come to see his war experience as the spur to his writing career. For the rest of his life he would feel, he said, a "need to represent people, give them a voice" (294).

After the war Logan was wracked by anxiety and restlessness. Over the next two years he served on merchant ships in Europe and South America and lived for a time in Mexico, returning only for brief visits to Wisconsin. Seldom Seen Farm was too calm, the trauma of the war too near. Ben recalled one visit home during which he remarked to his father that

I had no idea what I was looking for. He smiled and said, "Of course you do. You're looking for yourself." And suddenly I had a sense that my mother was there in the room, even though she was dead, and that she was smiling at me and I could almost hear her say, "So you were wounded after all." (294)

Logan continued moving, traveling and trying the writing life in New York City. The aspiring author who would later voice such a fervent bond to the land was rootless, disconnected, severed from any connection to place.

Logan's home state did pull him back when he returned to the University of Wisconsin to pursue a master's degree, which he completed in 1951. He then left Wisconsin again to seek his way in a wider world. To Mexico, where he studied anthropology and met his wife, Jacqueline. To try his hand at fiction, writing a never-published novel. To New York, where he and Jacqueline finally came to settle, rooting themselves north of New York City in a pre–Revolutionary War house. Logan eventually built a successful and varied career in public relations, editing and writing, and film, radio, and television production. Through the 1950s and '60s he and Jacqueline raised three children and enjoyed a life amid America's postwar prosperity.

In the early 1970s Logan was working as senior producer for United Methodist Communications, the outreach arm of the church. Although he was now far removed in space, time, and circumstance from his childhood on a Depression-era farm in western Wisconsin, it seems that the seeds of *The Land Remembers* were restive. Over the years memories kept returning him to Seldom Seen Farm. Scenes and sensations from his childhood came to him at unpredictable moments. It began after the war, when he was excavating a piece of ancient pottery in Mexico. "Then, the smell of the newly turned earth came up to me and I was not there at all. I was walking a furrow of my boyhood, watching the endless ribbon of sod turning over behind a walking plow."[8] Such "flashbacks" came to him regularly. The creaking of an old windmill's wheel evoked his father's oil can. The chuffing of a one-cylinder engine on a banana barge in Ecuador suggested the farm's deep well pump. A certain shade of blue conjured his mother in her garden, looking to the sky.

Logan described how these moments, recorded in a growing file, came to congeal into story:

> [A] little confused about when I was remembering and when I was being remembered, I began an intensely personal journey into a past that was much richer than I had realized. I found I could again be any age I had been. Recalled images triggered other layers of images. Voices, sounds, smells, textures, laughter and tears came back, vividly clear. Ever pull on a dangling end of yarn and find if you pull long enough you'll unravel a whole sweater? It was that way for me as I pulled on bits of memory in the writing of *The Land Remembers*.[9]

But why did Logan feel the urge to pull on that yarn? In *Wolf Willow* (1962), his description of life on the Saskatchewan plains, Wallace Stegner wrote of "the queer adult compulsion to return to one's beginnings." In so doing, "a contact [is] made, a mystery touched. For the moment, reality is made exactly equivalent with memory, and a hunger is satisfied."[10] In *Trace* (2015), her exploration of history, landscape, and identity, Lauret Savoy crosses the same threshold. "We may find," Savoy writes, "that home lies in *re-membering*—in piecing together the fragments left—and in reconciling what it means to inhabit terrains of memory, and to be one."[11] At midlife Logan was still wounded, still looking for himself, still reconciling. He acknowledged as much. He remarked that he found writing therapeutic. "Graham Greene once said, 'I can't possibly understand how those who don't write can deal with the anguish of life.' I think that's a good definition. It allows us to deal with things directly that are very personal."[12]

Perhaps Logan's urge to revisit his childhood had something to do as well with the times. Viking Press published *The Land Remembers* in 1975, as the cultural tremors of the Vietnam War and Watergate rattled the nation's sense of its core values. As an offshoot of the environmental movement, a countercultural back-to-the-land movement was underway. Aldo Leopold's *A Sand County Almanac* had recently been reprinted—resurrected—in paperback and found a large audience across generations. Wendell Berry had just published *A Continuous Harmony: Essays Cultural and Agricultural* (1972) and was at work on *The Unsettling of America: Culture and Agriculture* (1977). Voices of this emerging literature of a new American agrarianism were leap-frogging back to the time of Logan's boyhood to find perspective on what had been so quickly lost in American agriculture and rural life—what had changed and what might yet be reclaimed.

The Land Remembers became part of this larger conversation. Logan's story of life on Seldom Seen Farm met the narrative needs of a nation that, like Logan himself, was outwardly successful but increasingly cut off from its rural roots, experiencing flashbacks, and looking for itself. Ben Logan was remembering for others, not just himself. "I cannot leave the land," Logan writes at the end of his opening chapter. In his mind and memory, he had not left. Now, in print, he testified to the land's hold on him and its role in shaping his identity. Not so evident to its first readers was how, in the process of writing the book, he was recovering his past.

The book met with healthy sales and widespread critical acclaim. Reading the reviews now, one senses that reviewers—especially those from urban publications—were prepared to dismiss the book politely as a standard bucolic memoir but then found themselves drawn in. The reviews sounded a consistent note. *Kirkus Reviews*: "Somehow Logan manages to describe that simpler, more wholesome life, without succumbing to excesses of nostalgia and sentimentality." *The Christian Science Monitor*: "He reviews his growing up years in the 1920s and '30s less with nostalgia than with a naturalist's eye for detail, wary of the distortion of memory and sentiment." Logan's storytelling skill lifted the book above the level of comparable accounts of rural and farm life. William Sumner's goading, Helen C. White's critical editorial eye, and Aldo Leopold's caution had left their marks on Logan.

In 1985 the Madison-based publishing house Stanton & Lee brought out a new edition—the book's fourth. In an afterword, Logan expressed his satisfaction and made an announcement: "This edition brings publication of *The Land Remembers* home to Wisconsin and I will soon follow, returning to 100 acres and the tired buildings of our old farm." It may have seemed to some that, in returning to Wisconsin, Logan was attempting to recapture a past that was lost forever. "But it's all right," he wrote. "I know I can't go home again." He now recognized that in writing *The Land Remembers* he had "re-gathered" his family and himself. And with the book's publication he was able to let them go, "saying good-bye to them one by one." Later, on a return trip to the farm, he realized he had one more farewell to make. "I had to say goodbye to the earlier version of me I had recreated in the book. . . . I waved to him. I said goodbye. And I was back in the present, ready, like Thoreau in *Walden*, to go on to other lives I have still to live."[13]

Logan was not going backward. He was coming back around, through another open door. In 1986 Ben and Jacqueline purchased Seldom Seen Farm and retired there. They returned to a place much changed since Ben's youth, yet in returning they created continuity. Many of Ben's old friends and neighbors remained. They were aware of his breakthrough book and provided a welcoming local audience of readers. They had lived his story with him and nodded in appreciation of his bringing it back to life. Younger readers also found connection in it to their families' rural past. Yet other readers were newcomers to the region. The Driftless Area and the Kickapoo River valley in particular had begun to attract some of the back-to-the-land "hippie farmers" and other seekers of a simpler life (including a recent influx of Amish farmers). *The Land Remembers* resonated with them as well. At a time of accelerated cultural and political change in the rural Midwest, the book reached improbably across generations and ideologies.

Ben Logan enjoyed twenty-five more years at Seldom Seen Farm. He lost Jacqueline in 1990 but found company in a revived circle of local friends and neighbors. He devoted himself to new writing projects while enjoying the continued popularity of *The Land Remembers*. Local bookstore owners report that it still remains among their most requested titles. Wisconsin Public Radio's venerable "Chapter a Day" program has featured it more times than any other book. Several new editions of the book were published, including a twenty-fifth anniversary edition in 2000. The 2006 edition included an expanded, more personal afterword (reproduced here on 291–302) and a never-published ("too academic") account of the deeper history of Seldom Seen Farm originally meant to serve as a foreword to the book (302–11).

And then there were the pilgrims, those who felt so moved by Logan's writing that they wanted to touch the land that had touched them. If it was an imposition, he did not let on. He always welcomed them. He poignantly noted how many of them were men who came alone, and who were most interested in sharing stories from their own lives. "Here I get a message of loneliness. They don't believe anyone else in their lives would listen or would understand even if they did listen. But they are sure I will listen. I find a cultural warning in all this" (293). Logan understood. He had heard his own father's instruction to take the time to find himself. He had sensed his mother's insight. "So you were wounded after all."

Ben took his leave of Seldom Seen Farm in 2009, entering an assisted living facility in nearby Viroqua, Wisconsin. Before he did so he worked with the Mississippi Valley Conservancy, a regional land trust, to place an easement on the farm, ensuring that it would not be developed and stipulating that it remain an active farm.[14] "A farm is a process, where everything is related, everything happening at once"

(6). Logan's commitment to conservation—gained through his mother and father, through Leopold and others—embraced the notion not only of protecting places but of sustaining the relationships that enliven them.

Ben Logan died on September 19, 2014, ten days after he turned 94.

For those of us who live in the driftless "hill country" that Logan depicts, it is easy to appreciate *The Land Remembers*. We smile to ourselves when he lightheartedly points out the difference between ridge and valley people; when he describes how the weather works over the bluffs and how morning fogs "lay heavy and white" in the valleys; when his father takes him by the hand "to the edge of the oats and pointed across the rolling field, turning bright, deep yellow in the strong July sun." We know these scenes. We recognize the attitudes and the characters, even a generation or two removed.

We also understand how the region yields paradoxical feelings of confinement and comfort. On the one hand, some of our neighbors (then and now) "didn't have a chance unless [they] found some way to get out of that country" (193). On the other hand, the hill country had, and has, "a feel of home about it" when compared to flatter places; its intimate contours "didn't keep leading a man on toward a horizon that was never there" (309). That tension between the urge to leave and the urge to stay (or return) is also characteristic of the Driftless Area landscape and of other authors who have written of and from it. We can see ourselves in Logan's life within, away from, and ultimately back to the land.

And what of the land itself that Logan remembered, and that remembered him?

On the one hand it faces a range of threats, old and new. The Driftless Area, because of its topography, still supports smaller diversified family farms that are increasingly disappearing as agriculture in the Midwest trends toward ever larger and more consolidated operations. Yet, even here, extensive row-crop monocultures—ever more corn and soybeans—replace pastures and strip crops. The soil and water conservation measures that Logan's generation of farmers first put into place are easily taken for granted. Meanwhile, intensive rainfall events and major floods occur with increasing frequency, in keeping with projections of climate change trends. The region's cold-water springs and streams, having suffered from the accelerated soil erosion Logan saw in his boyhood, now support thriving trout populations; if trends continue, though, they are predicted to warm along with the climate. The rural communities of the region struggle, like so many rural communities across the country, to retain their wealth and their youth. Where economic opportunities are limited, a new option now sounds its siren call. Since the boom in the hydraulic fracturing industry began, the Driftless Area has been directly affected—not by the "fracking" itself, but by the extraction, processing, and exporting of the fine sands used in the process. The sandstones underlying Logan's hill country are an especially accessible and profitable source for these industrial sands.

On the other hand the hill country continues to inspire, as it did in Logan's youth, a strong commitment to conservation, land stewardship, and community resilience. Farmers and other landowners across the region have developed new approaches to restoring and sustaining their woods and streams, soils and watersheds. Smaller-scale agriculture, although challenging, is still economically viable and socially desirable for many farming families. As the movement toward local and organic food production has grown, the region has become a vibrant landscape of innovation and responsible investment. That movement has helped retain and attract younger people—countering the recent trend of their migration toward urban centers. People are still, as Ben Logan noted, "looking for something," and some continue to search for it—and find it—in the landscape he portrayed with such care.[15]

Of course, the search for meaning in our lives and places is not confined to Logan's hill country, or to Wisconsin, or to rural settings. Every place holds memory and hope, and invites exploration and reflection. Land, whether wild or rural or suburban or urban, both supplies and tells our stories. In his last afterword Ben Logan looked back on his life and on his story of Seldom Seen Farm and its people. He peered back and forth through his open door. He saw there "a microcosm." He saw that "the land cradles all life. The land outlives us all, forever remembering us and writing an epitaph for the good and evil we do to it" (302). *The Land Remembers* is a gentle book written around this enduring core. Forged from personal loss and grief and dislocation, but realized through a determination to stay connected to one's origins in the land and his family, Ben Logan's story brought him home to himself. We find ourselves drawn in the same direction.

Notes

1. Howard Sherpe, "Remembering Wisconsin Author Ben Logan," *Jackson County* (Wisconsin) *Chronicle*, October 1, 2014, http://wdrt.org/wp-content/uploads/2014/10/Tribute-by-Howard-Sherpe_Westby-Times.pdf. I am grateful to Ben Logan's friend Howard Sherpe, whose accounts of his late conversations with Ben have been so useful in preparing this introduction.

2. *The Land Remembers* has been published in several different editions. The numbers following passages quoted in this introduction refer to the page numbers in this volume.

3. Quoted in Howard Sherpe, "Ben Logan Will Always Be Remembered," September 30, 2014, http://sherpeacrossthefence.blogspot.com/2014/09/ben-logan-will-always-be-remembered.html.

4. My thanks to David Null, director of the University of Wisconsin–Madison Archives, for tracking down these details on Logan's academic career and his interactions with Aldo Leopold.

5. Quoted in Sherpe, "Ben Logan Will Always Be Remembered."

6. Ibid.

7. Online sources indicate that a Landing Craft Tank (LCT-242) was "sunk by a circling torpedo off Naples, Italy" on December 2, 1943. See http://www.uboat.net/allies/warships/ship/19243.html.

8. Ben Logan, "Afterword," in *The Land Remembers: The Story of a Farm and Its People* (Madison: Stanton & Lee, 1985), 279.

9. Ibid., 279–80.

10. Wallace Stegner, *Wolf Willow: A History, a Story, and a Memory of the Last Plains Frontier* (Lincoln: University of Nebraska Press, 1980), 19.

11. Lauret Savoy, *Trace: A Journey Through Memory, History, and the American Land* (Berkeley, CA: Counterpoint Press, 2015), 2.

12. Quoted in Sherpe, "Ben Logan Will Always Be Remembered."

13. Logan, "Afterword," 280–81.

14. See Timothy S. Jacobson, "Editing 'Hopelessness' Into 'Hope': The Story of Ben Logan's Farm and Its Protection," http://www.visjonaer.com /blog/editing-hopelessness-into-hope-the-story-of-ben-logans-farm- and-its-protection.

15. See Curt Meine and Keefe Keeley, eds., *The Driftless Reader* (Madison: University of Wisconsin Press, 2017); Kevin Koch, *The Driftless Land: Spirit of Place in the Upper Mississippi Valley* (Cape Girardeau: Southeast Missouri State University Press, 2010); Stephen J. Lyons, *Going Driftless: Life Lessons from the Heartland for Unraveling Times* (Guilford, CT: Rowman & Littlefield, 2015); Sascha Matuszak, "The Driftless Manifesto," *Roads & Kingdoms*, September 22, 2015, http://roadsandkingdoms.com/2015/the-driftless-manifesto.

Part One

GENESIS

1 The Land Remembers

Once you have lived on the land, been a partner with its moods, secrets, and seasons, you cannot leave. The living land remembers, touching you in unguarded moments, saying, "I am here. You are part of me."

When this happens to me, I go home again, in mind or in person, back to a hilltop world in southwestern Wisconsin. This is the story of that farm and its people. That land is my genesis. I was born there, cradled by the land, and I am always there even though I have been a wanderer.

I cannot leave the land. How can I when a thousand sounds, sights, and smells tell me I am part of it? Let me hear the murmur of talk in the dusk of a summer night and I am sitting again under the big maple tree in the front yard, hearing the voices of people I have loved. Mother listens to the whippoorwills with that look the sound always brings to her face. Father has just come from the oat field across the dusty road. He sits with a half dozen stems in his hands, running his fingers along the heads of grain, asking the oats if tomorrow is the day harvest should begin.

Let me hear drying plants rattle somewhere in a cold wind and I am with the corn-shredding crew. Men are talking about the hill country. "Why, my father used to say he dropped a milk pail once. By the time it stop rolling, couple days later, it was all the way down in the valley. Fellow who lived there said he hadn't bought a new milk pail in thirty years. Didn't know where they came from, he said, they just rolled in any time he needed one."

There is laughter. A big man slaps his thigh.

"Never happens to me," says another voice. "I got me some square milk pails."

Let me feel the softness of ground carpeted with pine needles and I am lying on my back in the middle of a great grove of trees, looking up to where the swaying tops touch the blue. Around me are my three brothers, and we argue endlessly about the mystery of the pines. Where did they come from? How old are they? Could a tree that's three feet through and eighty feet tall come from a seed not much bigger than the head of a pin?

Let the smell of mint touch me. I am kneeling along a little stream, the water numbing my hands as I reach for a trout. I feel the fish arch and struggle. I let go, pulling watercress from the water instead.

Let me see a certain color and I am standing beside the threshing machine, grain cascading through my hands. The seeds we planted when snow was spitting down have multiplied a hundred times, returning in a stream of bright gold, still warm with the sunlight of the fields.

Let me hear an odd whirring. I am deep in the woods, following an elusive sound, looking in vain for a last passenger pigeon, a feathered lightning I have never seen, unwilling to believe no person will ever see one again.

Let me look from a window to see sunlight glitter on a winding stream and I am in the one-room schoolhouse in Halls Branch Valley. A young teacher has asked me to stay after school because of a question I asked. Voice full of emotion as it seldom is during the school day, she reads to me of an Indian speaking to his people. He sweeps his hands in a circle, taking in all lands, seas, creatures, and plants, all suns, stars, and moons. "We are a People, one tiny fragment in the immense mosaic of life. What are we without the corn, the rabbit, the sun, the rain, and the deer? Know this, my people: The *all* does not belong to us. We belong to the *all*."

Let me hear seasons changing in the night. It is any season and I am every age I have ever been. Streams are wakening in the spring, rain wets the dust of summer, fallen apples ferment in an orchard, snow pelts the frozen land and puts stocking caps of white on the fence posts.

I cannot leave the land.

The land remembers. It says, "I am here. You are part of me."

2 Hilltop World

There is no neat and easy way to tell the story of a farm. A farm is a process, where everything is related, everything happening at once. It is a circle of life, and there is no logical place to begin a perfect circle. This is an unsolved paradox for me. Part of the folly of our time is the idea that we can see the whole of something by looking at the pieces, one at a time.

Yet how else tell the story of a farm?

There were two hundred sixty acres of cultivated fields, woods, and pasture land sprawled out along the narrow branching ridgetop. There was the cluster of buildings, dominated by the main barn with its stanchions for dairy cows, stalls for work horses. Attached to the barn was a tall silo, which oozed the strong smell of fermented silage when it was filled and made a marvelous, echoing place to yell into when it was empty. A second barn, mostly for hay and young cattle, had a machine-shed lean-to. An eight-foot-tall wood windbreak connected the two barns. Across the barnyard, like the other side of the compound in a fort, was the great tobacco shed. It stood on poles rather than foundations and it creaked and groaned in the wind.

There were the bulging granary, with bins for oats; a slatted corncrib with white and yellow ears showing; a hog house with roof ventilators turning restlessly in the wind; a milkhouse next to the tall steel-towered windmill; and a woodshed with sticks of oak for the kitchen range and heating stoves.

There was the house. It had two wings, the walls of the old one very thick because the siding hid what it had once been—a log house.

"You can say you grew up in a log cabin, even if it doesn't show," Mother used to tell us.

In the yard around the house were lilacs, elms, box elders, junipers, white pines, and one immense soft maple tree that looked as if it had been there forever. On the east side of the yard was the orchard with its overgrown apple, cherry, and plum trees. On the west was the rich black soil of the garden.

The farmstead stood on a hilltop, like a castle, like the center of the world. A dusty road went straight into the woods to the west and wound over knolls and swales to the east until it disappeared down the big hill that led to Halls Branch Valley. Look in any direction and there were other ridges, with dots of houses and barns, and the blue shadows of other ridges still beyond them, each a full world away from the next narrow ridge. Down below, in the valley, was yet another world. The valleys had different trees and animals. Even the seasons were different—watercress stayed green all winter in the valley springs.

Below our orchard, a ravine led down to a timbered hollow which broadened and joined the crooked valley of the Kickapoo River. That ravine and hollow brought to us the whistle of the "Stump Dodgers," the steam locomotives of the Kickapoo Valley and Northern Railroad, so loud on foggy nights the engine seemed to be coming right through the house. That whistle was joined sometimes, when the wind was in the west and the air just right, by the sound of trains along the Mississippi, nine miles to the west.

The nearest neighbors were a half mile away and seemed farther because the buildings were half hidden by a hill and because each farm was its own busy place.

In our own hilltop world there were Father, Mother, and four boys: Laurance, the oldest; then Sam (Junior); then Lee, and me, the youngest. There were two years between each of us. We were as alike as peas in a pod, as different from one another as the four seasons.

There was someone else to make seven of us. Lyle Jackson came as a hired man the year I was born. He stayed on and became such a part of us that even the neighbors sometimes called him the oldest Logan boy.

If the farm had a name before Lyle came, it was soon lost. Lyle, who had grown up near the village of Gays Mills, was used to more people. He took one look out along that isolated ridge, shook his head, and said, "Hell and tooter. We better call it Seldom Seen."

From then on Seldom Seen was the only name ever used for that farm. The seven of us, and the land with all its living things, were like a hive of bees. No matter how fiercely independent any one of us might be, we were each a dependent part of the whole, and we knew that.

Father was the organizer of our partnership with the land. Because he had come from out beyond the hill country, I was always searching for his past, but I could not easily ask him questions, nor could he easily answer. It was as though his earlier years did not belong to us. That part of his life had happened in a foreign language and did not translate into a new place and time.

He came from the Old Country, as he put it. That meant southern Norway and the community of Loga, which was once a little kingdom. "You are descendants of royalty," our Uncle Lou used to tell us.

Born fourth of eight sons and daughters, Father was named Sigvald Hanson Loga. The year was 1880. I know his world included the rising and falling of the tides, storms along a rocky coast, midnight sun and winter snow. I know he fished in open dories, offshore and up into the canyonlike fjords. And always at Christmas there was a sheaf of grain for the birds. What kind of birds in his childhood land? What color? Which ones stayed all winter? I never knew. I didn't ask.

There is a picture in my mind of Father, in the incredibly long summer evenings, running along dark paths close to the cold North Sea. He ran sometimes toward an old mill to surprise whoever, or whatever, made a light shine from the window of that long-deserted place. He would get to the mill and find nothing, no light, no sound except for the rushing water that was no longer harnessed to work for man.

"Yet," Father would say, "my brothers watching me from home said the light never left the window."

"But I was there," he would tell them.

"So was somebody else," they would say.

They pursued that light summer after summer, one running, the others watching, but the end was always the same.

"Maybe it was the reflection of the moon or the Northern Lights," I once suggested.

Father nodded and smiled. "We thought of that. There was no glass in the window."

It was one of the few stories he told me of his boyhood. I loved the mystery of it, though another mystery was even greater—the idea that my father had once been as young as I.

Father ran away from home and went to sea when he was fifteen, on an old schooner sailing with timbers for the coal mines of England. "Windjammers," he called the ships, with a mixture of ridicule and pride. For three years he lived with the windjammers. Then there was a voyage when a great storm took his ship. For eleven days it was carried far out into the open Atlantic. Finally the storm ended. Half starved, the crew rerigged enough sail to get the battered schooner headed back toward Norway. Almost every crewman was from that one little community. They came home to families who thought they were dead.

Father was eighteen then.

Here glimpses of his mother appear, the grandmother I never knew, though she lived to be ninety: a stern-faced woman in a metal picture with mountains in the background, a brass candlestick, a tin box for matches, a letter in a foreign language each Christmas, and a silver spoon inscribed with the words *Sigvald, fra Mudder.*

She gathered her sons after that stormy voyage and told them, "I would rather never see you again than to have you lost, one by one, to the sea."

She brought out the box. To each son went passage money to the New World. To the village silversmith she took a pair of old candlesticks. He melted them down and made for each son a silver serving spoon.

Father and three brothers landed in New York in 1898. At Ellis Island an immigration official suggested they add an "n" to the name Loga to make it "more American." They didn't know if they had a choice or not, so they left Ellis Island with the name Logan.

Father also left that island with "not a word of English, ten dollars in my pocket, and the whole country before me." The ten dollars took him to south-central Wisconsin, where his first job was grubbing stumps from newly cleared land. His pay—fifty cents a day. "Young Norwegians were cheaper than blasting powder in those days," he told us.

Father had worked as a hired man on many different farms. He and Lyle talked about their experiences sometimes on summer evenings under the big maple tree. It was endless, adult talk. I could run a mile into the dark woods and come back to find the talk still going on.

They had seen what happens on farms given mostly to tobacco, with the other fields going to ruin. They learned about different combinations of beef, dairy cattle, and hogs. They had worked for men who loved the land, treating it with respect, working with it. Other farmers seemed to hate the land, taking a living from it, giving nothing back.

They found people were different on ridge and valley farms. Some were happier down below where the days were shorter, the wind gentle, storms hidden by steep hillsides. Others were happier on the hilltop, where you could prove yourself by standing against the summer storms and winter blizzards, enduring the stony fields and loneliness, with other ridges beyond yours, like great rollers on the sea.

When he was ready to buy land, Father chose the ridge.

People who came to visit us on our hilltop talked as if they were on an expedition to the end of the world. A cousin of Mother's always drove miles out of the way to avoid the steep hill coming up from

Halls Branch Valley. Outsiders just weren't used to the ups and downs of southwestern Wisconsin. It was a small area, missed by the glaciers that had flattened out the country all around it.

Lyle nodded when he first heard about the glaciers. "That figures. Even the ice had sense enough to stay out of these hills. Now wouldn't you think people would be as smart as ice?"

Some of our visitors were from towns. They climbed carefully out of their cars, looking down at the ground with every step, expecting a bear or timber wolf or rattlesnake to get them any minute. They recoiled from every leaf because it might be poison ivy, and they asked questions we couldn't answer. It would have meant educating them about a world they didn't even know existed.

One of the summer-night voices I remember is that of a bachelor neighbor who shaved once a month, whether he needed it or not. He didn't care much for town people. "I got relatives," he said, "that come when the strawberries are ripe and leave before milking time. I guess it must be different in town. Don't know. Never lived there. I guess in town a man can be a banker, barber, storekeeper, just be good at one job. A farm needs a man who's some kind of revolving son of a bitch. You got to help calves get born, nursemaid a dozen different crops, be your own blacksmith, cut the testicles out of male pigs, fix machinery, keep the windmill going..."

"Of course, that's just before breakfast," Lyle interrupted with his cat-that-ate-the-canary grin.

The hill country was filled with voices that I remember. Some of them, the older ones mostly, were forever trying to put the past in proper order. I heard them at ice-cream socials, at school picnics, at stores in town, and under our own big maple tree.

"Was it eighteen ninety-five that we didn't get but fourteen inches of rain?"

"I thought it was twelve inches."

"When was it frost came in the middle of August? Never saw so much soft corn in my life."

A small group might come over to Father. "Say, Sam, we been

talking about your farm. Wasn't it Banty McPherson who broke the first land?"

"That's what we been told."

"Well, when was that?"

"The deed says eighteen sixty-four."

"There, I told you! I said the Civil War was still going on."

"Well, I thought Pat Mullaney lived there then. He used to tell about Indians crossing his land just below where the buildings are now. They was carrying lead from some little mines down in Halls Branch. Carried it down to the Kickapoo and took it by canoe clean down to Illinois someplace. Was lead still that scarce after the war was over?"

The voices went on and on, putting events and past years together.

Years were hard to separate on the farm. A year is an arbitrary, calendar thing. Our lives revolved around the seasons. Spring was each year's genesis, the beginning of new life, the awakening of the sleeping land. Summer was heat, sun, harvest, and always work, with muscles aching, shirts covered with dust and sweat and the white rings of salt from earlier sweat.

Fall was the end of harvest, end of the growing season, a glorious burst of color and sun-warmth before killing frost turned the land gray and cold. Fall was a moody time, full of both life and death, a time when we were reminded of the power outside us, reminded that the seasons happen to us. We do not invite the change to come.

Winter was in-between time, the frozen land resting under blowing snow. The farm seemed to shrink in winter, with the farmstead bigger and more important. The animals were inside the barns, the fields were empty. Even the winter birds gathered near the buildings. We were in the house more, and it was a time when we reached out past the frozen fields to explore a bigger world in our books and conversation.

Then, magically, spring again, the rebirth of the rolling seasons, the unfailing promise of the awakening land.

Part Two

SPRING

3 The Awakening Land

Spring was a contradiction. It was both creeping change and explosion. Because the soil was frozen solid, four or five feet deep most years, and covered with snow, it held the cold. The air warmed ahead of the soil in a false feel of spring that was only of the air—not of the entire land.

The days lengthened, the sun going higher, the rays striking the earth more directly, delivering more light and warmth. At the one-room school, down in a narrow part of Halls Branch Valley, we began going outside to eat our lunch, leaning back against the south wall, protected from the wind, the sunlight hot on our faces and reflected warmly off the white wood onto our backs.

Buds swelled. The stubborn leaves of the white oaks finally fell and blew along the snow, forced from the twigs by new growth. Crows gathered into noisy groups, black and arrogant, strutting on the white fields. Sometimes an early robin would sit huddled against the cold. In a few protected places, open to the sun, the land would bare itself, thawing a little each day into a treacherously slippery ooze, then freezing again each night. Below the schoolhouse, close to the creek, the willows began to show a fringe of yellow-green.

But all this was only a quiet message of promise. The land was still and dormant, snow-covered and frozen. It waited.

Then, the explosion.

In the night, the wind would go around to the south. It was a soft wind, moving the tops of the bare trees, but not giving the deathly cold rattle of winter to the branches. In the morning, put your feet out of bed and the floor was warmer than it had been for months. Go outside and there were new sounds. First a faint, rustling, restless sound, always familiar, always half forgotten, always a new discovery. It was the sound of running water, a thousand trickles on all sides as the melting snow began to form streams, seeking lower ground, beginning a journey toward the far-off sea.

By evening the little swales, dry runs, and ditches were roaring torrents of ice water, carrying miniature icebergs, running clean and clear because the still-frozen earth was erosion-proof.

I can remember an old man, whose name I have long since forgotten, shaking his head. "Didn't used to be like this. How things going to grow when the water's all getting away from us? Drought on the ridges, floods in the valleys. I tell you we've cut too much timber in this country."

Anyone could see the old man was right. In the thick woods the snow melted slowly and went into the thawing soil. The runoff was dammed by brush and a thick cover of leaves, the water cycling back into the soil right there instead of running into some river, lake, or ocean to be cycled back, maybe, someday by rain.

Mostly people just laughed at talk of too much timber being cut. "Ever try feeding trees to a dairy cow?" someone would ask. And someone like the old man would say, "Ever stop to think that this may not be the right kind of country for dairy cows? Timber's a crop, too, you know, and it's been here a whole hell of a lot longer than your pot-bellied dairy cows."

It wasn't the kind of talk people wanted to listen to. Letting some of the land go back into timber meant smaller crops and fewer livestock. And that meant less money.

⚘

Sometimes the explosion of spring stopped as suddenly as it had begun. The wind went around to the northwest again and the cold shut it all down. Then we waited for the immense process we did not control to decide when spring would come.

Early or late, explosive or creeping, it always came, and it was its own force and did not care what the calendar or the weatherman said. People talked of "a year without a summer" back in the early 1800s when volcanic ash from the eruption of a volcano in the Orient filled the atmosphere and blocked out the sun. But no one ever talked about a year without a spring. It was as unthinkable as trying to convince someone that they had never been born.

The coming of spring changed us, each in a different way. My three brothers and I would burst forth from the house like caged animals, leaving open doors behind, scattering a trail of mittens, scarfs, and stocking caps as the warmth got to us. Sometimes one of us would run back to the house to see if we could also discard our scratchy long winter underwear. The answer was always "not yet." I can't remember ever getting permission to take it off, yet I know we didn't wear winter underwear all summer.

We made dams on icy streams, searched for lost possessions that had vanished into the snow, found warm niches full of dry brown leaves, dug ice caves in the deep snow—drifts still unmelted, like leftover glaciers with the land bare around them. We also found softening soil, oozing acres of it, and Mother surely must have thought of early spring in terms of mud.

The mailman knew all about the spring thaw. On days when the road was too muddy for his Model T, his horses would be lathered with it, his wagon spattered from top to bottom. But George Holliday liked spring. It was warm enough to stop and talk to people again, and he always had a story. Every spring there would be the one about a farmer named Dave Twining who claimed he'd killed a deer with a hoe while he was chopping weeds out of a new cornfield. "Maybe you wonder how it happened. Deer jumped over the fence into the cornfield and got stuck in a five-foot snowdrift."

We would hoot with laughter and George would pretend to be

very insulted, saying, "Ain't going to bring you folks any more mail."
A hot cup of coffee would always end that threat.

For Mother spring really began with the coming of the birds. We
would awake one morning and find the outside world alive with their
voices, unbelievably rich and varied after the quiet birds of winter. It
seemed to be contagious. The cardinals, bright, but silent, flashes of
red during the winter, began joyously singing. The call of geese came
from far overhead where the V-shaped and wavering lines moved
slowly north. Sometimes, strangely, a lone white gull winged majes-
tically by. We often wondered if they had been blown to us from one
of the Great Lakes by a storm.

Fat robins hopped and "listened" and pulled worms out of the
lawn, which was turning green even in those spots where our feet
seemed to have trampled the soil into a lifeless mud puddle. Always a
robin built a nest in exactly the same spot in a juniper tree next to the
garden. Mother liked to think it was the same robin each year, or at
least a child from that same nest who had come home again.

Noisy grackles strutted around the yard, trying to claim it from
the starlings and English sparrows. High in the limber branches of
the big soft maple were the rusty blackbirds, their voices like old
hinges that need oiling. And sharing those high branches, a meadowlark or two, singing over and over again, according to Mother, the
phrase "This-is-the-spring-of-the-year!"

She would stand on the porch or under the trees, listening to the
birds, smiling at them, welcoming them back by name. They were her
promise that the world wasn't always white and frozen. The winters
were long for her. Lyle once said, "Wisconsin has six months of winter
and three months of late fall." Mother smiled and nodded. It was how
she felt sometimes. But all that changed with the coming of the birds.
I would hear her singing at the zinc-covered kitchen table, the door
to the porch open so the sound of the birds could come in.

It is strange and seems almost unfair that I know so little of my
mother's life in the years before my age of awareness. She was just as

important to me as Father, just as real, but she lacked the exotic background that made me search for Father's past.

Mother was of that hill country, just as I was. Perhaps we who are born to the land take it too much for granted. Father, coming from the Old Country and from the sea, discovered the wonder of the land as a remembering adult. He chose it, then deliberately put all the parts together. Mother and I and my brothers discovered it as children, beginning at an age before memory. The land was there and we were there, a part of it, without thought or question.

Mother had been a teacher. I know of her in those years only from pictures—with young men, girl friends, schoolchildren—a slim, beautiful girl with great eyes and a young and innocent look. They are only pictures. I *know* her on the farm, where she was warmth and music, a dream of other horizons, a keeper of the rituals of special days.

She was locked to that ridgeland, yet her books and college days had told her of wider worlds. I am sure she was often lonely, though I doubt if Father ever knew. He had finished his wandering before he came ashore on that high ridge. She was still earthbound. In some way the migrating birds were the roaming, adventuring side of her. Part of her went with them in the fall to strange lands where she would never go. Part of her returned with them, refreshed and reborn each spring.

For Lyle, spring was an awakening. He lost his dark, winter-morning sleepy look and went striding out to meet the new day, eager to be behind a team of horses in the fields again. He kept looking out along the ridge for farmers starting work, afraid that we'd be left behind.

When to start the field work was Father's decision. Lyle would fret about the calendar and how the oats had been in two weeks by this date last year. Father's calendar was the land itself. He walked out into the bare fields, feeling the soil, testing it for moisture and warmth, smelling it. When the soil said it was ready, then he was ready to begin.

There was something wonderfully mysterious about Father's decisions. I walked with him sometimes, feeling and smelling the soil in imitation of him. There is still a certain feel and smell of warming land that says seedtime to me.

The planting decisions were neatly organized each year by a long-range rotation of crops. About a third of last year's hayfields were plowed up and planted with corn. Oats were sown in last year's corn-fields. Sown with the oats was a hay crop, usually alfalfa. When the oats were harvested in mid-summer, the alfalfa thrust up through the stubble, lush and green, a promise of a new hayfield for next year. After several years in hay, a field was plowed up for corn and the cycle started all over again.

Corn or grain was never planted in the same field two years in a row. It left the hillside more open to erosion. And the land needed the nitrogen-building roots of the legume hay crops to enrich it for the corn.

When the soil was ready, the seed oats and barley were waiting. During the winter we had shoveled bushels of them through the hand-cranked fanner—a miniature threshing machine that blew away the chaff, weed seeds, and the light grain seeds. We wanted only plump and heavy seeds. Those germinated better and would make another crop of plump and heavy grain.

For each crop there was a special way of planting, some of the techniques going back thousands of years, with machines duplicating what had once been done by hand.

For planting the oats there was the drill, a handsome, bright red, two-wheeled machine that was like a wide cart, with a ten-foot-long axle and seed box between the wheels. The seeds ran from the box down through tubes to the disks, spaced a few inches apart, which opened the soil. Chains dragging behind each disk smoothed the soil and covered the seeds. Down through smaller tubes, from another seed box, ran the tiny alfalfa and clover seeds. The planting rate for each kind of seed was set with levers.

I was always amazed by Father's sure remembered knowledge when planting time came. We could play a game with him, half fun, half awe. How many bushels of oats do we plant to the acre? How many pounds of alfalfa or clover in with the grain? How many kernels of corn per hill?

Father answered with utter confidence. He had come from the sea, but it seemed as if he'd been born knowing about planting. To have to look it up in a book would have been like asking someone how to breathe.

One spring a new type of oats was advertised, with claims that yields would be double. Farm magazines had articles recommending the new seed. Father bought a few bushels, enough for one field.

"Why not plant all that kind?" we asked.

We were sitting, the seven of us, in the warm lamplight at the dining room table, the chores done for the day.

Father laughed and flipped the pages of the farm magazine. "Oh, I know what the paper says these new oats will do. I want to know what the land says."

The land said the new oats were better, though not as good as the advertisement claimed. They stood up straighter in the storms and the yield was higher. Next year we planted all that kind, using as seed the oats from that first small field. It was Father's way. Trust the land. Look to it for answers.

Still, he was uneasy with such changes. "What happens," he said, "if the oats do fine for a season or two, then turn out to be killed by rust on a wet year? We know the old kind always gave us some kind of a crop. And if we want to change back, can we do that? How many people have saved any of the old seed?"

After the oats were planted it was time to think of the corn. Day after day old hayfields were turned under, the gangplow pulled by four horses turning two wide ribbons of sod at once, the walking plow leaving a single moist furrow which was a path for the plowman, and for me. The horses walked quietly. The loudest sound was the tearing sod as the roots were cut or torn up and turned over. The sod talked. It said whether or not the roots were thick and healthy or weak and winter-killed. The soil underfoot talked, too. Good soil had a spring to it. Bad soil was hard and packed, with very little humus in it. Sometimes, on a slope where erosion was carrying the land away, the plowshare went to the bottom of the rich topsoil, scraping on the hard subsoil.

It was an incredibly busy time. Horses and men were going from dawn to dusk. Everything was happening at once. While one field was being plowed, another was disked and dragged. And all the time chores had to be done, cattle fed and milked. Calves and pigs were being born, and there were fences to be mended where posts had been heaved out of the ground by frost. Manure had to be hauled out to be plowed under, along with old hay and straw-stack bottoms and corncobs. It all went back to the land it had come from.

Even in late spring, the weather was full of surprises. A day would seem to have trouble deciding if the sun should shine or snow should fall. It reminded me of a story from one of our books, with the sun and wind having a contest to see which one could take off a man's coat. In the story the sun was the winner. In our spring, we wanted the sun to win, too. Mother laughed at our complaining and quoted a line from Shakespeare, something about "the uncertain glory of an April day."

Frost might come even after the first of May. It was not unusual to be plowing or planting with snow falling, or for the new green of the grainfields to be covered with white. Coming home from school in one of those changeable weather periods I would sometimes find a horned lark's nest with the lark sitting on her eggs and held to the nest by ice and snow. I'd free her and run away, watching her soar straight up into the sky and then fall back toward the nest.

May was corn-planting time, the horse-drawn planter putting in two rows at once. Sometimes the corn was "drilled," the planter dropping one kernel at a time, a few inches apart, along the rows. I liked planting time best when Father decided to "check" the corn. He would stretch a long knotted wire down the length of the field and each time a little tripper on the planter hit one of the knots, several kernels of corn dropped in a cluster, which we called a hill. The hills were aligned so that the corn rows ran both lengthwise and crosswise.

I walked behind the planter on its slow trips over the moist soil, hearing the click-click of the tripper as it hit the knots —and I never believed it was going to work. Each morning I would run out to look at the newly planted field. Finally the slim leaves of corn would be there, a checkerboard of green against the brown of the land. Even today when I walk along a theater aisle and notice how the perfect spacing of the seats makes rows in many directions, I am reminded of corn-planting time.

One crop was different from all the rest. Tobacco didn't seem a normal part of the process of land and seasons. It was our only cash crop, and a backbreaker—hard on the land, hard on people, demanding our time when alfalfa needed cutting or corn wanted cultivating.

"Closest thing there is to bringing up a baby," Lyle once said. The first step was forcing thousands of tiny black seeds to germinate between two wet cloths. When they began to show growth, they were carefully scattered into a seedbed and gently raked into the soil. Then the bed was covered, about a foot above the ground, with the light cloth we called tobacco canvas.

Those beds of sprouting seeds were watered, weeded, and fertilized—all by hand.

Finally, almost as summer began, the six- to eight-inch-tall plants were pulled one by one from the seedbed to be transplanted into the tobacco field. In addition to the driver, perched high on the water barrel, the tobacco-planting rig carried two men sitting low to the ground at the rear, each with a lapful of plants. As the planter moved slowly, slowly down the row, it made a little furrow, water squirted down, a plant was inserted into the furrow, and then the machine hilled soil up around the stem of the plant. It was all slow motion, a steady click-click with the two men adjusting to the rhythm of the machine with no time out for talk or even a sneeze or nose wipe.

It took a steady team of horses to keep the speed right, and it took the whole family to keep it all going. Three men on the planter, someone hauling water for the barrel, someone hauling plants, and everyone else leaning over the beds hour after hour, pulling the tender plants.

That was only a beginning. Missing plants had to be replaced. As the plants got a start, there was hoeing. Later there was the job of picking off the big fat tobacco worms and throwing them down on the ground with a green splash.

Almost everything about tobacco, except smoking it, meant working with your back bent into a circle. Break off the suckers, break off the tops, cut it, pile it, spear the stems onto four-foot wooden laths, pile it again, load it onto the tobacco wagon, hang it up in the tobacco shed to dry. Months later, during "case weather" when the leaves were damp and wouldn't shatter, we took it down again. Then, pile it again, haul it to the stripping shed, pile it once more, strip the leaves off one by one, sort the leaves, pack them into bundles wrapped in brown paper, and finally haul the bundles off to market. The endless circle of work began in late spring of one year and didn't end until early spring of the next.

We didn't like tobacco much. It took a lot out of the soil, and left only the stalks. We hauled them back to the land, but the real richness of the crop had gone to market to be burned into ashes.

Many a farm went slowly to ruin in that country because of tobacco. On some, all the manure and attention went to the tobacco field. Slowly the other crops got poorer, and the tobacco field got bigger and bigger to make up the difference. The vicious circle of land misuse went on until it broke the farm and its people. In the end, the buildings were half falling, the dairy cattle thin, the cornfields full of nubbins, and the people worn out and bent into a permanent half circle.

One year a new tobacco seed came in. People said it would give a much bigger yield. Some of our neighbors planted it, but Father stuck to the old seed. The yield was bigger all right, as it had been with the oats. But when it came time to sell to the tobacco-buyers who roamed the country like Gypsy horse-traders, our smaller crop sold for much more money than any of the new crops. There was no pleasure in it for Father. "You just can't go rushing into something like that," he explained. "Those things have to be checked out. You see, it wouldn't burn right for cigars. I was afraid of that the first time I put my hands on a leaf and felt how thick it was. The tobacco companies will have to chop it up for cigarettes or chewing tobacco."

Later, when the dairy herd was built up, we stopped raising tobacco. Summers were happier after that, more of a piece. Tobacco had been an alien to us. I don't think it had anything to do with whether or not it was right to smoke—Father liked a good cigar. But it may have had something to do with a larger, more subtle morality. Other crops completed the cycle from growth to new growth with enough of the crop going back to the land in manure or waste to keep the soil healthy. Other crops worked with the land, building it. Tobacco used up the land.

4 Four Boys

Something about the spring brought out an aggressive cussedness in us four boys. We were suddenly able and willing to argue endlessly about anything under the sun. There was no lasting hostility in it, just a constant sparring. Laurance had the superior position of the eldest to protect, so he was always partly a third parent to us, or at least trying to be. Junior was the skeptic who always wanted proof and didn't like quick and arbitrary decisions. Lee just seemed to like to argue, which was handy because he was willing to take any side and keep things even. I, of course, had the rights of the downtrodden, the put-upon young to protect and became a master at making up instant facts to protect my views.

We never realized how much our bickering must have irritated Mother until one spring morning. We were sitting at the breakfast table with a second cup of hot cocoa, a special luxury because it was Saturday and we didn't have to race off to school. Father and Lyle had left the table. The argument was about whose turn it was to take the cows down the lane to the day pasture and close them in.

It was a quick and easy job, a chance to run and be in the woods. We all liked doing it, but not if there was any chance that someone else should be doing it.

"Who did it last Saturday?"

Everybody remembered doing it last Saturday.

"Who did it the Saturday before that?"

"Last Saturday was the first time the cows were there this year."

"All right then, who did it the last Saturday last fall?"

26

Everybody remembered doing it the last Saturday last fall.

We were off. Should the oldest still be doing such childish jobs? Should the youngest do it as often as the others? How soon should whoever did it have to come back and get busy with other things? If we waited awhile, would Lyle maybe take the cows down?

On and on we went, never a silent moment, never any word that wasn't protest, accusation, or defense. Mother sat there sipping her coffee, staring straight ahead. I didn't even realize she was listening. Then she put the coffee cup down, put her arms full length out ahead of her on the table, and fanned one to the right and one to the left, sending dishes, pitchers, cups, and silverware crashing to the floor.

We stared at her, shocked into silence.

She didn't say a word, just picked up her cup, which had somehow escaped the disaster, and went on sipping coffee.

"I think I'll go take the cows down," Junior said. "I believe it's my turn."

We got up and tiptoed away. Lee and Laurance went outside. I went into a bedroom and threw myself down on the bed. I felt the world was coming to an end.

At some point Mother realized where I was. She came to the door of the bedroom and spoke very gently. "You know you're not supposed to be on the bed with your clothes on."

"I didn't think it made any difference now," I said.

She was somewhere halfway between laughing and crying when she came over to the bed and took me in her arms.

I don't suppose we bickered any less after that, but I know we were a little more careful about where we did it.

5 The Magic Seeds

Much of the magic of each spring was in the miracle of the germinating seeds. The corn, oats, barley, tiny alfalfa and clover seeds, the garden seeds—they all looked so inert, with nothing about them to say they were living things. The planting machinery moving across the land seemed like part of a game. The drill, putting in the oats, was only mechanical. My mind could not accept that each click of the corn planter was placing a little group of *living* seeds into the soil.

Proof of the miracle always came. Each seed joined the earth, entered into some mysterious partnership with soil, water, air, and sun and began to grow and become part of the living land. A fringe of green appeared one morning where yesterday there had been only the dark soil of a newly planted oat field. The neat, checked hills of corn sprang up, right where we had put them. In the garden, the tightly rolled leaf of a bean plant pushed up, carrying the spent case of the bean with it, to open under the sun like an umbrella. In all of these, because we had prepared the land and planted the seed, there was an assurance that the crops needed us.

But all around were reminders that the land was more important than we were. The land could do without us, reseeding itself. The winged seeds of the maples came whirling down in a dry, singing rattle, thousands of them competing to start a new tree in the already crowded soil. Sometimes almost all failed. But each year they were there, seeds in the late spring of one year, brave miniature maple trees a year later.

The weeds were a constant reminder that we were latecomers with our cultivated crops. They came, year after year, undeterred by our battle against them. It was as though the weeds tolerated us. Always we knew that if we left the land untended for a year, they would all be there, ready to take over.

Time was on the side of the weeds. Tear down an old building that had covered the soil with stone or concrete, let the sun and rain into that long-covered soil, and the same magic fringe of green would soon appear. Seeds that had lain dormant for a hundred years, alive and waiting all that time, would suddenly awake. Sometimes within that unbelievable miracle there was a second miracle. Perhaps from the site of an old building would come a beautiful wildflower we had not seen for years—a sobering reminder that we were changing things, taking a toll.

The miracle of the patient, sleeping seeds was controversial. Did they really lie there all that time? When you planted alfalfa and got half sweet clover, had the dealer cheated you with mixed seed, or had the sweet clover planted there five, ten, or twenty years ago finally germinated?

We found a 1931 report from the Michigan Agricultural College that helped set it straight. In 1879, a professor there collected seeds, mixed them with dry sand, put them in bottles, and buried the bottles eighteen inches deep in the ground. At five- or ten-year intervals, a bottle was dug up and the seeds tested. After ten years, in 1889, seeds of half the species germinated. The number dwindled each year, but on the fiftieth year, the seeds of five plants still germinated and grew—black mustard, evening primrose, smartweed, curley dock, and moth mullein.*

*This experiment is still going on. In 2000, 120 years after the seeds were buried, two species germinated—moth mullein and common mallow. Both of these species germinated in the 1980 test Five bottles remained

We read the article over and over again. It was hard to believe. Seeds buried in the ground before Father was born were still alive and able to grow. All they needed was moisture and light and warmth.

There were other reports after that. Sweet clover lived twenty or thirty years in the soil before germinating. Seeds were taken from old collections in the National Museum of Paris. Some of them grew after 158 years. The seeds had been collected in 1776, the year the United States was born. Seeds from the British Museum grew after 150 years. There was a report about water-lily seeds that grew after 250 years in storage.

We pored over these stories and argued. Junior was our skeptic. He just couldn't believe it. "You mean to tell me, I could go out and collect some common old weed seeds and put them someplace and they'd grow a hundred years from now? After I'm dead?" I think that was the part that shook us, the idea that a tiny seed could outlive us, could be here growing, if it wanted to wait that long, after we were dead.

One story was so incredible we didn't even argue about it. During work on a railroad cut in Manchuria in 1926, some lotus seeds were found, buried deep under an old lake bed. Geologists said the seeds might easily be four hundred years old. The seeds were planted. They germinated, producing lotus plants of a type no one had ever seen in that area. Later, when carbon-14 dating came into use, those lotus seeds were tested. They were at least eight hundred years old. They

---

buried. Dr. Frank W. Telewski, Michigan State University, reports that the next bottle will be dug up and the seeds tested in the year 2020. "I look forward to being here to unearth the next bottle, but beyond that, the experiment will be passed on to the next generation of botanists," he said. Those who wonder at the cussed persistence of weeds may be interested to know that the seeds of pigweed germinated after forty years and that each plant has an average of 117,000 seeds.

had dropped into the soil of Manchuria before the year 1200, and they were still alive.

Father was more interested in the kind of plant a seed would produce than in how long it would live, though the stories did make him think more kindly about seed dealers. He had his own ritual with seed corn in the days when we saved our own instead of buying the special hybrids. In the fall he walked through the cornfield with a bag over his shoulder, picking out the ears of corn he wanted to use for seed. He picked the big ones, filled out clear to the tip with kernels, from a strong upright stalk that had two ears.

He walked through the field until he had more than enough for next year's crop. But there was more to it. The ears went into a special drying rack with each position numbered. In the spring, Father took a few kernels from each ear, placed them on a dampened cloth, on a number corresponding to the ear, and waited. When any kernels refused to germinate, the ear they had come from was livestock feed again instead of seed corn. The rest we shelled, using the cobs for kindling and the seed for planting.

This was all very serious business for Father. For him there was a wild extravagance about nature's random seeding process. Take the maple tree again. Each year one tree might drop ten thousand seeds. It would do this for perhaps a hundred years. Yet all that was needed of those million seeds was that this one tree should be replaced with another when it finally gave in to the wounds of fire, lightning, wind, insects, drouth, disease, and man. To Father, who carefully weighed and tested his seed, this seemed careless. In a way I suppose he was right. Nature is careless with the individuals within a species, willing to sacrifice uncounted millions of individual plants. But it is a carelessness that reflects the tremendous effort nature makes to protect and preserve the species. For individuals there will be another year. If the species is not protected, the future is blank.

For me, no part of the miracle of the seeds was more impressive than the acorn. Red oak, black oak, white oak, bur oak—each had its own distinctive acorn. In the fall they pelted down at me as I ran through the woods. Sometimes I'd look up and find a squirrel peering at me. I would pick up the acorns, hold their cool smooth perfection in my hand, their stocking caps making them seem like unfinished small boys, waiting for a face and arms and legs so they could run and play in the leaf-strewn woods. I could not resist the acorns and I came home with pockets bursting.

Through the winter, the cache of acorns would lie unmoving, defying logic. I would pick them up and turn them until I had worn them smooth, the way I might turn an incubating egg, looking for the beginning of the pip hole made by the bill of the hatching chick. On the tree the acorns seemed alive. When they left that sturdy parent, how could I believe they had cast loose like children leaving home and needed only the right set of circumstances to wake them so they could begin to grow into a great oak tree, one day dropping acorns themselves?

Each spring I had to challenge the acorns. I'd plant them, or just lay them on the moist earth. The coat would swell and split. A white-red shoot would creep out through the crack and dig down for a foundation in the soil. Then another shoot would come out, turning toward the sun, already with a hint of green. For hours I would sit and watch them, the silent, unmoving acorns from my pockets now bravely putting out an oak leaf in imitation of a tree one hundred feet tall. Spring after spring I would do it. Each time it was a miracle and it was new.

"But how does a silly old acorn know to make one shoot go down and one go up?" I asked Laurance, who was already in high school and seemed to know everything.

"Light sensitivity," he said. "One seeks the light, the other is repelled by light."

"But how does a seed know that?"

"I just told you. Light sensitivity."

It wasn't the kind of answer I wanted, but I didn't know any other way to ask the question. It was one of those frustrating dead ends, like when a parent said, "You'll find out when you're older," or a teacher said, "I guess because that's just the way things are."

Once the persistence of the germinating seeds betrayed us. Lee and I went out with a bag of pumpkin seeds to plant between the hills of growing corn. The seeds were from last year's pie pumpkins. They were white and plump with some of the dried orange of the pumpkin still sticking to them. Father said to plant them all—they'd make good feed for the pigs. We went down the corn rows, bent over double, pushing a little hole in the ground with a sharpened stick, dropping in three or four seeds, then closing the hole over them. At the end of each row, we sat and ate seeds for a while, carefully biting off the edge so that the papery shell could be peeled away from the rich, dark green nut.

And, as usual, we argued.

Could a person survive eating pumpkin seeds? Would it take more energy to shell and chew them than you got from each seed? Could you do it fast enough to stay alive? It was an unending discussion. Somehow the troops of the Russian tsar got involved. Lee said they had lived all one winter on pumpkin seeds. The only time they weren't busy shelling and chewing was when they were sleeping. I wasn't convinced. Did pumpkins grow in Russia? The American Indians had raised them, so weren't they a New World crop?

"All right," Lee said, "maybe it was sunflower seeds. Same thing." We planted and rested and argued until finally we just couldn't believe anyone would want more pumpkins. We counted the corn rows, trying to estimate how many seeds we'd planted and how many pumpkins would come from each seed. It was almost frightening. Where would we put them all? Better that we stop planting now to avoid making the problem worse. We finally talked ourselves into doing something we rarely did—we disobeyed Father. Of course it was for his own good.

There was a woods nearby with a never-failing cold spring running from the hillside. We left the pumpkin seeds at the edge of the woods and went to the spring. After a delay while we drank and then had a contest to see who could hold his hand in the fantastically cold water the longest, we went back to the pumpkin seeds. We ate some more but there were too many for that. We didn't have all winter like the Russians. Finally, we just dug a hole in the woods, put the seeds there, and covered them up. Squirrels will get them, we figured. It's not as if they'll go to waste.

We went home and reported how many rows we had planted. No one was suspicious. We'd had a long unsettled argument about whether or not it would be lying to say we had planted them all, but no one asked.

The seeds grew, even there in the deep shade, the long vines crawling out toward the light at the edge of the woods. Lyle found them one morning late in the summer while he was hunting for the horses. He reported the discovery at the breakfast table.

Father sat, thinking about it. Click, click, click, we could see the various possibilities being tried out. Then his glance came to Lee and me.

"Could have been birds," I said.

"Birds?" Father said.

"It was like a whole batch of seeds was put there," Lyle said.

"Does a bird carry a whole pumpkin?" Father asked. He answered himself. "No, a bird doesn't carry a whole pumpkin. What does carry a whole pumpkin?"

"People do," Mother said.

"But who would be carrying a whole pumpkin around in the woods?"

"Kids might," Lyle said.

"That's right," Father said. "Or maybe somebody actually planted them, not knowing that pumpkins don't grow in the woods."

"Well," Mother said, "anyway we don't need them. More than enough in the cornfield."

Father smiled. "That's right. I guess it will just be one of those unsolved mysteries."

Did he know or not? We talked about it after breakfast. "You should have kept still," Lee said. "The minute you say something in a situation like that you're in trouble."

Then he forgot about being mad at me and started blaming the seeds. "Pumpkins got no right to grow in the woods. They just did it to get even with us for doing that to them."

The ones in the woods set some late blossoms, but they never did make any pumpkins. Nothing more was ever said about how it happened. Except that Lyle had a new phrase for his vocabulary, which already sounded as if it had been written for him by Robert Frost. When anyone suggested something he didn't agree with, Lyle would shake his head and say, "Hell, that's crazy as planting pumpkin seeds out in the woods."

6 The Garden

When the birds came back in the spring, Mother began to think about her garden. Out came the seeds—store-bought ones in neat little packages and those we had harvested last fall in unused Sears and Montgomery Ward order envelopes. With the packets spread around her at the dining-room table, she would shut her eyes and see the garden in front of her, then make a list of any additional seeds she needed.

The garden was a little field west of the house. Father was in charge of the rest of the land, but that little field was hers alone. I don't know how Mother decided when the time was right to begin. Maybe it was mostly a matter of when she could get to it. Maybe there were observations or signs that told her, so that a day would suddenly be the right one. Only now does it occur to me that the day always seemed to come on Saturday when I was out of school.

However it happened, she would announce at breakfast one morning that she wanted the garden spread with manure, then plowed and harrowed. It was always a surprise, maybe even to her, and she always meant today if at all possible. Father planned his work far ahead, so there was never really a right time for garden preparation. He would sigh, and we could see him reshuffling things inside his head before he said, "All right. We'll do it right after breakfast."

Mother would smile and say, "Thank you."

He would smile back, and there was something in the air between them, close and private, that made us stay very still.

For some reason it was always Lyle who got the garden ready, even though it made him feel foolish to be using the big horses and heavy equipment on such a little piece of land. "Hell and tooter," he would say, "the garden's so short I have to yell 'get ep' and 'ho' at the same time to keep from going right through the house."

Because I was the youngest and smallest, I worked more with Mother than my brothers did. For as long as I can remember, she and I planted the garden, though I'm sure my brothers had a turn, one by one, before me. There was a close warmth in it, a sense of being important and needed, knowing that I was a partner with her and the soil, sun, and rain in helping things grow and putting food on the table. Later, when I went out to get radishes, lettuce, and carrots for a meal, the smile of delight on Mother's face as I brought them in was the kind of payment that made me feel I'd grown an inch.

We were a busy family. Rarely did we sit down just for the sake of sitting and talking. Even meals tended to be rather silent. But when we worked together there was time for talk. It might begin casually, but when you are working with the soil, the plants, and the seasons, any conversation can lead you into philosophy.

It was in planting the garden that I felt closest to Mother. Despite the hard work, I was always sorry when the job was done and I could go back to other things. Partly, I suppose, it was a way of being something the youngest rarely is—an only child, with her undivided attention.

We began the garden by stretching a strong string across it near the north end, the cord lined up with a west window of the house on one side, with a plum tree on the other side. The section to the north of the cord we left alone. It was for volunteers, where seeds from last year's tomatoes and ground cherries would germinate and push up to the surface in the freshly turned soil. Volunteers that appeared in other parts of the garden would be transplanted there.

Under the string, we raked the surface smooth, then made a shallow furrow with the corner of a hoe for our first row of seeds.

Here a side of Mother appeared that was like Father. She did not have to look at the seed packages or in a book to see how far apart the rows should be, how close together to drop the seeds, how deep to cover. She was, though, a little more on the side of the extravagant maple tree than Father was. She liked to plant a few extra seeds, "just to be sure," and thin the plants after they came up.

It was all very personal, the planting. Each seed passed through the warmth of our hands. It was a thing to be done with great responsibility, this taking of living seeds from the envelopes where they had lain dormant and putting them properly into the soil so they could awake and grow. It had the richness of an annual ritual.

The years of garden planting merge into a kaleidoscope of images and feelings, without any chronology of time:

The firm, round radish seeds went into the soil, to be covered and patted down, so our hand prints ran the length of the row.

The big McMahon bloomed near the north end of the garden. It was an apple tree with a split personality. One side bloomed one year, the other side the next in an unfailing pattern.

"Why does it do that?" I asked, every year for how many years?

Mother smiled. "I suppose some horticulturist would have a scientific answer. I like to think the old tree just wants to be different from other trees."

The lettuce seeds were small and chaffy, covered with only a sprinkle of soil because they needed light for germination.

A robin was always building a nest on that same flat limb of the juniper tree.

"Where has he been all winter?"

"Down South," she said. "Maybe with a winter nest and winter babies in a live-oak tree way down on the Gulf of Mexico."

"What's a live-oak tree?"

"An oak tree that stays green all winter."

"Because there's no frost down there?"

"Yes," she said. "But partly because it's a different kind of oak tree. Maybe you've seen pictures. The kind that have Spanish moss hanging in them, like spider webs covered with dust."

"How does the robin know how to get back here like he does?"

"We don't know that. Some people think they can navigate, using the stars."

"Like sailors at sea? Like Father used to do?"

"Yes. Like that." She smiled, thinking about it.

We scattered the beet seeds very thinly, because each was really a clump of seeds that would make many beet plants.

"Is that how *you* think the birds find their way back?"

"I don't know how they do it," she said. "We don't have to know how they do it for it to be a kind of miracle. Maybe if we knew too much, everything would be scientific, all the questions answered, never any surprises, and nothing left to wonder about."

"Could that happen?"

She laughed. "No. It's like a wild onion."

"A wild onion?"

She told me about the Ibsen play, with Peer Gynt trying to get to the heart of a wild onion, but no matter how many layers he unpeeled, there always seemed to be another left to hide the beginning.

"Do you think we're not supposed to know?"

"I think we're supposed to know everything we can figure out. I don't think we're supposed to make up answers just because we can't stand living with unanswered questions."

"Oh."

We planted the big fat green beans and wax beans, placing them carefully two inches apart.

"If we plant the bean seeds and then gather them and plant them again, how long could it go on? A hundred years from now could we still be planting the seeds that started with one of these?"

"I don't think so," she said. "I mean, the seeds could still be here if someone kept them going, but I wouldn't be here. Probably you wouldn't either."

"Why not?"

"Because people die."

"Are you going to die?"

"Of course."

"When?"

She smiled. "That's one of those unanswered questions we have to live with."

"Oh."

The cool, gentle wind of spring seemed always to blow out of the northwest. Meadowlarks sang from the big maple tree. A cardinal called near the garden. Catbirds scolded us with their meow and imitated the cardinal. The peas went in, always two rows close together, then a space and two more rows. I don't know why we did it that way.

"Father's father is dead?"

"Yes. When your father was only four years old."

"People say the new neighbor made somebody die."

"Yes. In a fight. His own brother. I don't think he meant to kill anyone. That's one reason people shouldn't fight. When you fight you get angry and don't always know what you're doing."

I didn't know the man had killed his own brother. "It's like Cain and Abel," I said.

"Yes." I could feel her looking hard at me. "Do you believe in God?"

"I think so."

The knees of my trousers were damp from crawling in the moist soil as I covered up the rows. We were almost finished with the vegetables. I held in one hand seeds of the white turnip which would grow into a big white root underground. In my other hand I held seed of the kohlrabi, which was like a turnip except that the big part grew above the ground, with only the taproot underneath. How could all that difference be stored in little seeds that I could hold in my hand and hardly tell apart? I kept staring at them, immobilized.

I looked up and she was smiling at me. "What are you thinking?"

I shook my head. It was too complicated. "Can the seeds hear us talking?"

"Some people say the plants know when people are angry. They say some flowers won't bloom in a home where there's always quarreling and fighting."

"We kids quarrel all the time."

"That's different. You're just testing each other. It's not really meanness."

I remembered the time she sent the dishes crashing off the dining room table. "Sometimes our quarreling bothers you."

She nodded. "Sometimes I get sick of never hearing anything else. I'd just like to hear some good conversation. The way it is now. With you and me."

She had mentioned God. "There's something I never told you," I said. "One summer I wanted a gun. A Frontier Colt like in the Western stories. I prayed I'd get one. All that summer I kept turning over rocks. Looking under them. Because I thought that's where He would leave it."

"But you never found it."

"No. Then a funny thing happened. Lee whittled a beautiful looking gun out of wood. He painted it black like a real one and gave it to me. He'd never done anything like that before."

She stopped working and stood smiling at me. "Well, some people say that's how God works—through other people. It's a lovely story. Why did you want a gun?"

"I guess because in the Western stories all the important men carry a gun."

"Do you think that's the only way to be an important man?"

"Not anymore."

The south end of the garden, next to the road, was for the flowers. First, because they were the tallest, the dahlias, dead-looking clumps of dried roots from last year. Then the bulbs of gladiolus, heavy but with no sign of growth.

"What keeps them from growing during the winter?"

"Things just aren't right."

"But an onion sprouts in the house."

"Yes. Maybe it gets tired of waiting. Maybe if it waits any longer it will never have a chance to grow."

We planted the bright blue larkspur, the yellow and orange nasturtiums, the fernlike cosmos, the zinnias that never seemed to mind the drouth, and the impossibly fine seed of the moss rose.

"Will you ever teach school again?"

She put her hand on my head. "Maybe I still am."

"Oh."

Then we were finished and she stood up straight, head way back to stretch the tired muscles. "Look!" she said. "Look at all the different shades of blue."

"Isn't the sky just sky blue?"

"No, it isn't. Look straight up. See the color blue there? Now, bring your eyes slowly down to the horizon. There, didn't you see all those different shades of blue?"

"Yes. Yes!"

7   Black Grass

As the spring days lengthened, the sun dried out the dead weeds and grass that hid the green of new growth in the woods and hillside pastures. It was then that some farmers liked to set fires and burn off last year's growth. Light blue smoke spiraled up by day all across the countryside. In the evening we could see long uneven lines of flames moving slowly across a distant hillside. The pungent smell of burning grass and leaves was everywhere, day after day. As night dampness came on, the fires would fade and go out, only to be set again the next day.

When the burning was finished, an ugly black covered the land. "Black grass," Father called it. He would look at the smoke and his face would set.

A man on the farm north of us was a fire-setter. He seemed to love setting those spring fires more than anything else he did. Time and time again he started one close to our land, never seeming to care which way the wind was blowing. Soon the blue smoke was rising from our own woods. Whoever spotted it first would run to Father, who dropped anything he was doing and gathered us into a fire fighting team, each armed with hoe, shovel, or rake, a bucket of water, and a wet burlap bag. Carrying our clumsy load, we ran into the woods. Keeping the bag wet with water from the bucket, we used it to beat at the long line of flame that was creeping along our land. With the tools we tried to pull moist earth up onto the fire, or, if the flames were high, used them to hold the wet bag out in front of us.

The bags hissed against the flames. Sparks and burning leaves flew up around us. Pungent leaf smoke billowed, hiding us from each other, so sometimes I felt I was alone, with fire all around me.

When the flames seemed to be getting away from us, we built a backfire. That meant setting a fire of our own and forcing it to burn only toward the oncoming fire so they would meet and both go out.

Fence posts and dead trees caught fire and smoked for days. Birds and rabbits and squirrels went racing out of the woods. Sometimes the frightened quail would be right under our feet running in circles. None of the animals or birds seemed to be afraid of us. The fire was an enemy that blotted out all the rest.

Then it would be over. Because there were no evergreens, the fires stayed on the ground and didn't rage out of control like those in the north woods. The fire left behind a blackened, smoking, silent ruin, and the smell lingered for weeks. Slowly the new green would come again, but it seemed to me that land that had been burned over in the spring stayed silent, as though the birds and animals didn't trust it enough to come back.

Sometimes after a fire, Father went to see the farmer who set them. The man would laugh and say, "Nothing illegal about setting a fire on my own land, is there?"

"By God, there should be," Father said.

Once during a fire, the man's oldest son was suddenly there with us helping to put it out. "Can't that father of yours tell which way the wind's blowing?" Father yelled.

The boy went on stomping out the flames. "He can tell all right." When the fire was out, he came up to Father and said, "I'd just as soon you didn't tell anybody I was here."

Each year was the same. The man seemed to like trouble. Sometimes we thought it was the main reason he set the fires, hoping to start a good fight. He did it even more often as the years went on and his children all left him.

"Without them to fight with, he'd like to fight more with us," Mother said.

Once, coming home from school, I went by the woodpile on the man's land and found him splitting short blocks of wood into small pieces for the kitchen range. He was friendly and eager to talk with me. He split open a piece of black cherry filled with big, fat ants. Scooping them up, he pinched off the heads and ate the rest. I thought it was some kind of a trick, but he did it slowly for me, opening his mouth so I could see he was eating them, all right. He laughed at me when I wouldn't try one.

I told everyone about it that night at the supper table.

"Poor old man sounds lonely," Mother said.

"Which is just the way he wants it," Father said.

My brothers and I spent the rest of the meal arguing about whether or not people really eat ants. We ate busily as we talked, but Mother and Lyle didn't seem very hungry.

A week later the man set another fire that came onto our land.

"That because he's a poor lonely old man?" Father said to Mother.

"That could be," she said. "The fire proves he's there, doesn't it? Do you ever think of him being there otherwise?"

Father sat, silently thinking about that. When Mother had gone back to the kitchen, he looked at us, smiled, and said, "Well, I'll be damned."

Farmers who burned the land each spring claimed it helped the new grass get started and kept the weeds and brush from coming back into the pastures. Some said the Indians used to do it, west of the Mississippi, out on the prairies.

"Maybe so," Father said. "For all we know it maybe even works out there, though I doubt it. Indians can be wrong, same as us, you know. But this isn't prairie and it doesn't work here."

One spring when we had put out a fire, we sat down at the edge of the burned-over area to rest. We were breathing hard and covered with smoke and ash, white streaks down our cheeks where smoke tears had washed the soot away.

We started talking about whether or not the fires were bad. Junior, who never believed anything too quickly, was skeptical. He thought maybe we should do a test—burn part of a woods or pasture for several years and compare it with the unburned part.

Father scooped up a handful of soil lying almost bare under a thin layer of ashes. "Take a look. What's going to keep that soil from washing away first time it rains?"

He thrust the handful of soil up to my brother's face. "Look close. See the little pieces of stems and leaves? That's all the test you need. Old leaves make new leaves. Old grass makes new grass. They both make the soil. And fire? Tell me what fire makes?"

No one answered.

He let the soil run slowly through his fingers, sending up little black puffs as it hit the ground. "I'll tell you what fire makes. Fire makes ashes."

8 Which Came First?

The new warmth of spring meant the chickens could be let out to run free. When I opened the door for them, they poked their heads outside cautiously for the first time in four months or more, then with a wild flapping of wings they ran out into the yard.

"Just like you boys on the first warm day," Mother said.

The chickens chased and leaped and cackled for a few hours, then settled down and began scratching for seeds, eating the new grass and looking for insects. Almost immediately they began laying more eggs. These eggs were different, the yolks much darker yellow. Mother's cakes were a richer color and everyone said the eggs tasted better.

For me there was a problem in the chickens being let out. As far back as I could remember I had been the official egg-gatherer. In winter I had only to go into the chicken house and reach into the nests for the eggs, sometimes doing it twice a day in the coldest weather so the eggs wouldn't freeze and burst. But starting with spring the eggs might be just about anywhere. Something about being free brought out a secretive side of the chickens. At least half of them seemed determined to hide their nests from me. So with spring, egg-gathering became a battle of wits.

"All you have to be is smarter than the chickens, " Lee said, laughing at me. "That shouldn't be too hard, even for you."

It was, though. Either I wasn't very smart or the hens were a lot smarter than most people figured. Any sporting hen is supposed to cackle when she lays an egg. We had hens that would lay an egg and run halfway across a forty-acre field before they'd cackle, some that

laid eggs and never did cackle, and some that cackled and ran but
never did lay an egg. With hens looking pretty much one like another
it was hard to get very scientific about egg-gathering.

Some years we had two breeds of hens and that helped. The
smaller white leghorn had a more excited cackle and liked to hide
nests in high places such as the haymows. The heavier Plymouth
Rocks stayed on the ground and had a deeper-voiced cackle.

Mother helped by observing. "One cackled down in the orchard
today," she'd say.

"What kind of cackle?"

"Sounded like a Plymouth Rock."

That meant the hidden nest would likely be on the ground. But
the hiding places on a farm were endless. Hens used the soft sawdust
under the protruding ends of the post pile, sheltered fence corners,
feed boxes of unused horse stalls, hidden corners of the haymows,
and a hundred nooks and crannies in every outbuilding, weed patch,
and sheltered spot.

They especially liked dark and secret corners. Where one week
I reached in to find a fresh egg, the next week I might find the nest
taken over by bumblebees. Once, poking into a dark tunnel in the
haymow, I felt something cool and smooth. But the shape was
wrong. I took hold and hauled back. Out came a hissing, five-foot
black snake, lumpy with swallowed eggs. I jumped back. My full
bucket of eggs and I went crashing down the hay chute. I don't
know what happened to the snake (were the eggs inside him already
broken?). Mother said it was the best job of scrambling since the
time the buck sheep butted me when I was climbing over a board
fence.

There was a time she may have forgotten. That was when I was
coasting downhill toward the open barnyard gate, a bucket of eggs in
the wagon with me. Just as I got to the gate, the wind blew it shut.

I remember once at breakfast when it seemed everybody was
reporting cackling that I was supposed to investigate. I began to feel
the whole purpose of the hens was to give me a bad time.

Father laughed at my grumbling. "Ever stop to think those poor hens are just following their natural instincts? Probably all they want to do is get a batch of eggs together and hatch out some chicks. So the smarter you get, the smarter they have to get."

"Actually," Mother said, "it's kind of a compliment to you. It shows they respect your ability."

Well, that may have helped my bruised ego a little, but it didn't make the nests any easier to find.

For every reported and suspicious cackle I had to set up a strategy. Fortunately, each hen tended to lay her eggs at about the same time every day. I would hide and watch for one beginning to move in the direction of the reported cackle. They were very good at it. A hen would keep pecking and scratching, as if all she had in mind was more food, and all the time be slowly moving off from the other chickens. I shadowed the hen, keeping out of sight, trying not to make any noise. Of course, a hen never went straight to her nest. There was some kind of "natural instinct" that took care of that, too. She'd move off in one direction, double back, go around buildings, head into the deep weeds. At some point when she was half hidden, she stopped being casual and I knew she was getting close. Crouching low to the ground, the hen would creep forward so slowly that I might lose her if I took my eyes off her for a second. Then, if I was lucky, she'd move to her nest and I had won.

I didn't always win. There were hens that seemed to know I was following them. They just played a game with me. They would follow the standard routine, moving off casually, then beginning to creep, but after about fifteen minutes of leading me on they would walk out of the weeds and rejoin the other hens. Were they just practicing or did they know exactly what they were doing? I wanted to ask Mother if she knew of any way to tell if a chicken was laughing, but I couldn't think of a way to ask without giving away more information than I got back.

Sometimes hens were all too easy to outsmart. They overacted. I remember one who reminded me of how Lee and I tried to look very innocent when we were staging a raid on Mother's shredded coconut in the pantry. Sort of humming a little song, this hen would poke along toward the horse-barn door, acting as if she didn't have a thought in the world, or maybe was just out for a morning stroll. But she kept moving right toward the barn. Finally, with a little look, as though to see who was watching, she would hop through the door. About twenty minutes later she'd come walking out, still humming her little song. Slowly she would stroll halfway across the barnyard, and only then would she suddenly run and cackle. But I knew from experience that her egg would be where it always was—in the third horse stall from the door.

Other times, weeks went by before I located a nest. Then I'd find it, full of eggs. Such eggs were not to be trusted. I put them, a few at a time, into a bucket of water. If they didn't float, I took them to the house and put them in the basket reserved for what Mother called "the questionable eggs." Eggs from that basket had to be broken, one by one, into a cup for observation before they were used. For years I thought the phrase "don't put all your eggs in one basket" had something to do with separating good eggs and questionable eggs.

If the eggs floated, I either buried them or threw them against the side of the silo to see how they smelled. It was a way of checking the reliability of the water test. Usually they smelled pretty bad.

Sometimes a hen would be setting when I finally found the nest. Then I had to make a decision. How long had she been setting? Did we want more baby chicks? Was it too late in the season?

I had to sit down and think about it. If I took the eggs away from the hen maybe she'd stay on the empty nest anyway. Some hens were just natural-born setters.

One thing to do was see if the eggs were shiny. If they weren't, they'd been set only a few days and were worth putting to the water test. For the set-on eggs, the test was helpful but not conclusive. An egg that floated might be too old and going bad, or it might have a baby chicken forming inside. So when set-on eggs didn't sink, I had to run back and put them under the hen to stay warm while I made up my mind.

It was a weighty decision. How was the hen going to feel? Was there a beginning live chick inside each egg? I had to be careful about getting too sentimental. If I made a wrong decision too late in the season, there would be a whole bunch of little chicks running around in the frosty grass to feel sorry for. A late batch of chicks was always a mark of my failure, not easy to hide either, with chicks hopping and cheeping all over the place.

I can recall exactly how egg-gathering became a thing of philosophy for me. It was a warm spring day when I was in the second grade. All the boys were lined up at lunchtime, leaning back against the warm south wall of the schoolhouse. I carefully cracked a hard-boiled egg against the edge of the half-gallon syrup pail I used as a lunch bucket.

"Which came first, the chicken or the egg?" one of the big boys asked.

I hadn't been initiated to the riddle. I just stared at him.

"Which came first?" he repeated, laughing.

I thought about it. "The chicken hatches out of the egg."

"But the chicken had to be there already to lay the egg," he said.

I could see that all right, but where had that chicken come from if not from an egg? I sat there eating my hard-boiled egg, dipping it into the mixture of salt and pepper Mother had wrapped in waxed paper for me. The argument went on around me. The majority opinion was for the chicken being there first. Somehow chickens were more real.

I thought about it all afternoon. When I went out with my bucket that evening, I picked up a smooth white egg and turned it over and over in my hand. There was life in there. Inside that cool and motionless white egg, which made a silly hen cackle, was the start of a new chicken. And that new chicken would grow up, lay an egg and cackle, and the new egg would . . .

It was too much for me. I could see an unending line of eggs and hens stretching out of sight in both directions (I don't remember when I caught on to the importance of roosters). Still holding that white egg firmly in my hand, I went to consult Mother.

"Which came first, the chicken or the egg?"

She didn't laugh. She thought about it for a moment and said, "Neither."

She went over to my blackboard, next to the kitchen range, and drew a circle. "The chicken and the egg are both part of the same circle of life."

"Oh," I said.

I went back out and finished gathering the eggs. A circle was certainly better than a line. A circle stayed right where you could see it.

The next day at school I had a hard-boiled egg again and one of the boys asked me which came first. He started laughing.

"Neither one came first," I said. I picked up a stick, brushed the wood chips aside and drew a circle on the soft ground. "The chicken and the egg are both part of the same circle," I said with great authority.

"Oh," the boy said.

Everyone sat there looking at the circle. No one ever brought up the question again. There's something about a circle that puts a stop to things. Maybe that's all that philosophers really do—just bend the straight lines into circles, the lines coming back to meet each other so there aren't any loose beginnings or endings anymore.

Now that I come to think of it, I guess my mother was a pretty good philosopher.

9 Scrambled Eggs for Easter

There was a special Easter ritual connected with egg-gathering. In some strange way egg-hiding got turned completely around for us. We boys did the egg-hiding.

Since I was official egg-gatherer, we had control of the supply. Weeks before Easter, I began slowly tapering off the number I took to the house each night, reserving the others for hiding. There was a sure signal when I went too far. Mother, who probably knew to the day when hiding began, would look into my egg bucket and say, "I just can't understand why the hens aren't laying better. You know I don't even have enough eggs for a cake."

When that happened, we'd ease off, sometimes slipping extra feed to the hens, hoping for increased production.

There were lots of good hiding places for eggs on the farm. The hens themselves had taught me about some of them. There were the corn-planter seed boxes, the empty water barrel of the tobacco planter, dark corners of the haymows, the oat bins. We learned with the years never to put them all in one place.

Slowly we built our hoard. The night before Easter we gathered them from their scattered hiding places and early Easter morning put the buckets of eggs on the front porch to be discovered. Father and Mother were always appropriately surprised and we had a happy Easter.

After Easter, Mother could bake freely again and poor old Mr. Finley, who candled eggs in the store at Seneca, had to work overtime. Candling was the way he checked to see if an egg was all right. He used an empty oatmeal box with a hole in the top and a candle inside. By holding an egg over the hole, letting the candlelight shine through, he could see if the yolk was whole and good. I can see that old man yet, bent over the oatmeal box in his dark corner, a green eyeshade pulled down over his forehead. We were paid only for the eggs that passed. He always seemed surprised that he never found a bad one. What he didn't know, of course, was that I had my own way of testing eggs.

Once, in the early spring, a neighbor woman came to call when Mother was making a cake. "Get me four of the questionable eggs," Mother told me. I saw the neighbor woman's eyebrows go up.

I brought the eggs and Mother began breaking them, one by one, into a cup. "Those are the ones that haven't been set on more'n a few days," I explained.

The woman's eyebrows went up again. Lyle saw it that time. He was sitting in the kitchen mending harness, using the kitchen range to keep the sewing wax warm. "An egg is questionable only until it's broken," Lyle said. "People may fool you, but an egg can't."

Mother was busily beating the eggs and missed all this. The woman got up and said she'd better be going.

"Oh, I was hoping you'd stay for some cake," Mother said.

"No, thank you. I really couldn't," the woman said, backing out the kitchen door.

Mother watched her hurrying out of the yard. "Why, I wonder what's the matter with her?"

"Probably just didn't feel good," Lyle said. "Might have been something she ate." He winked at me.

Mother looked at him suspiciously and went back to her baking.

One of the things that makes egg-hiding interesting is the fragile nature of an egg. Eggs are a natural for a clandestine operation. When you lose, you lose with a dramatic smash.

Like the time we buried a nail keg full of eggs in the big bin of oats on the second floor of the granary. A few days later, Father sent Lyle up there to shovel oats. We didn't say anything, figuring they were buried deep enough to escape. Lyle was working away with the big scoop shovel when he hit the nail keg. He stopped whistling and began digging it out.

"Hell and tooter," he growled. "What's a nail keg doing in here?" He picked it up and gave it a heave. It landed at the top of the granary stairs and bounced down, spilling out scrambled eggs as it went.

Father, who had been working down below, looked up just in time to catch an egg on top of his head. He ran up the stairs, looking at the ceiling as though he expected to see a hundred hens up there that had all laid an egg at once. "Where the devil did those eggs come from?"

"Oats bin," Lyle said.

"For heaven's sake, why'd you throw them downstairs?"

"Now just a minute. If you was shoveling away and ran into a buried nail keg, would you right away suspect it had eggs in it?"

Father thought about that. "Well, no, but . . ."

"Figured it was empty as last year's bird's nest or just had oats in it," Lyle said. He scratched his head. "Well, that just might not be the truth. Fact is, I flung it out of there without doing any thinking."

"That makes sense to me," my short-tempered father said. He grinned. "Boys have to have their Easter egg fun, I guess." He was laughing as he started back downstairs. Then he slipped on the broken eggs. Down he went, bumping from step to step. He wound up with one foot stuck under the last step where the bumblebees' nest was.

It was a little early in the season, but the bees were out to give it a try. Father ran out of there, flailing away. When he got rid of the bees, he stuck his head back in the granary door.

"Clean up that damned mess!" he roared at Lyle. "Keep those damned eggs out of the oats!" he shouted at us.

Everyone said, "Yes sir!" at once.

We were a little short of eggs that Easter.

Right after that, Lyle began to be different about eggs. He was a short, wiry man with sparkling eyes and a sly smile. When he came to work on the farm, he was thin as a rail. It turned out he'd gone through a diet change. He'd been working in the Gays Mills creamery and he liked to drink fresh cream out of the farmers' cans. One day he dipped in and came up with a dead mouse. He cranked the telephone and started bawling out the farmer's wife.

"Oh," she said, "didn't I get them all out?"

He stopped drinking cream then. Stopped eating butter, too. That's why he was so thin. He liked eggs, though, but after the nail keg episode he didn't eat so many.

Eventually our egg-hiding reached a point where Father and Mother knew there would be eggs on the porch Easter morning. The only surprise was in the quantity, so we were trapped into topping ourselves each year.

One year we decided to make our greatest showing yet and quit. Easter was late and we coddled the hens into laying better than usual. But that wasn't all. We were going to fill two big washtubs three-quarters full of oats, then pile eggs on top. When Father and Mother saw those two heaping tubs of eggs on Easter morning, we figured they'd really be surprised.

It was a touchy business keeping all the eggs out of sight and the plan a secret. One night the weather turned cold. We gathered all the eggs into one place, then took turns sneaking out of bed to kind of sit over them to keep them from freezing. At the breakfast table next morning we had only to look at each other and the giggling would start.

Father eyed us suspiciously. "When boys start acting like that," he said to Mother, "there ought to be some kind of disaster insurance a man could take out."

Three days before Easter we heard Father tell Lyle to haul some old corn fodder out of the hay shed. That was where we had put all the eggs. We scurried out to move them to the woodshed, hoping no one would see. The eggs were already piled high over the oats in the tubs.

We made it all right with the first tub. Then, sneaking up the side of the yard with the second one, we all but ran over that same neighbor woman who had left once without any cake.

"Eggs," she said, looking at the full washtub. "Eggs!"

"We're just taking them to the woodshed," Lee said with a bright smile. We hurried on and left her standing there saying, "Eggs, eggs . . ."

When she went into the house, Lee sent me after her to try to keep her from mentioning what she'd seen.

Mother wasn't baking this time. Unfortunately, though, she brought up the subject. "I'm sorry I can't offer you any cake. We just don't seem to be getting enough eggs lately."

The woman opened her mouth. I caught her eye and shook my head.

In a moment, Mother went into the pantry to grind coffee. I went over to the woman and whispered, "About those eggs. We'd just as soon you didn't say anything. Our mother's kind of funny about eggs right now."

All I meant was that Mother was about fed up with the egg shortage. But maybe this woman didn't have any background in hiding Easter eggs. She shook her head at me and got kind of a wild look.

When Mother came back and began making fresh coffee, the woman watched every move. I had an awful feeling that I knew what was going to happen next, but I didn't know any way to stop it. Sure enough, Mother broke an egg and stirred it into the freshly ground coffee. She put the pot on the stove and got down two of her good cups to have them ready. The woman got up and hurried out, hardly saying good-bye.

"Why, that's the second time she's acted that way," Mother said with a worried look. I almost told her, but I remembered Lee, waiting outside, and decided a few more days of Mother and the neighbor woman each thinking the other was crazy wouldn't matter.

Father was the first one to see the two heaping tubs of eggs on the porch Easter morning. He shook his head, looked again, and shouted, "Holy smoke! Look what's on the porch!"

It was the best surprise reaction we'd ever gotten.

Lyle was just coming downstairs, his shirttail still out, his shoes in his hand. He was kind of excitable early in the morning before he really woke up. When Father shouted, Lyle dropped his shoes and went running out, yelling, "What is it? What is it?"

By the time he saw what it was, it was too late. One tub was closer to the door. He may have seen only that one, because he tried to jump over it. He almost made it, but one foot hooked onto the rim and went splashing down into the eggs. He slipped and danced for a while and finally crashed, bottom down, in the other tub.

That's a rare and beautiful sound, dozens of eggs breaking all at one time. It sounded like the ice going out of the Kickapoo River, and it was better than all the movie pie-throwing scenes put together.

Lyle wiped the splashed eggs out of his eyes and tried to get up. One foot was still in the other tub. He fell down again. The time it took him to get untangled from those tubs and wipe himself off was the closest thing to absolute silence I ever heard in that house. None of the four of us stayed around to see when the silence ended.

On the theory that the youngest child never gets punished as much, my brothers decided I should go back, two hours later, to see what was happening. I found everything quiet, the mess all cleaned up. Mother was baking a cake, so I knew some of the eggs had made it. She was singing. As I watched, she began to smile. The smile grew into a chuckle and pretty soon she was laughing so hard there were tears running down her face.

It seemed like a good time to reestablish contact. I went in and told her about the neighbor woman. She started laughing all over again. "I'd better go see her," she said. "I'll bake something for her and . . ."

I shook my head.

"All right. Something without eggs," she promised.

Next I tried to reestablish contact with Lyle. I told him no one was mad about him breaking all those eggs and that Mother was even laughing about it. What he told me took about ten minutes.

Every now and then during the next few days Lyle would start through a door, then suddenly stop and kind of freeze there with one foot in the air. Mother served cereal for breakfast for several mornings. Then she got tired of that and one day plunked a plate of fried eggs down on the table.

The four of us eased back in our chairs, ready to run. Father began to chuckle. Mother put a hand up to hide her face and retreated to the kitchen. Father gave up chuckling and began to roar. Lyle's face finally thawed out. He started laughing and helped himself to a fried egg. He never would eat his eggs scrambled after that Easter.

Part Three

SUMMER

10 First Day of Summer

Summer came more gently than spring, warm day easing into warmer day, the sun climbing higher, taking the chill from the light wind forever blowing out of the northwest.

But when had summer arrived?

Father paid no attention to the day on the June sheet of the feed-store calendar that said "first day of summer." For him summer arrived when everything felt like summer. That was not until the land was heated by a succession of sunny days so that it held the warmth and kept the nights from turning chill when the sun went down.

For my three brothers and me summer began with the ending of school, a day celebrated on a Sunday with a picnic in the schoolyard and a baseball game in the cow pasture across the fence. Everyone came right after church, bringing great baskets of food to be spread out on long tables made of sawhorses and planks. One whole table was covered with nothing but bowls of baked beans, potato salad, and Jell-O. It was hard to believe the variety—Jell-Os of every flavor and color, laced with bananas, oranges, apples, pears, sometimes with whipped cream on top, softening in the sun and running over the rich Jell-O colors in little golden rivers.

On another table were great stacks of sandwiches—egg salad, salmon, ham, roast beef, meat loaf, store-bought bologna. Once someone had the nerve to bring a batch of ordinary jelly sandwiches. They sat there in the sun untouched, corners curling up, as the other sandwiches vanished. I grumbled about them to Mother and she was angry with me.

"Sometimes that's all people have to bring," she said. "Not everyone's as lucky as we are."

A third table was covered with pies, cakes, and cookies. That was a good place to be helpful. If you could get yourself stationed there to keep the flies away, your waving hands were bound to get into the cake frosting now and then.

Over the years we learned whose food was the best. We hung around the tables as women unpacked their baskets so we'd know where to head when the signal to begin came. (We hated one fussy woman who kept rearranging the bowls to get a better color combination.) Some women brought big crockery jars with sweetened lemon juice in them, and we carried buckets of cold water from the spring for the lemonade.

Then, a short prayer by someone, some jostling for position, and go! The decisions were awful. Sandwiches weren't so bad. We could take quite a few and then trade and split with each other when we sat down. But which kind of Jell-O? And did I want angel food, devil's food, yellow cake, jelly roll, spice cake, marble cake, sponge cake, or white cake? And with which kind of frosting?

And pie. Did I want raspberry, blackberry, currant, raisin, apple, peach, cherry, lemon, banana, custard, pumpkin, or mincemeat?

The problem was never the supply. There was always food left over. The problem was our limited space. We gorged until not another bite would fit, then lay groaning, paralyzed with food, feeling suspended about four feet above the grass in the luxurious knowledge that school was out.

We half listened to the talk around us—about cars, threshing plans, and the past. Once, a man was telling how he'd driven his car all the way to California the year before. And an old, old man—the one who claimed he came up from Ohio by covered wagon—snorted and said "California! By God it's come a time when there ain't no place a man can go but what somebody's been there ahead of him."

Every year there was an argument (the same argument) about the weathered gravestone on up the valley from the schoolhouse. The inscription read: "Children of J. K. and H. A. Chapman—Ada, 1859, age 8 months, Calista, 1857, age 3 months." No one could quite trace things back to figure out who the Chapmans were, or which Chapmans they were, or who those Chapmans had been related to.

Men compared progress on planting, talked about crops, argued about whether it was drier or wetter, colder or hotter than the year before. Some of the older women kept trying to remember the names of all the teachers who had been at Halls Branch over the years. It wasn't easy, because as late as 1870 there had been three months of school in winter and two months in summer, often with a different teacher for each session. The women worked at the puzzle. Where were the teachers now? What was the name of the good-looking young man with wavy hair who had taught for a year before going off to be killed in the Civil War? And did Katie Kelley teach for three years starting in 1903 or for two years starting in 1902?

One year at the time of the picnic our dog had been missing for several days. Someone said the man down the valley who had the big moonshine still in his tobacco shed had shot him. My Uncle Lou, Father's older brother, came to the picnic that year, though he lived over on West Fork. He hunted up the seven-year-old son of the man who was supposed to have shot the dog. He smiled at the boy and let him look at his pearl-handled pocketknife. Then he said, in a quiet, pleasant voice, "Did your father shoot Sam Logan's dog?"

"No," the boy said.

Uncle Lou showed him his watch and let him click the case open and shut. Then he said in that same quiet way, "What did he use, a rifle or a shotgun?"

"Shotgun," the boy said. He bit his lip and ran away.

Turned out it was somebody else's dog, though. We discovered later that ours had been shot by the man who was always setting woods fires. The dog used to come to meet us when we came home from school, and one day he came too far and got on that man's land.

When we'd had enough talk and could move again, we got the ball game going. Once, when I was catching, I made a wild throw to third and hit a pregnant woman in the stomach. She fell right over. That stopped the game for a while. She was all right, but that night I had a nightmare about her having the baby right there on third base and me trying to help, still wearing my catcher's mitt.

The bases on the ball field were paper plates. Into the creek was out, and into the woods was limited to two bases. Anyone who hit the ball into cow dirt had to clean it off.

Once a foul went crashing into the roofless old house behind the schoolhouse. It landed on a little shelf in the empty case of a grand-father's clock. While we were fighting through the nettles to get the ball, the talk started.

"Say, who lived there anyway?"

"I think it was one of Peter Mullaney's boys."

"No. No. It was long before his time."

"That's right. When I went to school that house was already long gone empty."

"I figure it was Robert Nelson."

"No, I think it was Knute Nelson, same fellow who owned that field up on the ridge where the old orchard is."

Half of the players and spectators had moved to the old house.

"Play ball!" yelled the man who was umpiring. "By God, next time anyone hits a ball in there, he's out. Otherwise we might as well quit and have a 'remember when' meeting."

The game went on, but half the crowd was still standing over by the old house. While I was waiting my turn to bat, I could hear the quiet voice of Dennis Meagher telling how his grandfather, Patrick Meagher, had come from County Cork back in 1856 and bought land where the school road came out on the ridge.

The game ended when someone hollered that there was fresh lemonade ready. We crawled back across the fence to get our share and finish up whatever pies and cakes were left. Soon the sun began to slide down over the hills, leaving that narrow valley in shadow, though it still wasn't even four o'clock. Somewhere a cow was bawling and people began to start for home to get at the chores.

⁊

Something else had to happen before summer had truly arrived. We had to go barefoot, and that had to wait until we heard the first whippoorwill. It was Mother's rule. When we challenged her to give us a reason, she just said it had been her mother's rule, too. The waiting became a yearly ritual of summer. Any time I hear a whippoorwill now I feel I should kick off my shoes.

The whippoorwill was a secretive bird. No one we knew was sure he'd ever seen one. Some even claimed it was the same bird as the nighthawk. So each year we half believed they would not come at all and we'd have to wear our stifling shoes all summer. Then, like magic, on some warm, soft night, the call would be there, mournful and mysterious, from the dark woods—whippoorwill, whippoorwill, whippoorwill—always new and strange, always a familiar part of a summer evening with the last light of the sunset glowing in the west, or the moon bringing a ghostly silver to the oat fields out along the ridge.

The sound had to be verified by Mother. We'd race to her, yelling at her to listen, making so much noise she couldn't hear herself think, let alone hear a whippoorwill. Finally we would be still and the magic sound was there—whippoorwill, whippoorwill, whippoorwill.

"Yes," she would say. "It is summer."

Then off with shoes to go racing through the wet, cool grass, feet tender to the sticks and rocks. Out into the dirt road, the dust soft as face powder and still holding the warmth of the day, the dew on our feet gathering the dust, turning them black. Or if there had been rain, we found mud and tramped up and down, letting the coolness of it come oozing up between our toes. There was a wildness in us that almost frightened us. The whippoorwill's call went on and on, and we frolicked under the bright stars with Father and Mother and Lyle watching and laughing from under the big maple tree.

But the heart of summer was work.

There was fencing, old ones to fix and new ones to build by driving the sharpened posts into the ground with an eight-pound post maul. Or by digging deep with the posthole digger, setting in the white oak post and tamping the dirt around it. Then we strung the woven wire next to the ground, the barbed wire on top, and fastened it by pounding staples into the stretched, singing wire.

Some white oak posts lasted twenty years or more. Some rotted out quicker and were replaced, so a fence became a personal, well-known thing with posts in it that spoke of many different years of work.

Almost as soon as the corn came up, cultivation began. The cultivator straddled a corn row, the gangs of small shovels going on each side of the plants, throwing up a little window of soil around the stems. We walked behind, a curved wooden handle, smooth with years, in each hand, the lines to the horses knotted around our waist. Early in the season the horses had to be trained all over again to walk slowly or the soil would cover up the new plants. It was a lonely job, just you and the horses and the corn. If you were lucky there was shade at the end of the row, close to the woods, where you could rest yourself and the horses and keep your bucket of drinking water cool.

I remember the first time I cultivated corn. First, a trip across the field with Father showing me how. I walked behind him, and it all looked simple and easy. Father turned the team around at the end of the row and told me to take over. I looped the lines around my back, grabbed the handles, and yelled, "Get up!"

The horses jerked forward. The moist earth flew out to cover the young plants. The shovels hit a rock, and the handles were torn from my hands.

"Whoa!" Father yelled.

We went back and uncovered the plants.

"Look," Father said. "It's not a race. The only way a horse knows how fast you want him to go is by how you talk to him. You yelled. That means get out and go. Now, try again. Speak soft and easy."

I tried again. The team moved slowly along the row. Father walked behind, now and then saying "gee" or "haw" to the horses. I needed more hands. The handles vibrated and jerked like something alive as the feel of the land came up through them. I didn't dare let go to pull the horses right or left with the lines. I tried Father's "gee" and "haw" and again found that how I spoke was as important as what I said. I needed more eyes, too. I had to keep looking at the row up ahead and keep looking straight down at the same time to guide the shovels close to the plants. I also needed an eye in the back of my head to see how Father was reacting.

At the end of that first row, with the cultivator close against the woven wire fence, I breathed a sigh of relief and tried to turn the horses around onto another row. The horses couldn't seem to turn. I looked at Father. He was smiling. "You're going to have to back up a little. You've got the end of the tongue stuck through the fence."

When I finally got turned around, Father laid a hand on my shoulder. "You're on your own." He walked back toward the house. I watched him go. He never looked back to see how I was doing. That was important.

After a couple of days all the mechanics of cultivating corn became almost automatic. Then I had a chance to enjoy the feel of the turned earth, moist and cool under my bare feet. I was aware of the fresh breeze, the meadowlarks and bobolinks singing, crows cawing at me from fence posts. The sweet green smell of growing corn was mixed with the pungence of sweating horses. The team moved with a steady rhythmic creaking of harness leather, the cultivator shovels making different sounds in different parts of the field, scraping through rocks, running silent, or tearing and ripping in patches where quack grass had a start.

Occasionally, in a field near the farmyard, an adventurous old hen came out and followed behind the cultivator, singing away as she waddled along, seeming to be there as much for company as for the turned up insects.

I found that the horses could tell time. When I reached the end of a row at noon or at evening quitting time, they stopped and turned their heads to look at me, asking permission to turn toward home.

11 The Big Maple Tree

In summer, the center of our hilltop world was the big maple tree in the front yard. The tree was more than three feet through, with a main trunk that went up about twelve feet before it parted into many large towering branches. I could climb to the very top of my favorite pine tree and still I had to look up to see the top of the maple. It even dwarfed the windmill.

The big maple was part of every summer day. No matter how pressing the field work, it was a rare time when we did not rest there for a while after our noon meal. We gathered again to enjoy the coolness in the evening after chores were done.

Lyle always got very close to the tree, leaning his head back against the trunk. He had a tiny bald spot on the back of his head. I was convinced that the rough bark had pulled out the hair, but skeptical Junior differed. "He doesn't sit there in the winter, does he?"

"No."

"He still has the bald spot in winter, doesn't he?"

"Yes."

For Junior, that settled it.

In the long summer days, the sky was still light when we gathered under the tree. Even after the sun went down, a bright red glow lingered on the horizon for hours. Mother brought her sewing out to the tree, using the last light, postponing the end of day. The dog was there, curled up close to someone's legs. A barn swallow flew up from the barnyard sometimes to dive-bomb one of the cats. The wise cats pretended not to notice.

The last sounds of day came to us, a dog barking somewhere, a cowbell, a horse whinnying, a robin calling "cheer-up cheer-up," the last of the bees coming home, heavy with honey, wings thrashing the quiet air.

Then the night sounds began, whippoorwills calling endlessly from the orchard, the deep and lonely hoot of an owl, nighthawks circling, diving for june bugs, catching them in mid-air with a crunch that made me shiver.

It was then, in the growing darkness, that the talk began. It was mostly adult talk—about the old days, about tomorrow's work; about politics, religion, or the future; about a marriage or birth in the community. All of it was brought down to earthly size and measured against the reality of our own lives.

The four of us boys came and went, asking questions sometimes, getting answers, going back to our games. We played Little Joe Otter under the pines, hide-and-seek, and Andy-over; pushed each other in wagons; swung in the tire that hung from the elm tree. Even with our voices raised, yelling, arguing, we kept listening to the adult talk, living in two worlds at once.

Fireflies began. Some nights the moon would pop over the horizon, bright orange, lighting up the white fog that was already forming in the valley leading up from the Kickapoo.

When I was very young, the deep howling of the timber wolves came to us from the hilltop above Lost Valley. The sound quieted the talk under the tree. Mother would stare toward Lost Valley, a far-off look on her face. We all seemed to lean forward a little as though, if we concentrated hard enough, we might understand what the wolves were trying to tell us.

The howling always made me sad. The wolves had been there forever, long before man. I felt accused of having taken their land. That's how I remember it, but I find I cannot separate how I felt when the wolves were there from how I felt afterward. One summer they were gone.

"Where did they go?"

"Farther north, maybe," Father said.

"Why?"

"Too many people around here now. Your grandfather says a timber wolf needs a hundred square miles of hunting ground."

Grandfather was Mother's father, a game warden.

I thought about the timber wolves heading a little farther north each year, trying to escape from people. How far would they have to go? One day would they be gone from even the most northern part of Wisconsin? Would they disappear, like the buffalo?

Foxes and coyotes still yapped in the night from Lost Valley. It was not the same.

Anytime George Holliday, the mailman, came while we were under the maple tree at noon, we knew something had delayed him again. Sometimes it was a distraction, sometimes an accident. A horse might run away, scattering mail along the road. A car might break down. Mr. Holliday carried a roll of heavy wire in his Model T, and said you could fix most anything with it. He raised the hood for us once and showed how the engine was held in place with a big loop of wire.

One summer day we were almost ready to go back to the fields when George pulled his car up at the mailbox in a cloud of dust and yelled, "Hey! Look what I got!"

He joined us under the tree, carrying a snake in his hands. We saw the rattles and drew back.

"It's dead," he said. "Ran over it yesterday afternoon. Notice anything?"

He held it out. We came closer. The snake was about two feet long and looked normal enough. George winked and moved his hands, letting the head end of the snake hang down.

It had two heads!

George laughed. "Now don't that beat hell? Bet you never saw one of those before."

You could get a bounty of fifty cents on a rattlesnake by taking the rattles to the town clerk. George had tried collecting the previous afternoon. He told us how the conversation had gone:

"I got a dollar's worth of rattlesnake here," George said.

"How you figure that?" the town clerk said. "You know how it works. You bring in a set of rattles and I pay you fifty cents. Your snake's just got one tail."

"But dammit, man, why do they pay bounty? Because rattlesnakes bite people, that's why. And this here snake has got two heads to bite with."

"Not arguing about that," the clerk said. "Just telling you how it works. What you got to bring is the end of a tail, not a head. You bring me a two-tailed rattler and I'll pay you two bounties."

George got mad all over again when he told us about it. "Don't that beat hell? Ain't that just like a politician? Don't even know which end of a snake bites!"

He laughed and held the snake out to me. "Don't see many two-headed snakes, do you?"

I shook my head, knowing from experience I was being set up for something.

"You know why a two-headed snake don't live very long?"

I shook my head again.

"Well, I'll tell you why. Those two heads are kind of like a couple of kids, see? They get to fighting and snapping at each other. First thing you know that fool snake has killed itself."

George was still laughing when he went back to his Model T. In the end, he decided not to take the fifty cents bounty. He put the snake—tail, two heads, and all—into a jar of alcohol. About once a year he carried it along the mail route to show to people. We could count on him being about four hours behind schedule when he did that.

That night under the maple tree Lyle told the story of a man from Steuben who practically made a living hunting rattlesnakes. One day when he had a dozen or so live ones in a burlap bag, he started worrying about putting himself out of business. So he just cut off the rattles for bounty and turned the snakes loose again. The trouble was he turned them loose right at the edge of Gays Mills. Presented with a dozen deadly poisonous snakes that couldn't even rattle to warn anybody and were kind of irritated anyway, the town lived in panic for weeks.

The man admitted doing it. "Nothing in the law says I got to kill 'em. Nothing says I can't keep my breeding stock going."

The law was changed after that. From then on you had to bring in about eight inches of snake's tail to get the bounty.

There was also bounty on hawks, owls, foxes, ground moles, and wolves. Except for the bounty on rattlers, which killed people, and on ground moles, which started ditches, we thought bounties were a crazy idea. Maybe a few people did lose chickens to hawks, owls, and foxes, but that was nothing compared to the crops they saved by keeping mice and gophers under control.

As for the bounty on wolves, I didn't even like to think about that.

Sometimes it seemed that part of the purpose of summer was to make us seem smaller and less important. The wolves did that. The stars could do that, too. I would lie on my back under the maple tree, looking at the far-off pinpricks of light that came through the leaves, and I got smaller and smaller until I was pulled off into that endless space. I traveled the stars. Then, afraid I would get lost and never find my way home again, I locked my hands in the tangled grass of the lawn and pulled myself back to earth. I would find Father quietly talking about which cornfield to cultivate tomorrow. Mother might be saying she planned to can green beans.

Sometimes a falling star arced across the sky. Once there was a very big one to the east. A sparrow sang for a moment. The roosters crowed a few times, then went back to sleep. "You could read a news-paper," people said next day.

The falling star changed the talk under the maple tree.

"They say some of those stars we can see went out ten thousand years ago."

"Then how can we see them?"

"They're so far away the light they gave off before they went out is still reaching us."

"But light travels a hundred and eighty-six thousand miles a second."

"That's how far away they are. Or were."

"You mean a hundred and eighty-six thousand miles times how many seconds there are in ten thousand years? That many miles away?"

"Yes."

I looked up at the stars. They were growing bright again as my eyes adjusted to the darkness. There was a mumbling sound near me. It was Junior, working at the mathematics of it. "One hundred and eighty-six thousand times ten thousand years, times three hundred and sixty-five days, times twenty-four hours, times sixty minutes, times sixty seconds . . ."

"What does that come to?"

Junior smiled. "It's a mighty long ways."

A falling star brought a hush to the evening. Sometimes the talk never started again. On such a night, I always slipped quietly off to bed, wanting the shelter of a ceiling above me as I lay and worked at the puzzle. Where did they come from, those falling, dying bits of stars? Where does space begin and end? When I look up at the stars, does someone look down at me? Finally there would be just one question, over and over, "Who am I? Who am I?"

Once on such a night, I remembered a line from one of my books: "When I'm all grown up, will people know that inside I'm still just me?" In my warm bed, sheet pulled up despite the heat, I became me again.

There were conflicts on any farm. They were discussed sometimes under the maple tree, especially when company was there.

Take a piece of timberland with a certain hidden glade, like a fairy ring, where it was nice to lie on the grass or leaves and look up at your own private bit of sky. When it came time to clear that timberland for crops, a man didn't want to leave little corners here and there just because a woman or the kids took a fancy to them. If you did that all the time, you'd have fields crooked as the Kickapoo River. Pretty soon you might even be in trouble for cutting thistles. After all, they have pretty flowers.

Men liked to talk about the long-range view. They could see that the first thing to put up was a new barn and hog house. Without those, how did you make any money?

The women, those who were not captives, would answer back. "How can you raise a family without a house that's dry and warm? Isn't raising a family as important as raising pigs and cows?"

The conflict on our farm was the big maple tree itself.

The tree was important to each of us in different ways, but most important to Mother. I think she saw it as a place where we lived, an extension of the house, and the house was her domain. The maple tree was the first sign of the farm you could see as you came over the top of the hill leading up from Halls Branch Valley. When we'd been away on Sunday and there had been a windstorm, she would lean forward as the Model T groaned up the last steep pitch to the ridge. Then she'd lean back, smile, and say, "It's still there."

Most of all, the tree linked us to the migrating birds and the changing seasons. The new birds came to its leafless branches when its blossoms were a fringed silhouette of red and yellow, a week or more ahead of any other flowers.

The tree was more to her than we knew. Many times a day, looking up to where its high branches caught the breeze, she began to sing.

There was something very warm and right about that, reminding us that Mother, too, had her own private world.

I'm not sure Father realized how important the tree was to Mother. If he had, I don't think he would have kept wanting to cut it down. It wasn't that Father didn't like the tree. He did, and he enjoyed the good times we had under it, but he didn't trust the tree.

"Look," he would say, pointing at the heavy limbs, "soft maple trees don't belong on the ridge in the first place. They can't take the windstorms."

"This one's been taking it for a long time."

"It dropped a limb on the roof once."

"Only a small one."

"Maybe a bigger one next time."

"Look," Father would say, counting off the points on his fingers, "first of all it's going to drop a big limb on the house some day. Second, it cuts off the southwest wind from turning the windmill. Third, it makes the house dark."

Father was right, of course. The tree did stop the wind, and he often had to crank up the stubborn gasoline engine that ran the pump-jack for the deep well. It did make the house dark, and it had dropped a limb on the roof, just missing the chimney. The trouble was that all Father's arguments were based on logic. The rest of us just didn't want him to saw down something that was part of our everyday life.

The conflict had been going on as long as I could remember, the tree getting a little bigger each year. Even on a peaceful summer day, it might creak a little in the breeze. Father would look up to the spreading limbs.

"Where would you put the bird feeder in the winter?" Mother asked once when he did that. She hadn't even raised her eyes from her mending.

Father looked at her, totally surprised. "Bird feeder," he said. "I'll . . . I'll put it on a post."

"Where will you sit at noon on a hot day?"

"Under the pine trees."

"What about in the evening?"

"Well, we don't need a shade tree after the sun's gone down."

"It wouldn't be the same."

"No," he admitted. "It wouldn't be the same."

The conflict might have gone on like that forever if it hadn't been for summer storms that swept the ridge. When they came in the night, we would hear Father walking from room to room, closing windows against the driving rain. We listened, knowing he was worrying about oats being knocked down, windrowed hay getting wet, ditches being washed in the cornfields, tobacco getting holes knocked in the leaves. His footsteps would pause. We knew he was standing at a dining-room window looking up to where the top of the maple was swaying against the lightning-lit sky. During a storm, all his worries narrowed down to the one thing he could do something about.

Finally it happened. There was a storm. A limb split loose from the trunk. There was a crash. The house shook. Again, the limb had missed the chimney, but for Father the fallen limb was proof that the tree should go.

After breakfast, out came the crosscut saw. He sharpened it carefully, decided which direction the tree should fall, and called Lyle and Junior. He held out the saw. They hesitated. "I'm going to keep a roof over our heads whether anyone else wants one or not." His voice was ominously quiet.

Mother stood on the porch, face set, arms folded. She said nothing. It had all been gone over a thousand times. She wasn't the kind to say something like "if you do that, I'll never forgive you."

Lyle and Junior took the saw. I climbed up into my pine tree to watch. Junior saw me. He said to come down. "The tree might fall that way." His voice was flat, and he sounded like an adult.

"You mean you can't cut the tree while I'm up here."

There was a ghost of a smile. "That's right."

"Get down from there," Father said.

I got down.

Lyle and Junior knelt beside the tree to start the first cut, about eighteen inches above the ground. They swung the saw back and forth several times, just rattling the teeth against the bark to get their arms working together. The saw began to bite. The bark made red sawdust. White sawdust appeared, the sap making it ball on the teeth of the saw.

Father stood over them. Mother was still on the porch. I couldn't understand her silence.

The saw cut deeper into the trunk. It had eaten in about five inches when Lyle and Junior looked at each other and came to some agreement.

"Time for a rest," Junior said.

Father moved closer. "What's the matter?"

"We're tired," Junior said. His voice was polite but very firm.

Lyle looked around and met Mother's eyes. For just a minute his crooked grin was on his face. "As a matter of fact," he said, "we're damn tired. It just might be about fifty years before I'm rested up enough to try that again."

Mother smiled.

Father looked from Lyle to Junior to the tree. We waited, knowing how much he counted on being obeyed. For the first time he looked at Mother. She tried to hide her smile. She didn't quite make it.

"Look," Father said, "that damned tree ... I don't ... "

"I know," she said.

Father took a deep breath, and slowly let it out again. He took the saw out of Lyle's hands. We still weren't sure. One man could handle a good crosscut saw if he had to.

Tooth by tooth, Father brushed the white sawdust from the saw. He walked to the milkhouse and hung it up in its usual place. He brought a can of tar back and handed it to Junior.

"Good idea," Lyle said. He and Junior filled the saw cut with tar. The tree oozed sap for a couple of days. By the next spring, the wound was all healed up.

Only once after that do I remember any mention of the tree. The morning after a bad storm, Lyle looked into the yard and found no limbs on the ground. He forgot himself. "Hell, that tree's going to outlive us all."

"Maybe because it knows how we feel," Mother said, smiling.

Father looked at her for a long moment. He smiled. "Could be that. Could be I scared it a little, too."

12 A Place for Dreams

The four of us boys played together a great deal in the long summer days, yet we each had little worlds that were private and personal. We seemed to need secret places where dreams could grow. Dreams are fragile. A question, a frown, even a look can bring them crashing down before they have a chance to fly and roam and come back to reality in their own time.

One special place for me was a part of Denny Meagher's woods just to the west of our land. It became special and was almost destroyed for me on the same summer night.

I had started the cows out the road to the night pasture, running past them to open the wooden gate and head them in, then running back to drive those that were stopped, breaking their fool necks reaching over the fence for the grass they could have had anyway by going through the gate.

I swung the gate closed and sat on the top of it, thinking about the perversity of cows and watching darkness settle over the land. The air was warm and still. The last of the sunset hung close to the horizon, glowing red in the dust that was still settling back onto the road. In the meadow back toward the house a horned lark was singing.

There was another sound. It was an elusive whirring coming from Meagher's woods a hundred yards away. I walked slowly toward it, feet cushioned in the soft dust. I came up to the line fence. The sound was louder. The trees were filled with moving shadows. Suddenly I realized the place was alive with birds, hundreds of them, whirling, darting, singing, wings flashing in the last of the sunset.

They were redstarts, a bird all wings and motion. I had never seen more than one or two at a time. I didn't understand what was happening. It was like some fairy tale, with the birds trying to lift a piece of that land and carry it away. Hundreds of them would flutter down into a tree and come to rest. Hundreds of others would whirl up from the same tree. Then they would rise from all the trees at once until everything was moving again.

The sky darkened. The cool air was set in motion by the beating of wings. Slowly, more and more birds came to rest in the trees and did not rise again. Finally the woods were dark and back to the normal cricket and june bug sounds. Far off, a hoot owl was calling, a dog was barking, and there was the clanging of a cowbell. Someone walking past the dark woods would not know what was there or what had happened.

Feeling I'd been the only witness to some magical celebration, I ran back through the dew-damped dust to the house. Father, Mother, and Lyle were in the yard under the maple. I didn't know how to do it, but I had to tell them. I tried, using words I can't remember.

They listened carefully.

Father frowned. "What kind of birds?"

"Redstarts."

"They're beautiful," Mother said.

Father thought about it. "Trees in there are mostly white oak. Could mean the caterpillars are starting to come out."

Lyle banged his pipe against the tree. "You been out there all this time watching a bunch of birds?"

I felt the magic sliding away inside me. I wanted to make them stop it and bring the birds back.

I looked at Mother. It was all right. She was staring into the night, smiling, nodding a little. I knew I had put a picture in her head. Now we could both see it—trees blossoming with whirling red-and-gray flowers. The magic came back and I went off to bed.

Next morning, before anyone else was up, I raced out to the woods. The trees were quiet. The birds were gone.

Each year after that, in early summer, I checked the woods night after night. The birds never came again, or if they did, I missed them. It didn't matter. I had the picture inside me. Those slowly growing white oaks were never ordinary trees again.

13 Haying

Sometimes in summer when we felt dwarfed and stretched too thin by the immense diversity of the land, we might say, "Sure must be nice to raise just one crop. Like they do wheat, out West."

Whoever said it would find himself speared by Father's eyes. "And just how would we live if one summer the wheat failed? Even if it didn't, how happy would we be, working year after year with just one crop? Sounds like reading the same book over and over."

The hay was a taste of what one-crop farming might be like. The corn cultivating went on, the grain got cut and shocked, but the never-ending haying dominated the summer.

It began with the clicking, clattering of the horse-drawn mower, its five-foot sickle felling the bright red clover or the alfalfa with its dusty blue flowers. The ominous clatter of the mower shattered the peace of the birds and animals who lived in the hayfield. Bobolinks flew over the mower, scolding. Meadowlarks ran crookedly across the fallen hay, dragging one wing, pretending to be crippled, trying to entice the mechanical monster to follow them away from their nests, as they would try to fool the fox or house cat that hunted in the fields.

Once I remember watching the mower and seeing a line of black and white heading toward the fence row. It was a mother skunk, moving slowly, tail up, head high like some grand court lady. Behind her in a line were four young skunks, each a perfect imitation of the mother.

Almost always the noise and the tramping feet of the horses flushed everything out of the way. For every round of the mower hundreds of tiny migrations began—grasshoppers clattering off; butterflies floating up from the blossoms; mice running in circles; baby rabbits heading for the woods and turning somersaults in the fallen hay; gophers darting, then going flat and motionless when the call of the red-tailed hawk came or its shadow flitted across them. The hawks wheeled and waited, red tail feathers fanned out against the blue, then dropped like dive bombers to rise again with their prey dangling from sharp talons.

The bull snakes, usually eager to swallow whole the baby rabbits and mice, fled with the others, harmless in the shared danger of mower and hawk.

Perhaps once or twice a season, a quail or pheasant ran the wrong way, straight into the flashing blades of the sickle. The bright red of their blood spread over the bright green of the hay and the pleasure went out of the sunny day.

Once I carried a young quail to Mother, one of its legs gone. I was crying. "I couldn't find the mother. What do they think happened? Is it like the end of the world?"

She took the struggling quail and cupped it in her hands, and it was still. "We live here, too," she said very gently.

"How would you like it if a great big mower came right through the house?" I was yelling. "Right straight through! And big hawks outside waiting to get you if you ran?"

"The hawks are always there," she said.

That was true. They wheeled and dived in the blue of any summer day. I thought of the clattering mower. "Are we hawks, too?"

Mother looked at me for a long time. "Yes, I suppose to them we are hawks."

The quail stirred, blinking its eyes. Mother rocked it and the eyes closed. "I know how you feel," she said.

I didn't know if she was talking to me or the quail.

"If we got too sentimental we'd never raise a crop," she said. "Growing and dying, they're both part of life. We cut the hay, too, you know."

"Hay grows another crop. We don't kill the hay."

"The birds and rabbits grow another crop, too."

"It's not the same."

She tried again. "We kill chickens to eat them."

I didn't like to think about that. The squawking chicken, legs and wings held tight in the left hand, the head on the chopping block, the ax in the right hand. Then, chop! Without a head the chicken ran and flopped, blood squirting. Each time I swore I'd never eat chicken again. The vow never lasted. When the aroma of cooking chicken filled the house, it was somehow a different chicken.

"We raise chickens to kill them," I said. "It's not the same."

She looked at the tiny quail. "No, it's not the same."

After just a few rounds of the mower, the air was filled with the sweet, clean smell of hay drying in the hot sun. Before the leaves dried so much that they shattered and fell from the stems, the hay was raked into long, fluffy windrows and left for the stems to dry.

It had begun—the hot, dusty, complicated, and seemingly endless job we called haying. Morning after morning we woke to the knowledge that it was another haying day. Mow more fields so the fallen hay could dry and be waiting. Rake it into windrows. Twist the stems to see if enough moisture had gone out of them. Hitch up the horses to the wagon with its wide hayrack. Hook the hay loader behind the wagon and start slowly along the windrow, the loader lifting the hay in an endless ribbon and someone on the wagon spreading the hay. With the soft hay piled high, unhook the loader and head for the barn, riding cradled in the sweet-smelling green, wagon wheels crunching on the hard, dry ground. Pull the load of hay to the end of the barn, under the great opened door of the haymow. Pull the big, two-tined hayfork down from the mow on its pulley and double rope. Thrust the fork deep into the load of hay, pull the levers that lock it in place, then yell, "All right!"

At the other end of the barn, someone would move forward with the hayfork horse, pulling the heavy rope that dragged deep in the dust, hauling the great forkful of hay up from the wagon and in through the mow door, to slide along the steel track, to be tripped and fall. Then we'd yell "Whoa!" to the hayfork horse, or the fork would go right on out through the end of the barn.

In the hot haymow, whoever was "mowing away" had to pull and tear at the hay, spreading it in layers and tramping it down. Whoever was on the wagon would pull the fork back, set it, and it would all happen again. And again. And again.

When the hayrack was empty, there was time for a quick drink of cold water at the well, then back to the field for another load, trotting the rested horses, the moving air cold against sweat-wetted shirts despite the ninety-degree heat.

Each day was filled with agonizing decisions. Did we have enough hay cut to keep us busy? Had it cured enough so that it wouldn't mold in the mow, ruining it for feed and maybe setting the barn on fire? Were we behind, the windrows getting so dry the hay would shatter, leaving us with nothing but stems? Was a rainstorm coming? Would it be better to put the hay in a little damp and let it mold some, rather than letting the rain get it? There was nothing sadder than good, bright-green alfalfa slowly turning an ugly brown after a rain.

The decisions went beyond the hay. When did we break up our five- or six-man haying crew, which could keep two wagons going, so the corn could be cultivated? When were the oats ready for cutting? Could we afford to take a Sunday off?

There was no perfect way to farm. A field of alfalfa, beautifully blue in the hot sun and alive with bumblebees and honeybees, was not beautiful to Father. The full bloom of the flowers meant we were behind—the hay already past its prime, going more to fiber, losing its protein every day it was left to grow.

Every year during haying we got one of those stretches of heat when the thermometer went to a hundred in the shade day after day. Such days were like something out of another world. Heat waves danced up from the land; the green of the crops turned pale and dusty, reflecting the cruel sun back at us. The deep blue of the sky was gone, replaced by a hazy, almost white glare so that we worked with eyes squinted half closed. Everything was distorted, shimmering, washed out. To look at one another across a stretch of hayfield was to see a pale green ghost of a person.

At noon the house was dark and cool. All the green shades were drawn and a little breeze crept through, carrying the smell of dust. Our eyes adjusted. We began to look like flesh-and-blood people again. The hot food went into us. We ate without talk, like survivors who had stumbled in from the desert. Then we walked, half dazed, out into the yard. Under the shade of the big maple tree, halfway between the cruel sun and the dark house, we sank down and slept.

I used to think ahead to those after-meal naps and daydream of a time when we'd sleep on through the hot afternoon, waking only when the sun went down and coolness came back. That never happened. Some internal clock went off in Father's head when our hour of meal and rest was over. His voice came through the layers of sleep.

"All right, boys. Let us get a-going."

I'd start the long climb back into the day, aware first of grass under me making little whip marks on my bare arms. I'd feel the warmth on my face, the sweat between my skin and clothes. Then sounds would reach me—the dry vibrating scream of the dog-day cicadas, birds calling, a little rustle of wind in the trees. That rustle would slowly separate into the different songs of wind moving through pine needles, maple leaves, drying elm leaves, each song unique.

Finally I opened my eyes to the sun filtering through the leaves from directly overhead. Our day was only half over. The hay and the heat were out there waiting for us.

We would get to our feet, Lyle always limping a little from the time he'd been kicked by a horse. Like silent sleep walkers we moved back into the sun.

To think about such a day was to become a despairing observer. Step by step we moved in a non-thinking ritual of work. Load the endless ribbon of hay onto the wagon. Unload the wagon, forkful by forkful. Load the endless ribbon of hay onto the wagon.

Muscles automatically obeying the habit of the years, we worked on into the pale afternoon, storing the sun and green of summer for the long winter.

We stored something else. A time like that comes back now sharp and real with all its smells of dust, horse sweat, man sweat, Lyle's oozing pipe. There is the dry whirring of grasshoppers, steel wagon wheels ringing on the hard ground, the creak of the hay rope. There is the tepid smell of water as we drink from a bucket that has a taste of leftover lemonade. Above all is the sweet smell of curing hay.

Such days were agony, but there was a glory in them. It was as though, in proving ourselves equal to the harsh demands of the land, we glimpsed some hint of immortality.

In the eternity of hot days almost anything different was a relief. Like a hissing bull snake tossed into the hayrack by the hay loader, coiling and striking harmlessly, bringing a shout of laughter after that first tense moment when you made sure it wasn't a rattler. Like the hayrack toppling over on a steep hillside, spilling the hay, the rider jumping off, with a wild yell, just in time.

Even a bad storm was half welcome. The clouds built up in the northwest, the heat getting worse, the sweat no longer evaporating in the muggy air. We worked on, stealing glances at the sky, the clouds gathering, turning black, suddenly looming high and dark and threatening. White wind clouds boiled in front of the darkness. The sunshine was gone, the songbirds vanished, and a threatening silence came. The creaking of the harness was loud, the smell of sweat strong. We would go on piling hay high on the wagons, then race for home, the high load seeming to reach halfway up to the boiling clouds. Sometimes the sky came alive with nighthawks. Brought out of their daytime hiding places by the strange, midday darkness, they wheeled and dropped, catching insects as they flew before the storm.

The horses ran with manes and tails streaming, loose hay falling from the rack. We would race into the barnyard, open the great double doors of the tobacco shed, and squeeze the load in, the hay dragging against the top of the doorway. There was a tremendous satisfaction when we just barely beat the storm. We stood with the sweating, hard-breathing horses in the dark, the wind suddenly slamming against the creaking shed, rain pounding on the roof and sides, the cracks in the west wall turning wet as the rain came through.

When the storm was over, the newly mown hay dried and was ready to be put in. The uncut fields were waiting and the harvested fields were already putting up a bright new carpet of green for the next crop of hay.

On the farm nothing ever ended. Nothing was ever completed.

14 Tractors

One summer when I was about nine I fell in love with tractors. It began with a Sunday visit of the whole family to friends who lived in a little valley branching off from the Kickapoo River. There was a boy my age named Don and an older boy named George. They also had two sisters and I didn't, so I was interested in sisters. But they told me sisters were a pain, and I took their word for it.

I envied Don and George even before they got a tractor. A little creek ran practically through their barnyard, the riffles filling the place with the sound of water and the feel of a long lazy summer day. There were suckers and chubs in the pools, waiting to be caught, and slippery mud puppies in the banks, looking like foot-long dinosaurs.

And on the steep hillside above the stream was a giant prostrate juniper that made a great ground-hugging circle of dark green. I had never seen a tree before that grew out along the ground instead of up toward the sky. It had decided to be different, and was a fairy ring that invited me to race around it in the short grass of the hillside until I dropped to the warm ground, panting and dizzy, breathing in the rich pungence of the juniper, feeling the hot sun beating down on me.

Those people had those two things, and they had a tractor. On this particular day we walked, Don and George and I, up the narrow valley along the singing creek to find the tractor. Grasshoppers flew up ahead of us, some of them landing in the water. We stopped to look down at a grasshopper thrashing in the middle of a quiet pool, sending out little waves in a perfect series of rings that vanished at the edge.

We argued awhile about whether the rings would ever end. If the pool were big enough, would they go on forever, maybe even after the three of us were dead? If the whole world were water, would the grasshopper waves go clear around it and meet on the other side? And where would that be? In the China Sea, maybe?

Then we argued about the grasshopper's swimming ability. For me to float and thrash my arms at the same time was a newly discovered and death-defying accomplishment. "He's swimming," I said.

"He's trying to swim," said Don.

We waited for George's opinion. He frowned down at the struggling grasshopper. "He's floating because he can't sink even if he wants to. He's trying to walk, like he was still up here in the field."

All at once the grasshopper wasn't doing any of those things. There was a little swirl, a sucking, crunching sound, and the grasshopper was gone. A bigger series of waves spread to the edge of the pool.

"He can too sink," said Don.

George got a patient, older-brother look. "He didn't sink. He was sunk. One of three things happened. A turtle got him, a trout got him, or a chub got him."

"Sometimes you sound just like a goddamned sister," Don said.

"You're not supposed to say goddamn," George said.

"You just said it."

"That was only to tell you not to say it."

"Just the same you said it. And if you tell that I said it, I can tell that you said it, too. Anyways, what about a frog?"

"I don't think frogs eat grasshoppers," George said.

During all this we chased down another grasshopper and threw him in the water. He drifted slowly downstream. Nothing happened.

"Let's go see the tractor," I said.

It was a Fordson with cleated steel wheels, a steering wheel of wood and iron, and a crank hanging down in front, the same as a Model T. It smelled of new paint, grease, and gasoline, and it crouched there in the hayfield, ready to spring into life. I walked around and around that tractor, seeing the heat waves dance up from the broad hood, moving in to touch it sometimes, then moving back and walking around again.

"How do you start it?" I asked.

"We can't do that," Don said.

For some reason we were both whispering.

George was looking back down the creek. A bend in the valley hid us from the farm buildings. George turned around and looked at Don. "Look, when Papa was using it up here yesterday, could you hear it? At the house?"

Don swallowed. "I don't think so."

George smiled. "Tell you what, little brother, if you won't tell I started it, I won't tell you said goddamn. O.K.?"

"O.K.," Don said. "I won't even tell you said goddamn twice."

George fiddled a minute with levers and knobs. Then he went around front and started cranking. The engine wheezed and coughed a couple times, smoke came out of the exhaust pipe, and then it started and settled into a steady roar. George climbed up to the seat, throttled it down, got it into gear, and ran it forward and back a couple of times. Then he stopped and waved me toward him. "Want to steer it?" he yelled.

I didn't know if I wanted to or not, but he reached down and helped me up to the seat. He got it going and stood behind me while I steered that vibrating monster in a slow circle.

George shut it off. I was holding on to the wheel so hard I couldn't let go. Slowly the sound of the creek and the flying bees came back. I finally climbed down to the ground. A bell was ringing.

"That's dinner," Don said.

We raced through the sweet-smelling hay, sending the grasshoppers, bumblebees, and honeybees sailing off in all directions.

That afternoon, driving back up to the ridge, I started talking about the tractor.

"You boys didn't start it up, did you?" Mother asked.

While I was trying to think my way out of that, Father saved me. He looked at Mother and said, "If you want a boy to make a habit of speaking the truth, there's some things you don't ask."

I wanted to reach across the seat of the Model T and hug Father, but then I thought about how that might say we had started the tractor. The moment of warmth passed.

Mother sighed. I knew exactly what she was thinking. Any time a bunch of women got together they talked about tractors as if they were some kind of monsters that roamed the country eating people. Those women had all the news for a hundred miles around about tip-overs, broken arms from cranking, fingers cut off in gears, and some poor man over in Iowa so chopped up and scattered it wasn't even worthwhile to buy a coffin. Some of it was true, of course. There was no arguing with the fact that one of our neighbors got confused and sat up there on the tractor seat pulling back on the wheel, yelling "Whoa," and drove right out through the end of the machine shed.

I read about tractors in the farm magazines that summer and talked about them until everybody was disgusted with me. The trouble was nobody else got excited about them except maybe Mother and Lyle, and they were on the other side. Lee liked the idea of getting the work done faster. Junior would have liked another engine to tinker with. Laurance dismissed the whole idea with such older-brother phrases as "Just not a practical possibility."

Just mention the word tractor to Mother and she could see one tipping over, wiping out a whole family. Father listened to the talk and smiled, saying very little.

Lyle was the anti-tractor spokesman. I would bring up the subject and then it would go something like this:

"We don't raise gasoline. We raise hay. Ever try feeding hay to a tractor?"

"But a tractor doesn't eat hay when it isn't working."

"Doesn't make any manure either."

"But a tractor would save a lot of time."

"Sure, and what happens when you need a new one? We going to take the old one next door and breed it to a neighbor's tractor and wait for it to have a little tractor?"

It was no use. Lyle always got the last word.

Late that summer I was with Father when he stopped to talk to an old man named Abe who had a little farm out near the end of the ridge. Abe was standing at the edge of a hayfield watching a red tractor and a two-bottom plow roar across the field.

"Never thought I'd see a tractor on your land," Father said.

"Had to get one. My boy wouldn't stay with me otherwise. He's the last one I got. Dammit, Sam, a man gets old."

Abe picked up a clod of dirt and slowly crumbled it between his fingers. "I broke this land. This was the first field. I cut off the timber, grubbed out the brush. I put an old breaking plow behind three of the best horses that ever lived. I followed that plow around this field, dodging stumps, turning up rocks bigger than a man could lift. And goddammit, Sam, last year a man from the government was out here telling me I shouldn't be farming this hillside."

"You mean the county agent?" Father asked.

"Hell, I don't know. Could've been. It was one of those government men from somewhere. I told him it was the closest thing to a level field I got. Hell, he might as well tell me I should never made a living all these years."

The tractor roared by us in a cloud of smoke and dust, throwing up two fourteen-inch furrows of sod. Abe's son—I guess he must have been about twenty-five—waved down to us. He had a smile going that just about took up his whole face.

"He's got a glory all right," Abe said. "I had one, too. Mine was making this farm out of nothing. But that contraption—that's his glory."

"Well, things change," Father said in that way he had sometimes of just saying enough to keep somebody else talking.

Abe nodded. "Things change all right. That don't mean I have to like it. Seems to me a tractor gets a man up in the air too high. I figure I got to be down on the ground where I can get dirt on my hands and get the smell of it. I got to walk and get the feel of it under me. Then I can say when it's too wet or too dry. I can say what it needs. You can't tell me that boy of mine's going to know all that going across a field hell bent for election way up there on a tractor."

We left him there with a handful of earth running through his fingers, his eyes locked on the red tractor.

We got in the car. I was very quiet. Father looked at me. "What's the matter?"

It isn't easy when you're nine—or any age—to say you've thought of a man as being old and foolish and have suddenly found out he's not only not foolish but almost a poet of some kind.

"I didn't know he felt like that," I said.

Father nodded. "Still think we should have a tractor?"

I could feel the steering wheel of that Fordson jerking against my hands. I could smell the gasoline and hot oil smells and hear the roar of power I had commanded from way up on that swaying seat. I still wanted a tractor. But it wasn't the same.

"Not as much," I said. Father smiled.

15 The Fertile Land

The land was almost cruelly prolific in summer, crops bursting from the soil, buds bursting from the stems, flowers bursting from the buds. Oats ripening, hay ripening, corn ripening. In a series of long, hot summer days we sometimes began to feel like slaves, bound to the earth, captured by a process of growth and fertility that we had set into motion by our planting and could not control. The crops decided how long our day would be, whether we would work on Sunday or not. We could go to bed at night with the warm satisfaction that all the windrowed hay was in the barn. Then wake into the blazing sun of a new day, the heat already a solid promise at six in the morning, knowing that more hay was inexorably ripening, always just a little ahead of us.

Some farmers could not learn to live with this tyranny of the crops. As the years went by, men like old Frank Kelly went faster and faster, bent lower and lower as though the land reached up to pull him under while he was still alive. No time for talk when he went to town. "Hurry, hurry, blacksmith, there's work to do. There's weeds in the corn. The oats are turning. Fence posts rotting in the hog pasture. I need another wife or two damn good hired men."

Once the pattern was set for men like Kelly they could not seem to stop. Winter was like summer, running, running. Feed the cattle, slop the hogs, fix the machinery, cut logs for bigger buildings. "Hurry with the food, woman, there's work to do. Come on, kids, that's enough talk. Hell, you can talk when you're dead."

On such a farm, life became a Greek tragedy—a man and his wife locked into mortal combat with the land, headed for inevitable destruction. "Victims of the land. Victims of the hard life of farming," people said. I don't think they were victims of the land at all. They were victims of their own folly. They could not accept and surrender to the superiority of the land. They had to keep trying to beat it, keep ahead of it, become its master. They tried. They sacrificed themselves, their sweat staining the land like blood. They died. Their bent bodies were forced straight in coffins and the immortal land went on.

This race with the land was sometimes conversation under the big maple tree on a summer night. Father would be talking about tomorrow, trying to plan our work, and running headlong into the truth that he could not organize the land. He could decide what crops to plant in which fields, but the land was alive, a being that made its own decisions, based on rain and temperature and sunlight and all the other factors of growth that were hidden under our feet. The hay didn't wait until the corn was neatly cultivated. The oats ripened for cutting when the hay needed our attention. The thistles bloomed and went to seed whether we were ready for them or not.

Father would talk about it, frustrated, but accepting it, too.

Once Lyle, leaning back against the maple, banged his pipe against a root. "Well, you know what they say—'a farmer works from sun to sun and a woman's work is never done.'"

Mother straightened suddenly, eyes big and startling in the dusk. "I don't like that. It makes it all sound so inevitable. Like we're puppets who can make no choices of our own."

Lyle sucked busily on his empty, split-logged pipe.

Father stared, his head tilted way back.

Mother reached out toward him, as though to touch him across the six or seven feet that separated them. "I mean, why didn't a man like Frank Kelly ever ask himself if he was planting more than he could handle? Why does owning twenty cows this year mean thirty cows next year? Is there some law saying everything has to get bigger? Break more land. Plant more crops. Get bigger machinery. Bear more sons. Work longer days. Forget Sunday is a day of rest . . ."

There was a strange silence under the maple tree. The cry of the whippoorwills seemed suddenly louder.

Father moved closer to Mother and found her hand there in the safe near-darkness. "I don't mean you," she said. "I don't think you could ever sacrifice yourself and us that way."

Father nodded. "I remember once in the Old Country. There was a captain of a little ship. A good captain. He was offered a bigger ship. He turned it down. He said he liked that little windjammer. He said they understood each other. Everybody said he was crazy not to want to be captain of a bigger ship and make more money. I was just a kid at the time. I thought he was crazy, too."

Again, silence under the tree, the darkness filled with the pinpoint flashes of fireflies.

"Things are different for a man," Father said. "We have to look for something, try to be important. And anyway, the prices of what we buy keep going up. We have to raise more each year just to stay even."

Mother sighed. "That's what I mean. Why is it like that? Are prices going to keep going up forever? Is it because all over the world men are trying to be bigger and bigger?"

"Maybe. A man feels more important when he farms three hundred acres than when he farms two hundred acres.

"Isn't he the same man?"

"I don't know. A man is what he does. I could never be a Frank Kelly, but I have to admit there's something about an unplowed field, an unthreshed oat stack, or hay lying in the windrow that starts me thinking. If we just worked a little faster, got up a little earlier, quit a little later, why maybe we could catch up and . . ."

Mother laughed. "And break up a little more land and next year plant more crops."

"All right. I was thinking that."

"A person finds importance in other people." Mother said it like a teacher, and Father laughed. "For a man," he said, "that's not enough."

"And I will never understand why."

"And I can't tell you why."

Lyle put his pipe in his pocket and went into the house and up the narrow stairs to bed. The whippoorwill and the other night sounds took the place of the voices under the maple tree.

16 Rainy Days and the Sea

There was a certain magic in waking on a summer night and hearing a storm begin. The wind came first, scraping bushes against the side of the house, sweeping the treetops across a lightning-lighted sky. Then the rain came, rattling against hastily closed windows. I would stretch luxuriously under the covers, knowing tomorrow would be a different kind of day, the ground too wet for haying or cultivating corn. Even when the oats might be knocked flat or the windrowed hay hurt by the rain, there was no regret. Rain was one of the things beyond our ability to control. We accepted it when and as it came, as happy to have it as was the land, which drank it in to surround the millions of roots it cradled.

The next morning, we waited at breakfast for Father's decision on how the day would be used. We knew the possibilities—working on machinery, cleaning out or repairing buildings, fixing fences, hauling in wood to the woodshed, cutting thistles.

Those were the unexciting things, though even they were a welcome change. There were two other possibilities. Father and Lyle might work and the four of us get a day off to do anything we wanted. Or, best of all, we might all go fishing.

Sometimes we tried to influence the decision, saying things like, "Somebody was saying the bluegills are really biting down at Cold Springs." Or, "Been a long time since we had a day off."

Now and then Father would give in, but never if the thistles needed cutting. If Father hated anything in the world, it was that stubborn perennial weed we called the Canadian thistle. Devilishly

prickly and bearing a deceivingly beautiful pink flower, the thistles
spread in a field, crowding out anything else that grew there. To Father
they were an enemy. The four of us and Lyle were the army he marched
against them. It was an all-summer fight. When the thistles were
young, we hoed them out of the corn and cut them in the pastures
and grain fields with corn knives and scythes. If they escaped us and
went to seed, we picked the heads before the wind scattered them on
their umbrellas of fluff. We went all through our early years with
pockets full of prickly thistle heads. Even in a game, we'd come to a
sliding halt in the middle of a field and snatch a ripened head. The
neighbor children thought we were crazy. But when we emptied our
pockets into the kitchen stove, Father's smile and nod of approval
made it worth the trouble.

Once, after a rainy night, Father let us know how the day would
be spent by getting out the corn knives and sharpening them on the
grindstone.

At the breakfast table, Lyle looked at him a couple of times
and then said, "I guess them being from Canada don't make any
difference?"

Father looked at him suspiciously.

"I mean," Lyle said, "I wondered if you might feel different about
them if you stopped to think you have something in common with
them?"

Father was listening all right but he still didn't say anything.

"I mean," Lyle said, stirring his coffee very carefully, "since both
you and the thistles are kind of immigrants . . ."

Father had his "I dare you to say one more word" look.

Lyle drained the hot cup of coffee in one swallow. He pushed
back his chair. "You know, I was just thinking. Being it's too wet for
anything else, maybe we better go cut some of those damned Canada
thistles."

If, after Father had felt the soil and twisted the hay for moisture, the decision was for fishing, the day suddenly had an exciting new tempo. He would get the long bamboo poles from the machine shed and tie them onto the car, arching them over the top from the radiator ornament to the back bumper. The rest of us ran for manure forks and buckets and started digging angleworms in the moist soil at the edge of the barnyard. Mother fixed us a lunch, happy with the idea of staying home alone on a day when she could read or do whatever she pleased.

Then we headed for the Mississippi, nine miles away. It was a different world in the broad river valley. The high bluffs towered above us on the Wisconsin side. Far across, in Iowa, were green, rolling hills. There was a strange quietness, no wind in the trees, the vast river moving slowly, silently. Even the trains, which roared into the quiet and then roared out again, didn't seem to change the silence. The sun boiled down, bringing new moisture up from the wet ground, turning the day hot and steamy. Even the people from along the river seemed different, quiet and lazy, moving slowly as if time didn't exist. Father used to say it took twice as long to get the car filled with gas in Lynxville as it did up on the ridge at Seneca.

On fishing days, we became part of the lazy, timeless feel of the valley. If the fish were biting, that was fine. If they weren't, that was fine, too. We sat in unpainted, flat-bottomed rowboats, rocking gently, watching our corks floating on the smooth, dark water. Often enough so that we could call it fishing, a cork would start to dance, then disappear, and we pulled a flopping sunfish or bluegill into the boat.

We ate our sandwiches, drank our sun-warmed water, and forgot there was such a thing as a cornfield or hay to be put up. Trains crashed through. Hawks circled high up next to the bluffs, sometimes diving at something on the hillsides.

There was one tall pillar of rock, sticking out from a high bluff, that we called "Lovers' Leap." A legend said that an Indian girl had jumped from there because her father, a chief, would not let her marry an ordinary brave. The legend seemed to change with the years. Last time I heard it, someone had given it a Romeo and Juliet ending.

We fished in the main river and in the little lakes, called sloughs. Before the dam was built at Lynxville and the timber was cleared, there were hundreds of tree-covered islands with channels between them. Going out among the islands was like exploring an undiscovered world. The rowboat nosed silently through the dark water, great elms and willow and maple trees towering over us, birds singing far above in the sun. Father liked to row in the narrow channels, sending the boat skimming through the water with his long sweeping pulls, the oars carefully feathered on the backstroke as though still cutting through the waves on the sea.

Sometimes when the sun was directly overhead, the fish quit biting. Then we'd pull the boat ashore and lie on our backs on an island and take a nap or watch the white clouds drifting by. "Those are this morning's fog," Father would say.

In mid-afternoon the fish usually started to bite again. By the time the sun was low over the water we'd have enough to make a good meal or two. As we headed home to clean our fish, everyone was very quiet, as though we had caught the river-valley laziness. We would do the evening chores, then eat our fish along with potatoes boiled in their skins.

For me those days after a rain were linked with a search for the sea. Because of Father's past, the sea I had never seen was part of my life, even there in the landlocked Midwest.

My search was a lonely one. On a rare day when there was no work I packed some food and went to the upper end of Halls Branch Valley. There the creek was just a spring flowing out of the hillside, and I followed the cold, crystal-clear water downstream. It swelled in size, picking up color as it ran over steep riffles and oxbowed lazily through meadows. In most places there were willows along the edge and grass and weeds hanging into the water. There, I could see fish. In meadows where the pools had no shading trees, the water was warm and seemed lifeless. There were places where the creek had been straightened and was nothing more than a rocky ditch with only a shallow run of water, no fish and no weeds or willows. Yet give that straightened area a few years and I would see it change. Pools began to form, willows caught hold along the banks, and finally it was a living stream again with fish, frogs, turtles, crayfish, and the tracks of raccoons who came to hunt and to wet their food.

The creek grew broad and slow as I followed it down the winding valley. Different farmers used it differently. Some fenced it off from the cattle so the young willows and weeds could grow and protect the banks from crumbling. Some kept the stream clean. Others used it as a dumping ground for old cars, tires, tin cans, and rusty machinery, even old rolls of barbed wire.

The water kept pulling me on its slow journey. Finally I stood at the mouth of the creek, watching the water move out into the darker brown of the Kickapoo River and become part of the water flowing down to join the Wisconsin River, much too far away for me to explore. And the Wisconsin carried the same water to the Mississippi at a place called Wyalusing, and the Mississippi carried the water ponderously south toward the Gulf of Mexico.

For hours I watched the moving water of the creek merge with the moving water of the river, and I tried to go with it in my mind and get a glimpse and feel of the far-off sea with its great ships, raging storms, and restless tides.

As color came into the western sky, I headed home, tired and hungry and with no place to say I had been except "along the creek."

On a day when I was still very young I was alone with Father in a rowboat out in a very wide part of the Mississippi. The water seemed all around us. "Is this the sea?" I asked.

Father laughed. "No, but it runs into the sea, more than a thousand miles to the south."

A thousand miles!

Father sat for a long time looking out over the water as the slow current carried us a little way downstream toward the sea. His cork danced and jiggled, went under and came up again.

"You have a bite," I said.

"So I do." He pulled in a glistening sunfish, and we were back on the Mississippi River.

The sea stayed with Father in other ways. On rainy days people came from miles around bringing their broken hay ropes for him to splice. In his stubby fingers the frayed ends vanished to be magically rejoined, so smoothly it was hard to tell where the rope had been broken. I remember that once a man watched him work and asked him about the sea. Father said maybe twenty words about storms and sailing ships and then gave up.

"It's a different world," he said. "Too much I'd have to explain."

Despite how little Father talked of his sailing days, I came to understand an essential fact about the sea. Once a man has known it, the sea is forever a part of him, brought back by so simple a thing as the taste of salt on the lips or the wind moving in long green waves across a grainfield.

Often when we went out early in the morning to do the chores, the fog lay heavy and white in the valley leading down toward the Kickapoo. The white twisted off into each little ravine and hollow, leaving the lines of the hills outlined above it. Father told us once that the fog looked like the white-capped sea coming in along the narrow Norwegian fjords.

There were mornings when Father would stop at the milk-can rack to look at the fog and would stand there, his hand lying forgotten on the handle of a can. We would go to the barn, careful not to rattle the milk pails, leaving him there. There was something very natural and right about it. When he came to the barn a little later, he would milk silently for a time, then begin softly singing the mournful Norwegian songs which were a mood rather than words, forever reminding us of that part of Father we could never really know.

Then the milking would be done. The warmth of the climbing sun chased the fog away. The evaporating dew brought the smells of new-mown hay and growing corn to us. Father was again back on the farm, looking happily ahead to a day of work in the fields.

17 Drouth

There was a gentleness in most summers, the land staying green and moist even in the boiling sun of August. The summer the drouth was at its peak was different. That summer had violence in it. The thirsty land dried, cracked open as though to better receive the rain—and the rain didn't come. The stunted corn curled up its leaves, trying to save moisture. The oats, which needed cool weather when the grains were forming, cooked in the hot dry sun, producing grains light as chaff. The alfalfa was short-stemmed and had the pale green look of cured hay even before it was mowed.

Down in the valleys the creeks ran warm and sluggish, half clogged with moss and slime. The leaves on the elm trees in our yard rattled like the dried oak leaves of fall and began to turn yellow by the middle of July. By then the pastures were brown as old straw, the cattle thin, ribs showing halfway across a forty-acre field, and we could milk any two of them into one twelve-quart pail.

As the land dried out the days grew hotter. The sun came up a violent red through the dust and smoke, heat pulling at the moisture in us before we had finished the morning milking. For the first time anyone could remember, there was no morning fog filling the big valley that led down to the Kickapoo.

The bawling of cattle woke us at night. Any other summer it would have meant a cow had been left in the barnyard by accident when the others were put out to night pasture. This summer it meant they wanted to get back into the barnyard for water.

"Even the grass doesn't have any moisture in it," Father said. The drouth was not ours alone. Day after day the northwest wind carried the soil of the Great Plains to us in a never-ending cloud of yellow-brown. The fine dust that rode the wind was everywhere. It gritted between our teeth when we ate. Freshly washed clothes turned brown on the clothesline. I could draw faces on the dark wood of a tabletop that had been wiped clean an hour before.

Newspapers carried pictures of houses half covered with dust, roads being cleared of dust drifts with snowplows, and caravans of farmers leaving the land, possessions piled high in old pickup trucks. There was talk that half the soil of the Great Plains was going to end up east of the Mississippi.

The endless summer went on. Father suffered with the suffering land. Each morning his eyes swept the horizon, looking for some sign that rain might come. He walked out into the fields, feeling the wilted plants, poking at the concrete hardness of the dry soil. He would come back to the house, face drawn, shaking his head. "My God, if there was just something a man could do. I don't know anything to do but wait for it to rain."

Lyle tried to cheer Father up. "Hell, you always said it would be nice to have one of those rich Iowa farms. Few more weeks of this dust and you'll have one, delivered right to you."

The old men at the filling station, who whittled and argued their days away, compared the summer to the ancient-sounding past. Any time we stopped there they were at it. "Figure it's the worst one we ever had," old Charlie said. "Lot worse than back in ninety-five. I tell you, there's never been a summer like this one before."

He said it with great authority, and no one argued. I had never seen that happen before.

Men reacted to the drouth in different ways. Some gave up and moved away. Some prayed to God for help. Some went through the days cursing steadily at the Devil, the weatherman, the Republicans, and the son of a bitch who ever invented farming in the first place.

Some, like Lyle, kept trying to make jokes. "Joking about it's a lot better than shooting yourself," he said.

A neighbor offered Lyle a chew of tobacco one day.

"Nope," Lyle said. "Had to give it up."

"How come?"

"Too dry. Last time I tried some, I chewed all day. It was seven o'clock that night before I worked up enough juice to spit. Going to try it again some day if it ever rains."

It didn't rain.

The grasshoppers came in a horde, as though they were blown in from the West with the dust. There was a story about them, too, passed on by one of the men at the filling station.

"I heard a fellow over by Mount Zion was out cultivating corn. He noticed the grasshoppers was pretty thick but didn't pay them no mind. Finally he got thirsty. He was in a field close to the house so he left the horses there and started to go get some water. It was when he was climbing over the fence he noticed them grasshoppers had gone through all the grass along the fence row and was starting on the fence posts."

"Wood fence posts or steel fence posts?" someone interrupted.

"Fellow didn't say. Anyway, he went on to the house and got his drink of water. When he got back to the field, the cultivator and team of horses was gone. He figured they'd run away until he saw what the grasshoppers was doing. You know they'd ate up the horses and cultivator and was pitching horseshoes to see who got him."

As the summer went on, a new and pungent blue joined with the brown of the dust. Forest fires were raging out of control in the pine woods to the north.

Along the ridge wells began drying up. Neighbors came in wagons and pickup trucks to fill ten-gallon milk cans or sometimes drove a whole herd of cattle to water at our stock tank. Father kept checking the flow from our pump, but it held out, the windmill going steadily.

Storms rolled up in the northwest. We watched them coming, hopeful even when they looked violent and dangerous. White wind clouds boiled ahead of black clouds, the day going so dark the nighthawks came out and filled the sky with their whirling and diving. But the storms had a way of going around us or just seeming to dissolve into the dry air. Or they came on, driving us to cover, and turned out to be nothing but a giant wind.

"By God," someone said, "the wind's doing its best to bring us rain. It's like there just ain't any rain out there to bring."

We put up forty-eight loads of hay that summer. No one could remember a year when we had put up less than a hundred. One field of oats was so light we cut it for hay and made a stack behind the barn. That night one of the rainless windstorms came. Lightning struck the hay poles and set the stack on fire. The flickering glow coming through the window woke Father. We rushed out, but all we saved were the hay poles and rope.

Father reported the loss to the fire insurance company and a check came in the mail. He opened the letter at the dinner table, looked at it, and started shaking his head.

"They didn't pay very much?" Laurance asked.

"They paid too much. They must think that was good hay—like alfalfa."

And in that violent summer, when the crops were a failure, the cows drying up, money short, and it seemed it might never rain again, Father sent the check back to the insurance company and said he'd take half that much.

Mother suffered through that summer, worrying about Father, worrying about her garden and about a fall and winter coming with a family to keep fed. Her garden withered, only the brave-colored zinnias seeming to flourish in the drouth. Birds were scarce. "Gone on farther north maybe," she said, "to where it's cooler." And having said that, she began to worry about the birds getting caught in the forest fires.

Looking ahead to a lean harvest, we canned all the summer apples we could, even searching in the old orchards of deserted farms. Lee and I picked more than a hundred quarts of blackberries, still a decent crop, deep in the shaded woods along the moist ditches. When the ears of the field corn were in the milk stage, we picked bushels of them and cut off the kernels for canning.

"Good idea," Lyle said. "We won't be able to put it in the corncrib anyway."

"What are you talking about?" Father asked.

Lyle had on his deadpan look. "Why the ears are so small they're just going to come rolling out through the slats in the crib fast as we can shovel them in."

Father didn't even smile.

Rain finally came in the fall, breaking the drouth, and the land began to heal itself. But the costs of drouth were not yet paid. Ditches appeared where none had ever been as the rain pounded at soil that was cracked and protected only by the stunted plants and close-cropped grass. Hundreds of oak trees stood bare of leaves the following spring. Some of the wells and springs that had dried up never had water again.

We didn't farm quite the same after that summer. The reaction of the land to the drouth told us we had made mistakes, had taken the harvest too much for granted and left the land too little safety margin to allow for the dry years.

We learned to cultivate corn just deep enough to cut off the weeds, leaving the moisture protected instead of rolling it up to dry out in the sun.

Most important of all, we began laying out fields in long narrow strips, planted alternately in oats, hay, and corn so that a plowed field and a cultivated crop never laid open a wide piece of hillside to the rain. When water had a free run across a big cornfield, it picked up enough speed to carry the soil with it. In the new strip-cropping, water was slowed by running into the hay or oats before it could pick up the soil.

Laurance came home from high school with word that strip-cropping had been used more than fifty years before by farmers from Switzerland who lived in Mormon Coulee, near La Crosse, sixty miles to the north.

At first we laid out our strips in straight lines, but the hillsides were not straight. Later, we ran them along the contours of the hills and our fields began to look like pictures in my geography book of mountainside terraces in China.

From the drying up of the wells we learned that the need to protect the land was not just local. A state geologist explained what he thought had happened. Much of the well water in southwestern Wisconsin came from a layer of limestone buried three hundred feet or more below the surface of the ridges. That layer of limestone slanted upward, to the north, so that a hundred miles away, in north central Wisconsin, the limestone lay at the surface. There, it picked up water. That water seeped slowly southward through the limestone to our wells, taking perhaps seventy-five years to make the trip. And about seventy-five years before, the geologist pointed out, men had drained the surface water from the north central Wisconsin marshes to make more farmland.

The story of the seventy-five-year-old well water and the draining of the marshes made a deep impression on Father. "There's just too much we don't know," he said. "How could somebody way up there know he was draining away our water supply? For that matter, what are we doing right here that's changing things someplace else? We know what cutting off the timber has done—making floods in the valleys."

"I guess we can't be expected to know everything in advance," Mother said gently.

"That's right. But we can damn well go slow when we start changing things. We can admit that we're playing around with something that's a lot bigger than we are."

I suddenly remembered old Charlie Harding, teetered back in his chair at the filling station, fussing about the timber being cut out of the Mississippi bottoms. "I don't know just what it's all about," he said. "Might even be a good idea. But it's another thing being changed that ain't ever going to be changed back again."

An age of innocence had ended. Father had thought of man in general as being an enemy of the land. The summer of the drouth made him examine everything we were doing to see in what ways we, personally, were enemies of the land.

18 The Bees

One of the most constant sounds in the long days of summer was the busy humming of the honeybees coming and going from the hives in the orchard, ranging the countryside for pollen and nectar. They were already flying when we first came out of the house just after sunrise. They were still working in the evening when chores were done and the sun was on the horizon.

Laurance was the beekeeper, as gentle and patient with them as he was impatient with the three of us. Laurance loved the bees. We weren't even sure we liked them. They dive-bombed us when they were angry, scared the horses in the fields, and were forever getting their stingers into us. Walk through the orchard and they got caught in our hair. Reach down to pick a cucumber and they were in the blossoms. Pick up the tin drinking cup at the cistern and a bee was there getting a drink himself.

All we really liked about the bees was their honey.

Laurance laughed at our grumbling. "They sting you because you start trouble," he'd say. "Haven't they got as much right to get a drink at the cistern as you have?"

"No!" we'd yell. Our answer always seemed to surprise him.

Laurance tried to show us the bees were harmless by walking up to a hive and pulling the cover off. He would reach in and lift out a frame of honeycomb covered with bees. He rarely wore a bee veil over his head. Often he didn't even wear a shirt. The bees buzzed around his head, crawled on his bare skin, and never seemed to sting him.

"Come on up close," Laurance would yell. "They won't hurt you if you're not afraid."

"We are afraid."

"Well, don't be!"

I guess Laurance tried his best to educate us. Part of the trouble was his older-brother logic. Most of the trouble was the stingers of the bees. They were much more convincing than he was.

I remember a rainy day when Laurance was working at the dining room table, putting one-pound sections of comb honey into little boxes with cellophane windows. He kept holding up sections to show us how each swarm worked. "Look at that. That swarm makes the cleanest comb. This one makes the deepest cells. And this one always fills the comb out all the way into the corners of the section, like they're more careful."

Laurance talked about his fifty swarms of bees as if each one were a special family, as different as the families along our ridge.

"Fifty swarms," Junior said. "How many bees in a swarm?"

"At least fifty thousand. More in some."

Junior did the arithmetic in his head. "You mean to tell me you got two and a half million bees?"

"Maybe more than that," Laurance said, sounding like a king with that many subjects at his command.

"Then we also got two and a half million stingers flying around here."

"Not quite. Some are male drones. They don't sting."

"How do you tell which is a drone?"

"They're bigger. You can tell which is which by squeezing them, too."

We still thought of bees as dumb old gatherers of honey and said so.

"They don't gather honey," Laurance said.

"What do they do?"

"They gather nectar and pollen."

"Same thing."

"It is not. They use the nectar to make honey. They do that in their stomachs."

"I don't think I like honey anymore," Lee said. He was particularly fond of stirring honey into a glass of cold milk.

"Why do plants have nectar anyway?"

"To attract the bees."

"Why do they need the bees?"

"To spread pollen from one plant to another. Otherwise there wouldn't be any seeds. There wouldn't be any apples or plums or any kind of fruit."

I tried to get all that squared away with the barnyard-bulls and cows, hens and roosters. What if hen pollen and cow pollen . . .

"Well, how come it doesn't get all mixed up? Like corn with pickles? There's bees on all the flowers."

"A bee only works one kind of flower at a time."

"Do you mean to tell me," said Junior, "that there wouldn't be any bees if it wasn't for the flowers and there wouldn't be any flowers if it wasn't for the bees?"

Laurance smiled. "Maybe a few flowers. Like corn. It uses the wind."

Junior thought about it. He finally gave a big sigh. "I just don't understand that. I just don't see how plants and bees got hooked up together like that. It's like somebody invented bees and flowers both at once. Like motors and wheels."

Mother was listening. She smiled. "Why, that sounds almost religious."

Junior was still shaking his head. "I don't believe it."

"What don't you believe?"

"Any of it."

"I believe the stingers," Lee said.

Laurance went on working and telling how the bees flew from blossom to blossom, then flew back to the hive carrying a load half their own weight, making maybe ten thousand trips to gather one pound of nectar. Their stomachs worked on the nectar as they flew. Then they put the honey into the little six-sided comb cells. It had to be thickened, just like boiling down maple syrup. Bees assigned to that job fanned their wings until the honey was thick enough, and then put a wax cap over each cell.

"Wait a minute. Did you say assigned to fanning? Who assigns them?"

"Nobody. I guess they assign themselves."

That was too much. We were four competitive boys who worried constantly that we might do more than our share of the jobs. It wasn't the work we minded. It was a matter of justice. The idea of bees doing a job without anyone telling them didn't make any sense at all.

Still, there was an enthusiasm in Laurance that made us go on listening.

Each swarm had a queen. She flew out once or twice to mate with a drone, high in the sky. The drone died and fell to the ground. The queen went back to the hive and began to lay eggs, a thousand or more a day, each batch weighing as much as she did. Most of the eggs were fertilized when they were laid, and those turned out to be workers or queens. The unfertilized eggs became drones.

"The queen decides when she lays each egg if it will be fertilized or not," Laurance said.

"Decides?" Junior said. "She lays a thousand eggs a day and each time decides?" He looked at Laurance with his beautiful skeptical smile, giving Laurance a perfect right to be crazy.

The story got even wilder.

When the eggs hatched, the new larvae were fed pollen that was mixed with a chemical from the heads of older bees. After a few days, most were switched to a diet of honey. They became workers. A few were kept on the pollen mixture. Those became queens.

"Yes," Laurance said, before anyone could interrupt him, "I mean to say what they get fed makes them into workers or queens."

I was having trouble again with my barnyard sex education. I turned each new kitten over to check if it was boy or girl. Each new calf was bull or heifer. If we fed them different feed when they were first born, would they change?

While I worried about that, Laurance went on. Now it was division of labor. The new bees were like us, going through a whole series of chores before they were old enough to work in the fields. First, they did clean-up work inside the hive. Next, they were baby-feeders. Then wax started oozing out of their abdomens, and they built the perfectly shaped honeycomb cells.

"How come they know how to do that?"

"Nobody knows. Engineers say those cells are a perfect design. People have tried to improve them and can't."

Finally the young bees worked for a few days fanning their wings to cool the hive and thicken the honey. Only then, when they were about twenty days old, did the bees go out to gather nectar and pollen. They worked all the daylight hours and in the busy summer were worn out and died in six weeks.

"You mean in six weeks there might not be a single bee left?"

"No. There'd be just as many as ever. They keep on hatching out of the eggs."

"But all the old ones will be gone. Like the whole world having a new batch of people every month and a half?"

"Yes. Except for the queen. She may live five years or more."

"Does the queen run things?"

Laurance frowned. "Nobody runs things. It's sort of like the whole swarm is one animal. And all the individual bees are just parts of that animal. You don't expect a dog's tail to make decisions or run the dog, do you?"

There was a long discussion. Does a dog decide to wag its tail? Or does a tail decide to wag?

"But a dog has a brain to run things," Junior said. "What's the brain of a hive of bees?"

Laurance shook his head. "I don't know. They all seem to hatch out already knowing what they're supposed to do."

There was more still—how the bees communicated with each other. When a worker discovered a good supply of pollen or nectar, it told the other bees about it by the way it moved inside the hive. The bee ran in big figure eights if the pollen or nectar was close by. Running fast meant a big supply, and lots of other bees crowded around. They touched the bee to get the scent, then flew in circles until they found the blossoms.

When the discovery was more than a few hundred yards away, the signal was more complicated. The bee did a zigzag dance that told the other bees which direction to go and how long it would take. This meant a bee could carry the exact amount of honey needed for the trip, leaving the rest of its carrying space for nectar and pollen.

We listened to Laurance's talk about the bees communicating with each other, but I don't think we believed. If not, we were wrong. Some of his information came from a glass-sided hive where he could sit and watch what was going on. He had also read about a young scientist in Germany, Karl von Frisch, who was reporting on the dancing of the bees. Most people thought von Frisch was crazy. No one says that now. In 1973, he was awarded a Nobel Prize for nearly a half century of work on how bees communicate.

The rest of us helped Laurance only when the honey was being extracted from the combs. He took the frames from the hives without our help. Then, safely inside the garage, we used a heated knife to slice off the wax cappings sealing each cell. Two frames of comb at a time went into the extractor, which looked something like a greatly overgrown ice cream freezer. It whirled the frames, throwing the honey out. Extracting was a very sticky business, and naturally a few bees got stuck onto things. Naturally we squeezed them and they stung.

When we yelled, Laurance would say, "Your own fault."

"Yes, we know. Bees have just as much right to get stuck on the extractor handle as we do."

The honey from thousands of comb cells slowly rose in the extractor tank. It was strained just enough to get out the bits of wax without removing the flavorful pollen, and put into jars and ten-pound pails.

The containers were labeled "L.C. Logan—Pure Honey." It was strange to go into a store in Seneca, Gays Mills, or Petersburg and see Laurance's honey sitting on the shelves with all the other cans and jars of food. We felt superior. We knew how that honey had come to be.

One year we tried to get Laurance to change his label. We wanted to put on it "Two and a half million bees made this honey."

"No one would believe it," Laurance said.

"He's right," Junior told us. "I know it's true and I don't believe it myself."

19 Hunting for Bee Trees

Laurance added to his swarms and to our honey supply by hunting for hollow trees that bees were using for a hive. Laurance was oldest and I was youngest. There were six years between us. Hunting for bee trees was one of the few things we did together.

I remember being with him one sunny Sunday afternoon on a steep hillside above the place we called Lost Valley. It was south of our own land and so isolated we could sit there and not see any mark of people—no fences, no cultivated fields, not even a tree stump. We had come far enough away from the orchard so that our bees were not likely to find the feeding station we set up.

Lost Valley was narrow, with a dry ditch down the middle. Half-way across the bottom a giant cottonwood towered high above all the other trees. A cool breeze always seemed to come out of the heavy timber, creeping along the hillside, bringing up a moist earth smell to mingle with the dry summer fragrance of horsemint and wild roses.

Something about Lost Valley bothered me. It was always too still, too empty. Sometimes when Lee and I walked down into the bottom, we would find ourselves whispering, then realize what we were doing and shout our defiance into the shadows. Partly, my feeling came from knowing there were wolves there. It was from the hillside above the valley that their howls came to us on summer nights.

There was something else.

"How come nobody ever cut any timber here?"

"Too hard to haul it out," said practical Laurance.

"How come nobody ever farmed?"

"Too narrow. Floods would get the crops."

Hidden from any human noises, we sat in the hot sun and waited for bees to come. A hawk circled above us, screaming and diving every now and then at the hillside. Once it flew up with a squirming snake in its talons.

"There's a nest somewhere over on the other hillside," Laurance said. His eyes went back to his bee-hunting equipment. There was a little wooden box with bottles of sweet anise and sugar water for bait and a little door that could be opened for the bees, and there were two little pots of red and blue paint and two tiny brushes.

A bumblebee came and tried to get into the box. Laurance shooed him away.

"We could find his nest," I said.

Laurance gave me his disgusted older-brother look. "Bumblebees don't store honey. Don't have to. They all die, except the queen, every fall. Same thing with yellow jackets."

I was glad it wasn't that way with us.

The bumblebee had started Laurance talking. "Did you know there weren't any honeybees until the settlers brought them from Europe? The bees migrated west faster than the people. When settlers came west they thought the bees must be native."

Some little sweat bees flew around us, but they were after our perspiration, not the anise and sugar water. Then a honeybee came buzzing in, landed at the box, and began sucking up the bait. It was a golden Italian.

"Might be one of mine."

"This far from home?"

"Could be. More likely one that got away when a hive swarmed."

I never got over how complicated bees were. Sometimes when a new queen was about to come out of the cell, the old queen took a lot of the workers and swarmed out of the hive, buzzing so loudly we could hear them from a long way off. They would fly a little way and form a cluster, on a limb, fence post, building, or in the weeds. We were always hearing stories about them clustering on people. "If they ever do that," we were warned, "just stand still. If you fight with them, they could kill you."

Whenever we heard a swarm coming across the fields we fell flat on the ground and lay very still.

The cluster might stay where it first landed for hours, a crawling, buzzing mass of bees the size of a football, with the queen somewhere in the middle.

"They've sent out scouts to find a new home," Laurance would explain. "It's kind of like people starting out to begin a new colony, like the Pilgrims. When the scouts find a good place, the swarm will leave."

Sometimes when we were in the fields, Mother came running, calling, "Bees are swarming!"

Laurance would drop his work—that was another reason we didn't like the bees—and run for home. If he could get an empty hive on the ground near the cluster soon enough, he could often persuade the bees to start a new colony right there. If he failed, the swarm flew off to some hollow tree.

The bee that had come to our bait box might be from such a swarm. Laurance raised the glass lid of the box and very gently brushed a dab of red paint on the bee.

The bee got his fill, crawled to the entrance, and took off. We shaded our eyes from the sun and watched. It flew almost due southwest, a little to the right of the big cottonwood at the bottom of the valley, in the opposite direction from our orchard.

"It's a wild bee," Laurance said. He looked at his watch. He knew how fast the bees could fly and how long it took them to unload the honey that was being manufactured as they flew.

"Will that one tell the others?"

"Probably not. Not enough here to be important."

Minutes later the marked bee came back. Laurance checked his watch again. "About a half mile."

Several other bees came. Laurance marked one of them with blue paint. It flew off in the same direction and returned in the same number of minutes.

We had our "beeline" established, but it was not so simple as just walking in that direction looking for a hollow tree. Bees didn't always fly in a beeline. They often followed the contour of the land, flying along a hillside, turning to fly up or down a ravine, turning again at the other end.

We moved down the hillside and set up the bait box again. The bees still flew in the same direction.

"How do they find their way back?"

"People think they use the sun. They say if you lock a bee up in a dark box for an hour and then let him go, he'll get lost."

"But the sun would still be there."

"The bee won't know the sun has moved. It'll fly in the wrong direction."

"What if it's cloudy?"

"Makes no difference. Bees can still tell which direction the light is coming from."

We moved on down the hillside and into the trees. The bees still came to the box, but we had trouble. They flew straight up into the treetops and disappeared. The opposite hillside was heavily timbered, so we climbed to the top and set up again at the edge of the hayfield and waited.

"Why not just watch them when they leave a flower?"

"Can't tell when they're going home. They might stop at a hundred flowers to get a load."

Again the bees came. Again we marked them, timed them, and followed them. They led us along the hillside to the west, then back into the woods. Dozens of bees were buzzing around the bait box. We left it and began looking for hollow trees. When we found one, we'd stand with the tree between us and the sun, looking for flying bees.

"There it is," Laurance yelled, pointing. The silhouetted bees glowed like a cloud of amber smoke against the sun. We ran closer and could hear the loud buzzing. Hundreds of bees were going in and out of a hole about fifteen feet above the ground.

"Wow," Laurance said. "It's a good one."

The tree was a gnarled white oak, almost three feet through. It had been damaged by fire close to the ground and looked ready to fall.

The next Sunday we got permission from the owner of the land, Paul Paulson, and drove out through the hayfield to cut the tree, taking two milk pails for the honey and an empty hive Laurance would try to get the bees into. Lee, Junior, and Lyle were with us.

Using the same crosscut saw they'd tried on the big maple, Lyle and Junior started on the white oak. The bees went on working. The saw cut into the thin shell of the trunk, bringing out black-and-white sawdust. The top limbs began to move a little against the blue sky. In a few minutes, the white oak teetered slowly. It fell with a noise like thunder, echoing back and forth across Lost Valley.

The bees were everywhere. It was all Laurance's work now. He tucked his pants legs into the top of his socks, put on his veil, and began chopping open the hollow tree trunk. The bees swarmed around him. Now and then he moved back to take off his gloves and scrape stingers out of his hands.

The walls of the tree trunk were thin. Laurance laid open the big hollow space, exposing rows of amber-colored honeycomb. He was using his smoker now, a little can-and-bellows contraption that burned old rags and squirted smoke when he pumped the bellows. The smoke made the bees move out of the way and fill up with honey. A full bee was not so likely to sting.

Laurance went on chopping until he found a big cluster of bees, where the queen would be. He pumped smoke at them, then cut off the big piece of comb they were on, put it into the beehive we'd brought, and put the lid on. Some of the flying bees began going into the hive, following the queen. There was a trap at the entrance that wouldn't let them come out again.

Laurance filled one milk pail with pieces of comb heavy with honey. He filled the other pail and carried them both toward us. The bees followed him, and we backed away.

"It's a big one," he yelled. "Better go get the boiler."

Junior and I drove home for the fifteen-gallon copper boiler Mother used to heat wash water. When we got back, Laurance had chopped open five feet of the trunk and still hadn't come to the end of the honey. He filled the boiler, and Lee ran in to help him carry it.

"There's more. Get the big tub this time."

We went home again and got the twenty-gallon washtub. That too was almost full by the time the tree trunk was empty.

"They had enough honey in there they could have stopped working for ten years," Lyle said.

"Honeybees don't do that," Laurance said, still scraping stingers out of his hands.

We left the hive to be picked up later, dropped some honey off at Paul Paulson's, and took the rest of it home to Mother. She had two questions.

"All that honey out of one tree?"

We nodded.

"How am I going to wash clothes tomorrow?"

We hadn't thought about that. The rest of the day was spent getting the thick, dark honey drained out of the combs so we could store it away in jars.

That was the biggest bee tree we ever found.

Next day Laurance brought home the new hive of bees. They went right to work as if nothing had happened.

Sometimes the bees Laurance captured were German blacks. Those were mean bees. Even Laurance admitted that they went out looking for trouble. With them, he would kill the old queen and put in an already fertilized golden Italian queen.

The new queen was always in a little cage, the entrance blocked with hard sugar. By the time the bees ate their way in, they had accepted her. She began laying eggs and all the work of the swarm went right on. The difference was, in about six weeks all the black bees would be dead. All the new bees would be Italian.

It seemed to me there was something unfair about that. "Could we do that with people?" I asked one day at the dining room table. Mother blushed and hid a smile.

"No," Father said. "We couldn't. At least I hope not."

20 Some of the Blowing Dust Was Gold

One summer—I don't remember which summer—I listened to Mother and a young man and woman talking on the front lawn under the maple tree. The young man and woman were with a group of evangelists holding services at the Methodist church in Seneca. In the soft breeze under the maple, with the grass bright green beneath them, they could not seem to keep their eyes off one another. And the young man did something I did not know a young man did—he started reciting poetry. The lines I really heard and remembered were those from Robert Frost—"I was one of the children told / Some of the blowing dust was gold."

I heard nothing else that was said. The words became a surging circle in my head, playing over and over like the untended old crank-up phonograph at my grandparents' house. In the days that followed I made it into a little song. Father found me one day in the yard under the pine trees where the acid needles kept the grass from growing. I had pushed the carpet of brown needles aside and pulled together a little hill of soft dust. I would scoop up double handfuls and let the smoking dust trickle through my fingers, singing over and over "I was one of the children told, some of the blowing dust was gold."

I heard a sound, not quite a laugh. I turned.

Father was smiling at me. "Find any gold?"

I shook my head, the song stilled.

He reached out. "Come."

I took his hand, rough and hard from work, and he pulled me up. We didn't often touch that way. He led me out along the road to the west, the dust hoppers clattering out of our way, flashing red-orange as they flew, then landing and vanishing against the dust as they folded their wings.

He took me to the edge of the oats and pointed out across the rolling field, turning bright, deep yellow in the strong July sun. He stood a moment with his hand on my shoulder, then left me with the song starting again and ringing in my head.

A breeze came across the field in little golden waves as the ripening heads bent to the wind, then sprang back. A bluebird peered at me from the top of a fence post. Its head went back in song, but all I could hear was my own—"I was one of the children told, some of the blowing dust was gold."

21 Harvest of Gold

As the oats ripened in the warming summer, each plump grain filled with white milk. If the weather was too hot at this critical stage, the field would soon have a white-yellow look which meant the oat grains would be small. A change to dark orange-brown meant wet weather had caused rust. Then the stems might crinkle, letting the heavy heads fall to the ground, to rot if the weather stayed wet, to shell out and be lost on the ground if the weather turned dry.

We asked a lot of the land and the weather. We wanted warm weather for the oats to grow in, cool weather when the heads were forming, dry weather for harvest. We did not want a windstorm to knock it down, a hailstorm to crush it, a heavy rain to flatten it. If there had to be a wind, we wanted it to come ahead of the rain, before the ground was softened and the roots gave way.

All we wanted each summer was a miracle.

Most years the miracle happened. Day after day we watched the wind moving in waves across the constantly changing color of the oat fields. First there was velvet green, like a picture of the grass of Ireland in one of my books. The green changed to a pale yellow, to a deeper yellow, then to a rich gold. The gold color sent my father walking each morning out into the oats, legs hidden by the rich growth, fingers feeling the ripening heads to see when the old Deering grain binder should be brought out. We watched him and waited for his report.

"Another ten days maybe."

"Looks like next week."

"Another couple days."

On farms all through that hill country, people watched the grain and watched the sky. Stay away hail. Stay away windstorm. Stay away rain, wait a week, even if the corn does need it now. Sometimes in a Sunday service a minister who had grown up on a farm would petition God to give special care to the oats in the week ahead.

Then the day came when Father would finish his walk through the oat fields and say, "Tomorrow." He didn't have to say it. We knew from his face. We knew from the sheaf of grain he carried with him, cut stem by stem with his jackknife and tied into a little golden bundle. Each year he stored that first harvest away to be brought out on Christmas day for the birds, as he had done in Norway.

The heavy grain binder rolled out of the machine shed. We brought the cutter bar from the milk house, the wide canvas belts from the house, the tools and the oil cans from the garage. The heavy strong-smelling balls of binder twine, big as a man's head, went into the twine box. They were made in Mexico or the Philippines, and once or twice we had some made by men in the State Prison at Waupun.

Father filled grease cups, squirted oil into the mysterious complexity, pulled at wheels and chains until all the squeaks were gone and everything turned smoothly. When he was satisfied, two horses pulled the rig to the first oat field. The road wheels came off. The big bull wheel, almost as big as a tractor wheel, was cranked down so its steel cleats could bite into the ground and drive the cutter bar and the clutter of wheels, chains, and moving canvases.

The tongue was moved from the end to the front. Another horse or two was added, then the first round began, with all the mechanical parts singing and chattering in the warm summer sun.

The cutter bar trimmed off the oats close to the ground. The slowly turning fan pulled the stems back onto the wide canvas belt, heads to the rear, and the moving canvas carried the grain up and over the bull wheel to be gathered into a tight bundle. The long curved needle, threaded with twine, darted out. The knotter made its sudden twist, always too fast for me to see, and a bundle of oats, as neatly packaged and tied as an order from Sears, fell to the bundle carrier. When several bundles lay on the carrier, Father tripped a lever and the bundles rolled to the ground.

Soon, lines of bundles dotted the field, green in the butt ends from the young alfalfa or clover that was next year's hay crop. Then came the shocking. We gathered the bundles, first leaning a pair against each other, butts spread apart for air. Another pair was added, then a bundle on each side where the pairs joined; a final bundle fanned out on top for a cap that kept out the rain.

The binder moved around and around the field, spewing out bundles, no one trip seeming to make any mark, yet the field gave way to the golden shocks and the green stubble. Then we'd put the road wheels back on the binder, crank up the bull wheel—my job whenever I could manage it—and move on to another field to begin all over again.

Father ran the binder. He and the machine seemed to know each other and worked together in some special way. When Lyle or some-times Laurance, because he was oldest, climbed up onto the high seat to spell Father for a round or two, nothing ran as smoothly. The bundles were different sizes, or tied too close to the top. The knotter didn't always succeed in its magical twist and we had to tie the loose grain into a bundle, using oat stems for a rope. Each year, Father showed us how to do that. He took maybe two dozen stems in each hand, twisted the head ends together to make the rope longer, then tied it tightly around the loose grain.

"Like in the old days, before binders," Father told us, making it look very easy. He could never understand why the bundles we made came out looking like a tangle of old barbed wire.

On a year when the rust was bad, Father and the horses were orange-bronze by the end of the day. The dust crept through our clothes and up our pants legs. Washing for supper included taking off shoes and socks, putting our feet into buckets of water, ice cold after the heat of the day, and washing our legs to the knees, the itching, clinging dust giving way to the wonderful cold of the water.

In the early years, when threshing rigs were small and scarce, we often stacked the grain, hauling the bundles in from the fields and building tall round stacks that looked like giant old-fashioned straw beehives.

Father was the stacker. We threw the bundles down from the wagons one at a time and he began a bright ring on the ground, maybe sixteen feet across, each bundle placed just so, heads in, butts out. As the stack grew taller, we threw bundles up to him. He caught them with his pitchfork, placing them carefully, each circle a little smaller than the last and always higher in the middle to keep the rain from running in. When the stack was tapered to a peak, Father was far above us, moving carefully on the slippery grain. Then we threw him a sharp stick to push down through the cap bundle, and that stack was finished.

Stacking meant handling the grain an extra time, but the heads were safer from the weather. And in the fields, the hay that had been seeded with the grain could grow where the shocks had been.

The stacks sat, weathering into the color of old straw in the rain and sun, while we waited for the threshing rig to come.

The rigs seemed bigger and faster each season. The hissing steam engines were replaced by chugging gasoline-engine monsters—once an old Titan Tractor with rear wheels taller than a grown man, a giant one-cylinder engine, and a flywheel so heavy it ran long after the engine had been shut off.

Behind the clanking, steel-wheeled tractors came the threshing machine itself, the older ones made of wood, the red paint fading from the sun of other seasons, the newer ones shiny galvanized steel with bright red trim. We could hear the rigs groaning along the road long before they arrived. Sometimes the roar stayed in one place. Then Lyle would hitch up a team and trot them out to help a heavy rig up the hill. Lyle loved that. The threshing men hated it because they knew they'd be reminded for weeks that their mechanical monsters still needed the help of horses.

We knew long in advance which of the many threshing rigs that roamed the country would thresh on our ridge. How that decision was made was one of the little things that helped us know our Father was an important man.

In late spring the threshermen began their rounds, lining up their circuits. It was a touchy business. They had to know who the natural leader was in each neighborhood. Which farmer did the others look to in the decision-making?

On our ridge they came first to Father. The greasy overalled men came in cars and trucks filled with rattling oil cans. They were always big and heavy, with booming voices. At least I don't remember any who were quiet and slim. I would crowd in close when they talked, never thinking of them as ordinary humans. They were some special breed who rode their clanking monsters across the country, eating up the miles and grain, then vanishing over the horizon. The men talked with Father about when, how much, by the bushel or by the hour, and was it a rig that threshed clean or did it blow good grain into the strawpile?

If it all seemed right to Father, he climbed into the car with the thresherman—often it was the same man who got the job year after year—and they drove along the ridge talking with the other farmers. It had to be that way. No one could thresh by himself. We were bound together in those special times of the year into neighborhood decisions.

The threshermen had decisions to make, too. How big a circuit should they set up? How long would people wait for a good rig? Should they cut the price a half cent a bushel to get more jobs?

Once Father asked one of them, a man from Steuben, how he decided.

The big man laughed. "I set in front of a map. I make a list. I put down who pays me and who don't. I put down what places work together, with enough help to keep the wagons coming."

He laughed again and rubbed his stomach. "I even remember what the food's like, different places." He clapped Father on the shoulders and boomed again. "By God, Sam, I'll tell you something. Yours is one place I know the last bundle will still be rattling out the straw pipe and I'll turn around and there you'll be, your checkbook already out. You know there's people I chase half the winter trying to get my money. Hell, there's a man right here on this ridge—I don't have to tell you his name—won't pay me for last year 'til I pull in to thresh him this year. I swear one year I'm gonna pull right on past his place."

He never did that, even though he came year after year. He was my favorite thresherman.

I remember once picking up two fat bundles of oats that had fallen into the barnyard. I loaded them on my coaster wagon, hauled them out to the rig, and got in line with the other wagons. When the one ahead of me pulled out, the big thresherman saw me.

"By God, that's the smallest bundle wagon I ever saw. You got any more loads coming?"

I shook my head.

"Well, this could be the smallest job I ever handled."

He took the bag off the pipe, after tripping the measuring bucket to let the grain come out. Then he took me back, had me pick up one bundle, and held me up to the apron. "All right. Throw her in."

I dropped the first bundle. He swung me down for the other one and the moving apron carried both bundles into the jaws. There was a little roar from the tractor, the sound of something happening inside the threshing machine. A burst of straw came out of the pipe onto the strawpile. Grain rattled into the measuring bucket. The big man put me down, went back, tripped the oats into a bag, and handed it to me. "There you go. I figure your crop thrashed out at about seven pounds. That'll be a penny."

I reached into my pocket and brought out an old knife, a small fossil, and several nails.

"I don't have any money."

The man sighed. "Yeah, it's been a tough year. You'd be surprised how many ain't been able to pay. Tell you something. I'm a man who likes cold water. You suppose you could take that wagon and haul me out a bucket of really cold water?"

I nodded.

He handed me a battered gallon pail. "You do that and we'll call her even."

I put the pail into the wagon with the bag of oats and raced for the house. I could see the windmill running. That meant cold water in the pipe from the deep well. But it was slowing down, the tall wheel turning lazily, swinging from side to side, searching for the wind. I raced for the well and got there in time to fill the bucket. Mother saw me. She looked at the bucket and the grain bag in my wagon.

"What's going on?"

I told her, watching her face. She didn't laugh.

"Bring the bucket of water," she said and led me to the kitchen. She got out two lemons, cut them in half, squeezed the juice into the bucket, then added sugar, threw the four squeezed halves in, and stirred it all up. She poured out a glass and handed it to me. "You try it and make sure it's all right."

I drank. "It's good."

"Enough sugar?"

"Just right."

With a smile, she handed me the bucket. "There. You take that to him."

I raced back to the threshing rig, the bucket cold against my leg, condensation forming in little beads on the metal. I found the big, greasy overalled man and handed him the bucket.

"Took a while." He pulled off the lid, lifted it up, and took a great pull.

"Hey," he said. "Hey!"

He took another long pull and the lemonade was half gone. He lowered the bucket and wiped his mouth. "Man, that's good. You make that?"

"My mother did."

"Son, you got a mother that oughta be sitting on some fancy throne in Europe."

He took another long drink. Then he frowned at me. "Only one trouble. Now you're ahead of me. You went and overpaid me. I can't give you any back cause I just about drank it all up."

He pulled out a handful of chaff, coins, and nuts and bolts. He blew at the chaff and pushed things around with his stubby fingers. When he held out a buffalo nickel, I shook my head.

"Well," he said. "It's sure a problem. I could thresh your crop for nothing next summer, but I hate to owe a man for a year."

He blew on the handful again, sending the chaff flying. "Look at that. My wife claims it's spring before it's all gone."

It was the first time it had occurred to me he might have any life beyond the roaring machines. A wife? Children? Impossible!

He came up with an Indian-head penny. It was a good one, bright and shiny. "How about a penny, then?"

"All right," I said. "But only because it's not really money. Only because it's for my Indian-head collection."

He gave me the coin and shook hands with me. "It's a deal. Mighty nice doing business with an honorable man."

He drained the gallon bucket, put it down, and began greasing the whirling wheels of the threshing machine.

I went back to my wagon and considered the bag of oats. Should I build a little granary? Finally I decided the oats belonged to all of us. I hauled the bag down to the granary, got in line with the grain-wagon men, and dumped it into the big bin.

22 Rites of Passage

In a farm family without girls, each boy in turn helped in the house. Because I was the youngest, I worked with Mother longer than any of my brothers. There weren't any younger sons to take over and free me to work in the fields with Father.

At threshing time, until I was about twelve, my work had to do with meals. Mother made her plans—getting ready for as many as twenty-five men—and I helped her put them into action. I carried extra water, brought in fresh vegetables from the garden, carried canned fruit up from the cellar, sliced loaf after loaf of the bread she had been up half the night to make. I peeled great pans of potatoes from the bin in the cellar, or dug new ones from the potato field. I got all the extra leaves from the dark closet at the foot of the stairs and soon the dining-room table stretched almost from wall to wall, lined with chairs from all over the house.

I set up buckets of water, washbowls, and great stacks of towels on the outdoor work stand, under the dinner bell. I made certain the stock tank was filled with water for the horses from the bundle wagons.

The roar of the threshing rig and the rattle of the wagons were constant reminders of men building up a hunger. Finally, the table was set, extra dishes stacked and ready for the men who couldn't fit at the first table. Pots bubbled on the wood range and good smells began to come from the steamy kitchen.

Then I began going back and forth between Father and Mother. The conversation would go like this, with a lot of running in between:

"Mother wants to know when you'll be ready?"

"When will she be ready?"

"She says the potatoes need forty-five minutes."

Father might call to the man on the last bundle wagon in line. "Hey, how many loads left out there?" He'd get his answer and turn back to me.

"We got this field about whipped. Then we have to move across the road. Ask her if we could eat early?"

"But she says the potatoes need forty-five minutes."

"Ask her about that."

"He says could they eat early?"

"Well. Maybe I can cut the potatoes up smaller. Tell him twenty minutes."

"She says twenty minutes. And she wants to know if they'll be eating here for supper."

"I don't know yet."

"She said if you said that to ask you when you will know."

With the exact time set, Mother shifted her pots and pans, making sure everything came out even. And Father knew when to keep the empty wagons from going out for another load.

With the men beginning to look at their watches more often and measuring the height of the sun, the tractor would slow, the great belt slapping, and the hum of the threshing machine would slowly die.

In the strange warm quiet, after hours of steady sound, the men came to the yard, flapping chaff and dust from clothes and hats. They smelled of horses, grease, and grain dust, clothes stained with sweat and salt. Their straw hats made a pile on the grass. Once a puppy chewed some of them up while everyone was eating.

Four at a time, the men went to the washbowls, splashing and snorting like walruses, then rearing up, eyes full of soap, to feel for a towel. Every year, at least once, someone would hand a groping man a grease-filled rag brought in from the machines. The half-blind person would mop himself, not knowing anything was wrong until his face was black and a roar of laughter surrounded him.

Then to the house. Big, heavy bowls began to move around the table, forks spearing meat, potatoes, vegetables—sometimes a fork coming across from the other side of the table. One person was always the butt of all the jokes about eating too much.

"By God, George" (or "Tom," or "Spike," or "Dingy"), "we've been talking about you. What we decided is we ain't going to change work with you anymore. Nothing personal, mind you. Just can't afford it, you eating ten times what the rest of us do."

"He could bring his own dinner."

"Hell, to do that he'd have to bring two wagons."

George would go on shoveling, talking through the food. "You're right. I do eat ten times as much as anybody else. No argument about that. Figure I got it coming, seeing as I work twenty times harder."

A hoot of laughter. The bowls made a second round. George speared a potato, popped the whole thing into his mouth and couldn't talk, eyes bulging as if he might explode. Still working on the potato he filled his plate with dessert, taking pie, cake, Jell-O, and cookies.

The chairs scraped back from the first table. The men went out to the yard, sprawling under the maple tree, to light pipes and hand-rolled cigarettes or take a chew from a plug of tobacco.

The second shift came in, heavy eaters sometimes taking a quick look into the kitchen to make sure there was plenty of food. I scurried from kitchen to dining room with more bowls of hot food, more bread, more coffee. I refilled the sugar bowl, put it down in front of a fat man, and waited while he put half the bowl over freshly sliced tomatoes and the other half into his coffee, running it over into the saucer. With the cup in one hand, he lifted the saucer and drank with a loud, vibrating slurp. Each time, someone at the table would rise to the occasion, frowning, looking under the table and saying, "Damnation, sure sounds like there's pigs and a slop trough in here somewhere."

The fat man grinned, handed me the empty sugar bowl, and went on eating. I kept circling the table, grabbing the bowls and platters as they emptied. I carried more cream and milk from the cellar, the pitchers steaming as they came up into the hot summer day.

Finally, with the food almost gone, the tractor started up, calling the men back to work. Mother and I sat down at the great long table, not talking, sobered by a mountain of dirty dishes waiting and another meal to be ready in five hours.

Father joined us sometimes for a consultation. Would the threshing be finished today? That might mean supper should be earlier than usual or later. Did we need anything from town?

When a job was going to be finished during the day, the women got nervous. Would the men eat at this job or move on to the next one, thresh an hour, and eat there? The women needed a definite answer. The men hedged. A tractor could break down, some wet bundles plug the machine, the last load slide off a wagon and have to be pitched back on.

In a situation like that, my liaison trips between Father and Mother seemed like every five minutes and the telephone rang with questions from a woman who might, or might not, have to feed twenty-five men two hours from now.

It wasn't talked about much, but there were farms where the men tried to avoid eating. They might quit a little early and decide everybody should go home to eat. They might decide to eat early at the present job.

I remember eating once at a house with no screens on the windows. The flies were a constant hum over the table. We ate with one hand and waved flies away with the other. Ben Twining had brought some repair parts for the tractor from Gays Mills. He made the mistake of staying for supper. When it came time for dessert, he reached out for a pie, saying, "I think I'll have some of that raisin pie."

A swarm of flies rose as his hand came near. "Oh," he said, "I guess that's custard pie."

One year I began the passage from boy to man. We were short of help because another threshing rig was over on Pleasant Ridge, where we usually exchanged help. Father said he needed me. Mother made plans for a neighbor girl to come and help.

"What will I do?" I asked Father.

"I was thinking about the straw pipe. Think you could handle that?"

"Sure." I had a dim impression of cranks and levers.

"It's not easy. You have to pay attention every minute. Couple years back I saw a boy knock a man off the strawstack being careless how he swung the pipe. You got to stick to it no matter how hot it gets, how much dust and chaff comes back at you."

"I can do it."

The rig came in the late afternoon, a big chugging Rumely Oil Pull tractor with a square stack and a little box where black oil squirted mysteriously through glass tubes. It chugged through the barnyard to a field northeast of the barn, pulling the bright red threshing machine behind it.

The driver was my familiar big, greasy overalled man. He started getting ready for the next day, leveling up the threshing machine by digging holes for some of the wheels to drop into, then lining up the tractor and stretching the long belt from tractor pulley to threshing-machine pulley. Around the tractor were red milk cans filled with gasoline, unpainted milk cans full of water, and great boxes of tools and spare parts.

The long pipe that carried straw from the machine to the stack was cradled along the top of the thresher. I climbed up to the little platform where the straw-pipe operator was supposed to stand. There were three cranks and a rope. I didn't know which did what.

The big man swung the grain chute out and walked back along the top of the rig. "You going to run the pipe?"

I nodded.

"Ever do it before?"

I shook my head.

"You can do it. Let me show you. This crank here raises the pipe up and down. This crank swings her back and forth. This one makes her longer and shorter. And this rope—that opens up a little door at the end of the pipe. Pull that, the straw goes shooting straight out the pipe. Leave it closed, the straw goes down onto the stack. Got that straight?"

I nodded.

"All right. Let's try her. Raise the pipe off the rig a couple feet."

I turned the crank. The pipe lifted up.

"Fine. Now swing her around."

I turned another crank. The pipe began to swing in a great half circle, making a groaning noise.

"Hold it." He picked up his oilcan and gave the collar of the pipe a big squirt of oil.

"Try her again."

The pipe turned more easily and I swung it until it stuck straight out from the end of the thresher.

"Now get the feel of cranking her longer and shorter."

I did that, chain links rattling along the top of the pipe.

"You'll do fine." He winked at me. "Now then, put her back on top the rig the way she was. You can crank her around in the morning. Folks'll think you been doing it all your life."

In my mind I cranked that pipe half the night.

First thing next morning, when the dew was off, we went out into the fields to tip the oat shocks over, butts toward the morning sun so the dampness from the ground would dry out. As I worked, I remembered the first time I had ever done that. It had been early in the morning, the sun still low and red. In an hour or so I had to go back to the house and help Mother. I started tipping the shocks, the butts directly at the sun. Lyle was with me. He watched for a few minutes, then came over, shaking his head. "Nope. Not right at the sun. Tip them where the sun's going to be a couple hours from now."

I looked at the sun. I looked to the right along the horizon where I knew the sun was going. But how far to the right?

"Like the face of a clock," Lyle said. He pulled out the inch-thick old watch that bulged from the top pocket of his high-bibbed overalls. The hands stood at seven o'clock. He turned the face so the little hand pointed to the sun. He pointed his finger from the center of the watch to the number nine.

"That's where the sun'll be in a couple hours."

I went back to tipping the shocks, looking at the sun each time, aiming the butts at that certain angle to the right. I'd never before had such a feel of the sun's absolute route across our days.

That had been three years before. I turned the shocks casually now, automatically aiming them ahead of the sun.

The wagons, with their wide hayracks, began to arrive. I helped throw bundles—from shocks that had been tipped the day before—onto the first wagon and rode in on the high swaying load.

The tractor was already running. The wagon pulled in close to the feeder apron. I slid off and ran to the pipe—raised it, cranked it around in a half circle, then extended it. I gave the rope a couple of pulls, opening the little door and letting it clang shut. Everything went without a hitch.

I looked down and found Father watching me. There was surprise on his face. He looked at me a moment, then at the thresherman, then back at me.

I nodded.

Father smiled his approval and I grew about two inches up there on that high platform.

Another wagon pulled in along the other side of the machine. The thresherman pulled the drive lever on the tractor. The threshing machine came alive under me, vibrating, rocking back and forth a little, the chaff dancing on the metal top. Slowly it all built to a steady humming that was half sound, half feel.

The men on the wagons began feeding oats to the machine, their pitchforks swinging in an easy alternating rhythm. A steady line of bundles was carried by the moving apron into the hidden workings of the great machine. The tractor engine roared louder. New sounds began as bundles were ripped apart and oat heads shook loose from the stems. Straw rattled under me and went shooting out the pipe. The oat grains sifted through screens and fanners and poured into the measuring bucket on top of the machine. The bucket filled to a half-bushel weight and dumped automatically, registering on the counting dial. Then the oats poured down the grain pipe in a rich stream to the waiting sack.

As always, Father was there to meet those first oats. He reached into the sack and brought out a handful, still warm from the fields, bright gold in the early sun. He blew into his hand, checking for chaff and weed seeds. Satisfied, he nodded to the thresherman.

Father went next to the beginning pile of straw. He held his hat out in front of the pipe, then checked in it to see if any grain was blowing through. Again he nodded his satisfaction to the thresherman.

Father returned to the grain pipe and carefully lifted a full bag up and down. This was how he confirmed what his walks through the fields had told him earlier. Everyone watched his face. As he swung the first bag into the waiting grain wagon, we knew without a word ever passing that it was a good crop.

The bundle wagons came and went. The grain wagon raced off to the granary to unload and return. Straw spread out on the ground in a long pile as I swung the pipe back and forth. Father and a neighbor moved into the straw, which was next winter's bedding for the barns. With their pitchforks they began to form the rectangular outlines of the stack, motioning to me when they wanted the pipe moved.

Once, straw stopped coming out of the pipe. The machine groaned and thumped. Someone yelled. I looked around. The thresherman was running toward me. He made a pulling motion. I grabbed the rope that opened the door at the end of the pipe, and a wad of damp straw went shooting out beyond the stack. The machine smoothed. After that, the sound warned me when to pull the rope.

The sun moved across the sky. The dust and chaff settled around me. Once, when the bundle wagons got behind, I had a minute to climb down to earth and get a drink of water from the ten-gallon milk can, like the other men.

Finally, it was time for dinner. The machine whined to a stop, my little platform strangely motionless after hours of vibration. Father slid down from the strawstack and gave me a nod and a smile. There was a burst of laughter from the grain wagon. Lyle lifted a baby rabbit out of one of the bags. "Look at that," he said to the thresherman. "Can't understand how your rig can get the oats clean if a rabbit can go straight through."

The thresherman grinned. "You're lucky. Few days ago a skunk came through."

Lyle put the rabbit down and it hopped away across the field. He told me later that somebody had found it under a shock and brought it in.

I beat the chaff and dust off my clothes and washed up with the other men. For the first time in my life, I sat down at the first table. Mother put a steaming platter of food in front of me.

When the chairs scraped back, I went out into the yard with the others. There, under the shade of the big maple tree, I listened to the talk.

"Call this grain?" a hired man was saying. "Hell, you should see it out on the Great Plains. They got wheat fields that stretch from hell to breakfast. I've seen twenty horses hitched onto one combine. A man starts cutting and by God he's got to take a bed with him cause he'll only be halfway around a field by nightfall."

There was laughter. "You sure you're not stretching things a little?"

"Hell no. If anything, I'm holding back 'cause I didn't figure any-body would believe the truth. Fact is, those fields are so big, and it takes so long to get the seed in, that different parts of the field don't even get ripe at the same time."

Old Abe was there. He was listening and nodding. "My grandfather was out there once. He came west from Ohio back in the eighteen-forties. Tried to grub out a farm down in Haney Valley. Somebody came by and told him he was crazy. Said there was land out on the Great Plains level as a table, not a tree in sight. Well, sir, he went out there and just about went crazy before he turned around and came back here."

"What went wrong?"

Abe took a chew of tobacco and got it going. "Why, he said a man used to hill country could lose his soul out there. Said that country swallowed you up without even a belch. Said there was no surprises. Country shows itself to you all at once. No privacy either. A neighbor living twenty miles away can look out in the morning, see if you're up and got a fire going yet."

Abe raised his head. A long stream of tobacco juice went sizzling into the brown grass. "So he came back here, my grandfather did. Said hill country had a feel of home about it, didn't keep leading a man off toward a horizon that was never there."

From that year on I was part of the threshing crew. When the rig went to the next job, leaving our farm quiet again and sleeping in the hot summer sun, I went with it to run the strawpipe at each farm along the ridge.

23　A Day of Our Own

In spite of long days in the fields, something in the summer brought the four of us boys closer together. A day when we did not have to work was very special. It was ours. We were free. We could vanish into the child-hiding green of hundreds of acres of countryside and make a world out of a single day.

The bits and pieces of such days merge into one great whole so that I remember a day going on forever. We dug worms and put them into empty cans that would fit into our pockets, sometimes just a flat Prince Albert tobacco can, the tobacco gone into Lyle's pipe. We put lines, hooks, and sinkers into another pocket, and always a jackknife. We packed a lunch in a paper bag, ran down along the old hill road, then on down the dry hollow to Halls Branch Creek. We cut limber willow poles, bending them so our knives sliced quickly through the wood, tied our lines on, put a squirming worm on the hook, and were fishing five minutes after reaching the water.

Then the waiting, lying back on the grassy bank, the sun warm, the breeze rattling the leaves of the cottonwoods and bending the willows, the stream singing its way down the valley. Round-mouthed suckers and fighting chubs bit now and then, pulling our corks under. Sometimes we took naps, line wrapped around a finger or bare toe so we'd wake when we had a bite. As the fish bit or did not bite we'd wander downstream, trying each pool.

Once we found a burlap bag net along the bank. Two willow hoops kept it open, and a willow pole was lashed on to make a handle. Laurance put the net in the water at a narrow place below the pool.

The rest of us went upstream and loaded our arms with rocks, ready to drive the fish down toward the net. When Laurance called, we started throwing rocks into the water, each a little ahead of the last, splash, splash, splash, almost never hitting each other, and yelling at the top of our lungs as though the fish could hear.

Our rocks splashed right up to the net. Laurance lifted it out, the willow handle bending, water streaming out through the mesh of the bag. He put it down on the bank and peered inside. "Hey!" he yelled. "Hey!"

We raced across the creek toward him. He lifted out a two-foot-long rainbow trout, gleaming silver and red in the sun. Laurance stood with it struggling in his hands for a minute, then put it back into the water. It disappeared with a big swirl.

It was the biggest trout we had ever seen. We crowded around Laurance, ready to push him in after the fish.

"I had to put it back," he said, voice dry, almost a whisper. "It's against the law to catch trout with a net."

"Well, we could've kept him a minute just to look."

"He'd die in a few minutes."

"Well, how come it's all right to catch suckers with a net and not trout?"

"Because there aren't that many trout around. There wouldn't be any if people used nets."

Laurance's hands were shaking. He sounded angry.

We went back to our willow poles. Laurance sat a little apart from the rest of us. There was no talk. We knew he was right. That was part of the trouble. Older brothers always seemed to be right.

We fished. The day moved on, the sun higher, the lazy warmth surrounding us, the dew drying in the sun. The breeze rattled louder in the cottonwoods, and the wild morning glories opened up, a pale blue on the fence behind us.

My cork wiggled. It began to move along the surface. Sometimes that meant a big sucker had swallowed the worm and was swimming off, trying to get back under the bank. I jerked on the pole. There was no resistance. I fell over backward on the bank and a five-inch crawfish landed on me, one lobsterlike claw still hanging on to the worm. Everyone laughed at me. Laurance was sitting with us again and everything was all right.

We watched the moving sun, arguing endlessly about what time it was because time and opening our bag of food were the two most related items in the universe. A stomach's sense of time was not to be trusted. One look at the bag and our mouths watered, our stomachs growled and yelled, "Lunchtime!" We learned to ignore our stomachs and trust the sun. Otherwise we ate too early and were starving to death by midafternoon.

We argued, marked the travel of shadows with sticks, and searched for clues to support our arguments.

"Mailman hasn't gone by. That means it's not eleven yet."

"Maybe he went by and we didn't hear him."

"We always hear him."

"Maybe it was when we were using the net."

"Well, John Oppreicht's cows are already down at the creek drinking. That means it's at least eleven."

"Maybe he got them out early."

"He never gets them out early."

There was another clue we watched for with wicked pleasure. Had the veterinarian driven by, and how fast was he going? The vet drank a lot, and the more he drank the slower he drove. We had concluded that he never drove slow before 11:30 and almost always drove slow after 12:30.

On the day of the big trout, Laurance suddenly pointed to the shadow of the big cottonwood tree and declared it lunchtime. It seemed early, but we didn't argue. It would be his fault if we were starving later. We propped up our poles and moved back into the cool dark shade of the trees. There we went through our sandwiches, hard-boiled eggs, and cookies without a word. Then, on to the spring near that big pool and a cold drink, using a rinsed-out worm can for a dipper, the water tasting of mint and watercress. Only a little of worms.

We went back to our poles, but it didn't seem like a fishing day now with the sun almost straight overhead.

"Think the apples are ready?" someone said. We raced down the valley toward an old abandoned orchard on the south hillside above the creek, leaving our bag of fish in another little spring.

The apples were green. We ate them anyway, using salt left over from our hard-boiled eggs. Pockets bulging with apples we ran on across the hillside to the great grove of white pines.

The air was filled with the smell of pine pitch. Our bare feet were cushioned by brown needles, our sun-narrowed eyes blind in the deep cool shade. The trees were a mystery. There were no other white pines growing wild anywhere in the area. Why were they there? Who had planted them? How long ago? Had the three in our yard come from here when they were two or three feet tall?

The trees spread out along the steep hillside, big ones at the center, young ones at the edge, the whole grove growing outward each year like one giant tree.

We lay on our backs on the soft needles, gnawed at the rockhard apples, and slowly recaptured the strangeness of the place. It was like that each time. We gathered at the center of the grove surrounded by the biggest trees, some of them so big that two of us, hands linked, could not reach around them. We lay and listened and waited and waited for lost secrets to come back.

"Will they get so big all four of us can't reach around them?"

"Maybe."

"But we're getting bigger, too."

"We could come back and try it."

"Let's make a promise. Let's come back. When we're all big. We'll meet here on a certain day. We'll see if we can still reach around the biggest one."

"They might be cut by then."

"We can reach around the stump."

"Yeah. And count the growth rings."

"How long have they been here?"

"Longer than anyone can remember."

"Was there a house here once?"

We had long ago searched for a foundation, an old chimney, a mound. There was nothing.

"Somebody said the biggest one's got to be a hundred years old."

"More like two hundred."

Argue, argue, argue. Three hundred. Four hundred. Five hundred.

Across the valley, in a farmyard, were two pines that had come from the grove.

"Those two were five feet tall when somebody dug them up here. That was more than sixty years ago. Mr. Slade says so."

"Did you hear him say it?"

"No, but . . ."

"How do we know you're not just making it up?"

"We can go ask him."

Argue, argue, argue. "Well, I think the cabin's got something to do with it."

"That's newer. Not even fifty years old."

The cabin was on the hillside between the pines and the orchard. It was made of gigantic oak logs that were slowly sinking into the ground. The roof was falling in, the heavy plank door hanging from one rusted hinge.

"Who lived there?"

"No one remembers."

"Some old woodcutter, I bet."

"Why didn't he cut any pines?"

For some reason not a tree had been cut except for a little one now and then at Christmas. We were always angry when we found the little stumps. It wasn't our land, but it was our place.

"Maybe it was a bird."

"A bird built a cabin?"

"No, no, no. A bird carried one seed, maybe two hundred years ago, and dropped it here."

"Where did the bird get the seed?"

"Well, there's white pines up the Kickapoo by Ontario."

"That's thirty miles away."

"It could happen."

"Sure, some bird picked up a seed and said, 'Hey, I don't think I'll eat this seed. I think I'll take this seed to Halls Branch Valley and plant it.'"

"Anyway, Hall wasn't even here then, whoever he was."

"What do you mean—'he'?"

"I mean 'he' because everything is named for a 'he.'"

"It is not. There's a town up in northern Wisconsin that's named Ladysmith after a woman blacksmith."

Argue, argue, argue.

"So, you say one tree grew up and grew seeds and made all these trees?"

"Yeah."

"So how come one tree isn't a lot bigger than the others?"

"Maybe the bird carried a lot of seeds."

"Sure. Maybe a whole pocketful. Maybe even a whole pine cone."

"Maybe just one seed. Maybe a long, long time ago. So long ago that the tree is gone. Just the trees it seeded are left."

Finally, worn out with our words, we lay and listened to the wind way up in the tops of the pines. We felt very small and very young. We had all the time in the world on an endless day like that. If we waited long enough, we would find all the answers.

A cooler breeze along the hillside reminded us of the day outside the pines. The sound of the creek pulled us back to our fishing.

Evening came early in that narrow valley. When the sun went down behind the hillside, it was time to go. We each rolled up our line on the end of our pole, cut off that end with our knives, and discarded the poles. We wet our bag of fish in the cold spring water— suckers stayed alive for hours in a wet bag—and headed home, bringing the cows up the lane with us.

24 Something Hidden

Days like the day of the big trout were a search for something we could not name. We wandered for hours along the hillsides and in the dry ditches looking for fossils—snail-shell spirals and neat patterns of coral. We sat with them in our hands, staring at the living things that had become stone millions of years ago. We walked on land that had once been the bottom of the sea. As the day went by we became smaller and smaller, no more important in that immensity than one tiny fossil.

We prowled through a freshly cultivated cornfield in the northeast corner of the farm. Father said there must have been an Indian village there once because arrowheads and bits of pottery turned up behind the plow. Half hidden by the fast-growing corn, ignoring the crowing of roosters from the neighboring farm, we searched for the arrowheads and began to see tepees, smell the smoke of wood fires, hear the sound of voices in a language we couldn't understand. We turned the cold, smooth flint arrowheads in our hands, looking for clues. Each was different—different sizes and shapes, colors from almost white to gray to dull red, some crude and hurried-looking, some so smooth we could hardly find the chip marks. Each made by an Indian who was dead.

What were they like?

How did they die?

Were there boys, like us, roaming the woods, searching for an earlier time, just as we were searching now?

What were we looking for on such days? We didn't know. We only knew there was something hidden, something lost, some mystery waiting to be passed on to us. We didn't believe in ghosts, yet we searched for something left over from another time, as though the land might tell us what had gone before.

Suddenly, half afraid of being captured by the past and never getting back to the present, we ran from the cornfield to the wild plum tree, just in case the golden yellow plums might have ripened earlier than usual. They never had, but it was worth a try. Then on down the ravine, across the hillside with all the dead oak trees that were turned into constant drums by red-headed and pileated woodpeckers. On to the cold, cold spring flowing out of the hillside into a moss-covered trough for the cows.

The spring water splashed over the edge of the trough. We followed it down through a series of clear pools and miniature waterfalls, our bare feet numbed by the cold, our feet warmed again by the sand at the base of a small cliff. There, we found the present.

We made roads in the soft sandstone and raced bottles along them. The bottles were rectangular, usually Watkins vanilla and lemon extract. They were shaped a little like long Nash or Buick sedans, and that's what they were to us—cars. They were much easier to come by than real toy cars. They had no wheels to bog down in the soft sand. And they weren't too definite, so a large-sized vanilla bottle could be a car, bus, truck, or even a locomotive. It could even change from one to the other right in the middle of the road.

Because the cars were just bottles until we made them into something else, the exhaust noises had to be just right, the roar louder as a bottle headed up a steep pitch, easing off on the level and backfiring some on the downslope. The level exhaust noise was easy, just a rather moist booey-ooey-ooey-ooey, though if you wanted to be a stickler about it, that was the sound of a small, four-cylinder car like a Model T Ford.

My brothers were sticklers.

Nothing brought out the parent in them more than the sound of my bottle cars. Getting a car into motion was the most important of all. Shifting through the gears had to go like this: *brrooommm*— pause—*brroom*—pause—*brroooommmmm*.

The pauses and the short *brroom* had to do with something called double-clutching. One after another they would explain it to me. "You put in the clutch. You move the gear shift into neutral. You let the clutch out again and give her a little gas. Then you put the clutch in again, pull it into gear, let the clutch out again, and give her the gas."

"Why?"

"Because you'll grind the gears, that's why."

"Because you'll tear out the transmission."

"What's a transmission?"

Consternation. Long lecture about what's a transmission, complete with pictures drawn in the sand.

"Try it again."

I'd try again, putting in the big *brrooommms*, adding the double-clutching *brrooms* the best I could. They would listen, then huddle, trying to figure out what I was doing wrong, talking about me as if I weren't there or had maybe killed myself by not double-clutching.

"All right. You're driving a Dodge. It's got three forward gears. You got to double-clutch twice to get into high."

"Father doesn't double-clutch."

"That's different. That's a Model T. That's a different kind of transmission."

"What's a transmission?"

Back to the pictures in the sand.

"Try it again."

They coached me and *brroommed* for me as I pushed my Dodge bottle through the sand. Sometimes I got all the way into high and they would give a wild cheer. Then I'd head up a steep slope.

"Shift into second!"

I'd go *brroomm*. They'd shake their heads.

"Forgot to double-clutch."

"Probably tore out the differential."

"What's a differential?"

"It's the rear end!"

No more pictures in the sand. They would all get their biggest bottles to use as wreckers and haul me off to the garage, carefully double-clutching all the way, of course. And I would go sulk under a mulberry tree that grew at the top of the little cliff, a funny tree with no two leaves alike, growing frantically as if each summer might be all it had.

Being youngest got me into trouble with another game we played. We found places where young hickory trees grew tall and slim, trying to reach their way up to the sunlight through the bigger timber. We would climb way up to the top until they bent over, gently lowering us to the ground and springing back when we let go.

Once all four of us climbed one tall tree and swayed it down in a long, smooth descent.

"Like floating down in a parachute!"

"Like riding in a balloon!"

On signal, when our feet touched the ground, we were all supposed to let go. I was out at the far end. Everyone else let go. The tree whipped up, jerking me with it. It went straight up, then swayed the other way. I stayed with it, legs wrapped around the trunk, carried back and forth across the sky, leaves floating around me.

I looked down. The earth was moving, the white, upturned faces of Laurance, Junior, and Lee floating far below. When they saw I was all right, they started laughing.

"If coming down is like a parachute, what's it like going back up?"

"Like being shot out of a cannon!"

"Want to do it again?"

"No!"

"He's talking funny. Did you notice how funny he's talking?"

"I could've been killed!"

"But you weren't. Anyway, you were supposed to let go."

"My feet weren't on the ground yet!"

"He says his feet weren't on the ground. Let's do it again. This time we'll make sure his feet are on the ground."

"No!"

Still vibrating, I slid from the tree and ran down the ravine to where a big mesalike rock towered over the valley leading on down to the Kickapoo River. The valley was empty, guarded on the north side by a series of bald hills. For a while I was a lone rifleman keeping a line of riders from coming up the big valley.

The sun boiled down, the dry lichens scratching me. It was quiet and lonesome. I ran back up the ravine, all the anger gone. When I got to the hickories, the three of them were trying to tie down one of the trees for a snare, fighting over whether or not it would lift a bear.

That's the way it was. We were so far from home that not even the angriest yelling could reach the ears of Mother or Father. We played, hurt each other, made up, and played again. Then hurt each other and made up again, for to fight and not make up was to live out a day with no one to help you mirror back the joy of life. To hate and not love again was to be locked up forever in the lonely silence of the self.

It was the only way we knew. We could not find the flavor of a day in endless talk the way Father, Mother, and Lyle could in the shade of the big maple tree. A day could not be saved for later, the way we sometimes tried to save a perfect flower, pressing it in an encyclopedia along with gold and silver candy wrappers. So we pursued a day, chasing it through the woods and meadows, reaching for it, running as it sped ahead of us in the swiftly moving shadows of the sun.

Yet, when the day ended, we came home willingly, partly because we were starving, but also because we could not stay in our never-never land like Peter Pan. To do that was to lose a sense of belonging. To lose a nearness to Father was to lose some firm strength that gathered us into a unit.

Not to come back to Mother was to lose a warmth and peace that we could not make for ourselves. We crowded into her warm kitchen and showed her our fossils, scratches, arrowheads, and bruises. We tried to tell her about our day, the words pale and empty, just a listing of all the separate sights, sounds, smells, and feelings that we could not put together into a whole. One by one we tried and gave up.

But she listened and smiled. "I was a child once, remember."

"Did you try to figure things out?"

"Yes."

"Well, how does it all get held together?"

"Does God do that?"

She laughed. "You make God sound like some kind of glue."

"Well, does God do that?"

"I don't think God holds it together. I think God is the *it*—the everything. It's up to us to find out how the *it* all fits together."

"Oh."

The answer didn't help as much as she seemed to think it should, but we let it go at that and went out to do our evening chores.

25 My Brother Could See Inside Me

Even when we four boys were very young and so much a unit we hardly needed individual names, we knew that Junior was different. Laurance, Lee, and I had a quick and lasting stubbornness. Our anger could change an entire day. Junior's anger was quicksilver, one small cloud across the sun and then we'd have him laughing again.

The three of us were more restless, too, always running off through the woods, looking for something that was never there. We'd come back, tired and still restless. Junior would be whistling and building things of wood, tinkering with machines that needed fixing, or maybe playing his guitar and harmonica. He played them both at once, using a little wire frame he'd made to hold the harmonica up to his mouth. When he did that, the dog would sit beside him, nose in the air, howling. Junior called it his "three-piece band."

"Why is he different from us?" I asked Mother.

"Is he?" She said it almost absently as she sank her hand into a bowl of rising bread dough.

I tried to tell her.

She listened, studied the bread, and nodded. "I think you're right. Maybe it was his being so sick. That time at Christmas, with scarlet fever. I don't know if you knew or not. He almost died."

"I knew." I remembered it as the time we didn't have a Christmas tree.

Mother shaped the bread into loaves and slapped them. She laughed. "Did you know he used to cry when I did this? He thought I was spanking the bread."

I didn't remember.

"He was very young. Maybe you weren't even born."

"What about his being different?"

"People say it changes you, being that sick when you're young."

"How changes you?"

"I don't know. Maybe makes you understand life is very precious."

"I think life is precious," I said, feeling stubborn.

"You take it more for granted."

⚘

One summer, Junior and I worked with each other in the fields more than we had in any other year. We didn't know if it was just chance or a deliberate part of Father's planning. I don't think it ever occurred to us to ask. When Father told us what to do, no one ever asked why.

Junior was four years older, but we worked well with each other despite his skepticism and my talent for instant argument. Even so, I guess we didn't speak as freely with each other as we might have. I remember going to Mother that summer and asking about Junior's hair. "How does he do that, part it only halfway back?"

Mother looked startled. "Why, that's funny. He was just the other day asking how you did that, parted your hair all the way back."

As the summer went on, now and then I found Junior watching me in a certain way. I began to have the feeling he was looking inside me. It wasn't the way Father looked inside me. Father did it to see what needed fixing. Junior seemed to be looking just to see what was in there.

On a hot day in mid-summer, I asked Junior what time it was. He pulled out his dollar watch. While he was still looking at it, I heard myself saying "Ten of twelve."

His head jerked up. "How did you do that?"

"I don't know."

He cocked his head to one side, smiling and looking pleased. He showed me the watch. "You were right."

We played that game for the rest of the summer. Whenever he took out his watch, he would look at me and wait. A figure would pop into my head, but I would look at the sun and check the shadows, pretending to think a minute, because I was a little afraid of what was happening. Then I'd tell him what time it was. His big smile would light up his face. He'd nod and show me the watch before putting it away.

The others knew about our game. They thought I was doing some smart guessing, so we didn't always let them know how often I was exactly right. I did miss a little sometimes, as though our minds weren't close that day.

"Almost," Junior would say, smiling just the same as he showed me the watch.

～

That summer I heard some men at Petersburg arguing about whether or not you could hear the corn growing on a hot night. It seemed like a good idea to try on our own corn. I thought about telling my brothers so we could do it together. I eliminated Laurance because he was too superior for that kind of thing, Junior because he was too skeptical, Lee because he'd say it was a silly idea.

That left just me, and I went out into one of the cornfields after the chores were done. It's hard to believe all the noises there are in a summer night when what you want is quiet. Cows were bawling, a car rumbling somewhere on a gravel road, an owl hooting, the whippoor-wills going on and on, nighthawks booming as they swooped down. The insects alone added up into a gigantic chorus of squeaks, rasps, and whistles.

I knelt by a stalk of corn. Along with all the other sounds, I could hear my own heart beating. The ground was damp against my knees. The sweet, sticky smell of the growing corn was everywhere. A light breeze started the leaves whispering.

I put my ear up against the stalk. There was something there! It was a little stretching, popping noise that could have been the corn pushing upward. I moved my ear away from the stalk, and the sound was gone. I tried several times. Each time the sound was there.

I had heard the corn growing! I raced for the house, but when I came running up to the big maple tree, I lost my nerve and didn't tell.

I had heard the corn growing! It was a pleasant secret that I carried with me through the days. Junior watched me with a look that said he knew something was going on inside me. One day when we were hoeing thistles out of a cornfield, he said, "You've got some kind of secret about the corn."

I jumped. He was looking at me, head cocked to one side.

"You'll just laugh at me. You're always so damned skeptical."

"Me, skeptical? Oh, I don't know about that."

"See! You're even skeptical about being skeptical."

He waited.

I told him.

"It's possible." He knelt down by a cornstalk.

"They didn't say anything about hearing it in the daytime."

"Well, if corn grows at night, it must grow in the daytime," he said. "They probably just figured it's quieter at night."

"If they did, they're crazy."

He put his ear up against the cornstalk. I wanted very much for him to hear it, but I could tell he didn't expect anything. He wiggled the stalk back and forth. He pulled, his ear still tight against it. Finally he got up. He was smiling at me. "There's a sound there, all right. Same kind of noise as when I pulled, but not as loud."

We went on hoeing thistles, stopping every now and then to kneel down and listen. The sound was always there, louder in some stalks than in others. We got so interested we forgot all about how we might look to anybody who was watching.

"What were you two doing out there today?" Lyle asked at the supper table.

"Hoeing thistles."

"Well, from where I was, I couldn't tell if you were praying or maybe rolling dice."

Everybody was looking at us. We decided not to try any explaining.

Junior and I shared another secret, though he was not there when it began. In late summer, a spell of cool weather hit us. It felt like fall one Sunday afternoon when I took the single-shot twenty-two rifle out to get some squirrels.

I went down into the hollow that led to the lower end of Lost Valley. There were plenty of squirrels working in the tops of the oak trees, knocking acorns down on me, but because of the leaves I never fired a shot.

I decided to walk part way up Lost Valley before climbing the hillside toward home. It was half dark in the heavy timber, the sun hidden by the hills. When I had climbed a little way up the slope, I stopped to look around, again wondering why no one had ever lived there. A cold breeze blew along the hillside, rattling the leaves of the hazel brush. I shivered.

Suddenly I was afraid and wanted to run, but made myself stand still and listen. I remembered stories of how a bobcat or lynx will follow you and stare until you begin to know it is there. No one had seen a bobcat or lynx for years.

Nothing moved. There was no sound that did not belong there.

My hands began to ache. I realized I was holding very tightly to the rifle. I pulled the bolt back, took the shell out, and put it in my pocket.

I started slowly up the hillside. It was as cold as mid-winter. At the top of the hill I stopped and looked back. Everything was the same, but the cold was gone. I wasn't afraid anymore as I turned and ran along the sun-lit ridge to the house.

Because of the way things had been all summer, I told Junior, ready to say it was just a joke if he laughed at me. He listened and thought about it.

"You unloaded the gun?"

"Yes."

"Why?"

"I don't know. I just did."

"I think that makes it mean something."

"Mean what?"

He went on looking at me, thinking something, but I couldn't reach in there and find out what was going on.

The next day, while we were waiting for supper, Junior said, "Let's go look."

We walked out through the fields, along the rolling ridge, then into the brushy woods. He moved slowly, feet firm and noisy, not woods-wise like Lee and me. We started down the hillside. He slipped and knocked a rock loose. It rolled all the way to the bottom, banging on other rocks, the echoes clattering through the valley.

Halfway down, the cool breeze began. He looked at me. I shook my head. There was no fear now.

"Where did it begin?"

I took him to the place. There was just the cool silence and the lonely feel that was always part of Lost Valley.

Junior began to poke through the brush.

"What are you looking for?"

"Don't know."

He went down the hillside a hundred feet or so to a level place near the bottom. He stopped and stood there for a couple of minutes, looking down. He waved for me to come.

It was a pipe sticking up out of the ground, a galvanized pipe about six inches across with brush growing all around it.

"Old well casing," Junior said. "Somebody drilled a well here once."

I looked around. There was no sign that there had ever been a building or a road.

Junior nodded. "I know. Something must have gone wrong."

"Like what?"

"Maybe they just never moved in."

"Or maybe they did and something happened."

Junior sat on the ground beside the pipe and tried to look down into it. "Do you believe in ghosts?"

I jumped. "Of course not!"

"I mean if people go away from someplace, do you suppose there's something that stays there?"

I thought of Father's old deserted mill in Norway. "I don't know."

Suddenly Junior cupped his hands to his mouth and yelled down into the pipe. "Hello down there, ghost!"

The deep echoes went rolling back and forth across the valley.

Junior started laughing and yelled again into the pipe, "Leave my brother alone, ghost!"

I began laughing with him. "Come out of there and fight like a man, ghost!"

"Or come out and fight like a ghost, man!"

Still laughing, half expecting something to answer or follow us, we ran up the hillside, through the woods, and across the open fields. We got home just in time for supper. Whenever our eyes met across the table, we began laughing again.

Mother looked at us suspiciously. "What have you two been up to?"

Junior grinned. "Oh, just out looking for ghosts."

"God help the poor ghosts," Father said.

26 Wildflowers

The first wildflowers of the year, a startling white against the somber land, were only a brief promise of the long-lasting companion flowers of summer.

The lilacs were in between, half tree, half flower, too late for spring, too early for summer. They grew only where people planted them, yet we thought of them as wildflowers because we often found them blooming far from any farmhouse. Their fragrance spread through the woods. We searched around them, knowing a house had once been there.

A depression in the ground meant a house with a cellar had fallen in upon itself long ago. A slight mound might mean a dirt-floor log cabin. Sometimes we found a hint of a chimney or a foundation with wild grapevines crawling over the stones. Grass, brush, and even trees were growing, healing the land, where the house had been.

We would sit in such a place and try to find the past.

"I bet it's been eighty or ninety years."

"What do you think they were like?"

"You suppose Indians got 'em?"

"Or maybe smallpox or some kind of fever. People in books were always dying of fevers back then."

"You think there's anybody left anywhere, maybe way out in California or someplace, with the same last name, and they might know what happened?"

As the weather warmed, one of the pleasures of summer was to go running through acres of wildflowers, all the different colors alive in the sun, the different smells coming up, the bees a steady hum, pollen dust giving the flowers a halo. Sometimes a tall flower stem would bend all the way down to the ground with a heavy bumblebee. The stem would snap back, and the bumblebee would thrash and fight its way back up out of the grass to try again.

The cows ate and belched and rumbled through whole fields of flowers, the bright colors dangling from their mouths as they raised their heads to stare at us. A whole hillside would be purple with violets. An opening near the sandrock, where we played with our bottle cars, was filled with solid red. In between our double-clutching and exhaust noises, we argued half the summer about whether the red flowers should be called Indian paintbrush, red-hot poker, fireball, or scarlet cup.

On the hillside above the old road leading down to the spring were wild strawberries, with white blossoms that became red and tangy little berries.

The flowers were very different around the farm buildings. Brave blue chicory, used long ago as a substitute for coffee, survived along the road despite the traffic and mowing. Near the cistern there were plants with white flowers and clusters of seeds shaped like wheels of cheddar at the cheese factory. We called it cheese plant and in quiet moments sat there peeling away the little green husks so we could eat the nut-flavored "cheeses."

Yellow dandelions spotted the lawn, heads turning silver as the parachute-equipped seeds formed and were ready to drift away. People said the dandelions could tell you whether or not it was time to go home. Half believing, we knelt down by ripened heads, took a deep breath, and tried with one great gust of blowing to send every last seed drifting away on the wind. If we succeeded, it wasn't time to go home. We blamed the dandelions sometimes when Mother fussed at us for being late. She loved to see the seeds riding the wind, but she told us we'd just have to learn when to believe the dandelions.

The yard near the chicken house was filled with the white petals and yellow eyes of dog fennel (called May weed now), which people used sometimes for tea. The blossoms were perfect for the little game of counting petals one by one, saying, "She loves me, she loves me not." With fennel the answer was almost always "She loves me not."

I complained about the fennel to Mother. She thought about the problem for a moment and said, "Try it with a violet."

The violet, with its scanty number of petals, wasn't really proper for the game, but Mother was right. Each time, the answer was "She loves me."

This was one of my first glimpses of the stubborn way each variety of plant clings to its own identity. Dog fennel almost always has an even number of petals, violets an odd number, some genetic memory in the seeds keeping things that way. The new knowledge took all suspense out of the game. Soon I had classified practically every flower into a "loves me" or "loves me not" category.

Our best wildflower place was a night pasture for the dairy cows. Yellow lady's-slippers and trillium bloomed there in the deep shade along the ditch. Those we didn't pick. They were already scarce, disturbed by timber cutting and the grazing of cattle and horses. Beyond the woods, on an open hillside facing directly south, a rich variety of wildflowers bloomed all summer. My favorites were the elegant shooting stars, buttercups, columbine, wild roses, and blue- bells in the early summer. Later, there were brown-eyed Susans, field daisies, and wild peas. In late summer, goldenrod and horsemint (wild bergamot) formed a border around the woods.

Mother came with me sometimes to that hillside. We sat quietly in the warm sun, breathing in the mixture of fragrances, often leaving without picking a single flower from the thousands blooming there.

The night pasture was a small piece of land. Much of it had been cleared once, then taken out of cultivation. As the years went by, we used that pasture less and less. At first the wildflowers were better than ever. Then the protected land began to change. I watched it, puzzled. I had not realized how the land, if left alone, begins moving back toward some inevitable destiny of its own.

Goldenrod crept into the open land, beginning to cover the hillside with bright yellow plumes that moved in waves with the wind. A year or two later, black raspberry vines began to replace the goldenrod. Hazel brush moved out from the edge of the trees to compete with the berries.

Most of the wildflowers were gone from the hillside by the time the scraggly sumac trees began to grow there. In a few more years, the poplars, with their restless singing leaves, had started. Soon the young oak trees began to spread from the woods, edging into the sumac and poplar, a first hint of the day when the entire piece of land would be back in hardwood timber, as it had been perhaps fifty years before.

For the first time I noticed that the changes had already been happening, just too slowly for me to see. The only virgin oaks were next to the ditch. When I walked from there toward the open pasture, I walked through younger and younger oak trees, then into poplars, then sumac.

When I followed one of the little ditches from the edge of the woods up toward the cultivated field, I walked through a whole series of different kinds of growth. Each ditch was healing itself, with hazel brush next to the woods, then berry vines, then bull thistles, then grass, then weeds. Next to the field, where the water ran fast, the ditch was still bare ground, crumbling in at the sides.

It was all changing faster now because the cattle were gone.

The experience explained other puzzles. Black raspberries gave us a great crop in one place for a few years and then vanished. I looked closer and saw that the berries were being crowded out by other growth in an almost predictable pattern of change.

"Are we changing like that, too, not even knowing it?" I asked Father.

He laughed and pointed down to where my pants hung six inches above my shoe tops. "Well, your trousers didn't all at once get shorter."

I had picked the summer wildflowers and brought them in innocence to receive the reward of Mother's pleasure. Now wildflowers were part of a larger whole. I could never be so casual about them again.

27 The Hired Men

In late summer, Father often hired extra hands to help with the harvest. Some were local men who were crawling up the ladder—from hired man to renter, from renter to owning their own farms someday. Others were a breed apart. They were loners, single men of all ages who came like visitors from another planet to the steady ongoing world of the farm.

Lyle, of course, was different. He was one of the family and he stayed on year after year.

The others did not become part of us. They had almost no possessions and seemed proud that everything they owned, except their cars, could be put into one small suitcase. They lived with us, worked and ate with us, but remained strangers.

There was a man named Roy Wicks who hung up a World War I helmet and gas mask in the milk house when he came. He never spoke of them and we never asked. He worked hard all week, drew his pay on Saturday night, and drove off toward Gays Mills, seven miles away, in an old Nash without a muffler. Father sent me upstairs to see if his suitcase was still in the extra bedroom. It was there, a scratched and battered metal case. "Well, then, he'll be back for another week," Father said.

He came back early Sunday morning, just in time for milking, driving a different car, an old four-door Buick. He spent all Sunday tinkering with it, taking off the muffler first of all, looking very pleased when he heard the full-throated roar of the big engine. Then he bent the exhaust pipe so that it pointed straight down and hung only a few inches above the ground. When he took the car out for a test run on the dirt road, with powdery dust three inches deep, that bellowing exhaust stirred up a cloud that didn't settle for hours.

For several weeks that was the pattern. He came home with a different car every Sunday morning and spent the day tinkering it into shape. Sometimes I watched him work, handing him tools, as he bent over the engine. He was silent except for a constant and tuneless whistle from between his teeth. Once a wrench slipped and he scraped the skin off a knuckle. He straightened up quickly and hit his head against the hood.

"So that's the way you want it, is it?" he yelled.

He grabbed a heavy monkey wrench, stepped back a little, and threw it as hard as he could at the engine. The wrench crashed across the motor, broke off a spark plug, knocked wires loose. "There, you son of a bitch, how do you like that?"

Then, whistling between his teeth again, he bent back under the hood and began to repair the damage.

One Saturday night he came down from his bedroom carrying the battered suitcase. "I better be moving on," he said.

"Still a couple weeks' work here for you," Father said.

He shook his head and waited while Father wrote out a check for his wages. On his way past the milk house he picked up the helmet and gas mask, climbed into his car, and roared off to the east, leaving a great cloud of dust behind, the roaring of the exhaust coming back long after the car was out of sight.

I was used to hired men coming from nowhere and then disappearing into nowhere, but this time it bothered me, maybe because the helmet and gas mask gave him a past for me to wonder about.

"Why did he leave?" I asked.

I expected Mother to answer. Surprisingly, it was Father who said, "Maybe this was starting to be a home to him. With some men, it seems like they have to move whenever a place starts being a home. I don't know why it's that way."

I was fascinated by the wandering hired men, envious of their freedom and how they always seemed in command of their lives, no one forever telling them when it was time to gather eggs or bring in wood. They reminded me of the silent heroes in Western magazines. I wasn't supposed to read them, but I would stick one into my pocket and climb high up into a pine tree in the front yard. There, curled around a whorl of limbs, hidden from the everyday world and rocked by the cool wind, I read the stories and became a silent Western hero myself, riding into a troubled land to set things right, then riding on again at the end. One of the magazines was called *Ranch Romances*, and its stories were different. The hero stayed and settled down at the end, always marrying the daughter of a wifeless and grizzled old rancher. I never did figure out why Western girls weren't allowed to have mothers.

Sometimes I talked with Mother about the hired men.

"I think they must be very lonely," she said.

I thought of how they were always on the move, seeing all those different places. "How could they be lonely?"

"They never get close to anyone. You know, it's people that make a place a home. Ever notice how they always talk about places, never about people?"

When I thought about it, she was right. They liked to tell how things were different somewhere else—mountains with snow on them all year in the West, prairie land level as a pool table, the South with sidewalks so hot you could fry an egg on them. No one could top their stories about places. They had seen it all.

I puzzled about it. Mother watched me, smiling. "I think you wonder about them because they are a little like you. Small boys who never grew up."

I climbed up into my pine tree to think about that. I felt like two people. I could see the hired men through Mother's eyes, forever lonely when they could have been settled and close to other people the way we were. But part of me wanted to wander as they did, possessed by no one while I searched to find out who and what I would be.

I climbed down from the tree and tried to say that to Mother.

She nodded. "I know. But you don't find who you are all by yourself. We find out who we are with other people."

Back up into the pine tree to be cradled by the wind and think some more. The thing that bothered me was that everything had to be so definite. Why did it always have to be one or the other? Why not half of one and half of the other? Why couldn't I wander, free as the hired men, and still have the close warmth of other people?

One hired man, a carpenter, worked all one summer painting and fixing up the buildings, saying little, moving methodically from job to job. Something about the steady constancy of the tall slim man began to irritate Lee and me. We had never seen him enthused, excited, or rattled, so we decided to see if we could get a reaction. He was a slow milker, always the last one out of the barn. One evening we sneaked through the barn into the empty silo, each of us with a piece of steel pipe. Speaking hoarsely through our pipes in the echoing silo, we began our attack. "Walter Schnei-der—do you hear? . . . Wal-ter Schnei-der—destiny—calls you—away. . . . Evil—awaits you—here. Go—before it is too late . . ."

We stopped. The echoes died slowly in the tall silo. He just went on milking. We could hear the milk squirting into the pail as though he hadn't even heard us. We crept out, disappointed.

But a few days later he drew his pay and left without giving Father a reason. Lee and I were startled.

"Aw, he was going to leave anyway," Lee said.

We tried to think about it as a joke, but it wasn't funny. Certainly not funny enough to tell anyone about. There was something disturbing in knowing we might have influenced someone's life like that. It gave us a sense of power we didn't want.

Once two hired men came as a team, a big man and a little man we knew only as "Big" and "Little."

At supper the first night, Big was talking. "It's the only way we work. If Little don't work, I don't work. If I don't work, he don't work. We been together in every state of the Union."

Little shook his head. "Nope. Ain't been in Delaware."

"What do you mean we ain't been in Delaware? We came through it just two months back."

"Nope. Been meaning to tell you. Remember I was driving, that night we was coming north out of Virginia. Remember we cut over into Maryland so we could pick up Delaware. Well, I made a wrong turn and we went right past Delaware."

Big had a stunned look. "You mean we got to go all the way back to the East Coast just to pick up a little state like that? Why the devil—excuse me, ma'am—didn't you say we missed it?"

"Didn't know until I looked at the map next day. By then we was four hundred miles away someplace in Pennsylvania. Figured if I told you, you might kill me."

Big got halfway up out of his chair. "What makes you think I won't kill you right now?"

Little waved at the loaded table. "Aw, you'd never waste time beating on me and let all this food get cold."

Big sat down and started eating again. He looked as if he might cry any minute.

"My apologies, folks!" He gave Little a dirty look. "We ain't been together in every state of the Union! We only been in forty-seven!"

Little spread his hands in front of him. "So I made a wrong turn. And where were you? Asleep, that's where! With the map spread out on your big fat lap! Anyway, Delaware's a real little state. Anybody could miss a state that size."

Big and Little stayed two weeks, arguing the whole time about Delaware. On the second Sunday morning, Little asked Father for their pay and said they were leaving.

"Where you headed?" Father asked.

"Well, we got a job lined up harvesting wheat out in the Dakotas, but that's not where we're going, I guess."

Father gave him a sharp look.

Little nodded. "That's right. Damn me if we ain't going back East and pick up Delaware."

"And this time," Big said, "I'm going to stay awake."

Little gave me a nickel to fill the radiator of their Model A Ford roadster and wash off the license plates. I opened the barnyard gate for them. As they went through, they were arguing about what route to take. They stopped at the road, Little wanting to turn left and go through Chicago, Big wanting to turn right and go through the Upper Peninsula of Michigan.

"We already been in Michigan," Little said.

"But we ain't been in the *Upper Peninsula* of Michigan."

Little fished another nickel out of his pocket and flipped it into the dust at my feet. "Heads," he said.

I picked up the nickel and looked. "It's tails."

They turned right and went up the hill past the house. Big had the map spread out on his lap.

Part Four

FALL

28 A Time of Change

On the farm, fall does not seem like a true season. It never settles down into a steady sameness of days the way summer and winter do. Fall is a time of change, an end of the growing season, a preparation for the season of cold and snow that is coming.

Late summer always warned us. In August, yellowed leaves appeared on the walnuts and elms, coming down in a gust of wind like great flakes of yellow snow. Sometimes a walnut tree was bare long before first frost.

Nights grew cooler. There were reports of frost farther north in the cranberry bogs. The wild things knew, maybe because of the shortening days. One morning the whole yard would be filled with feeding robins, too busy to sing. Blackbirds gathered in noisy flocks. Suddenly the goldenrod and the bright blue wild asters were in bloom.

In the woods, acorns covered the ground, rolling under our feet like marbles when we tried to run along the cowpaths. Squirrels ran ahead of us, hanging upside down on tree trunks to scold us for disturbing their harvest. They even climbed into the hazel brush, the slim stems bending down to the ground as the squirrels clipped off clusters of nuts. Sometimes when a stem flipped back it sent a squirrel rolling. They just sat up again, front paws holding the clusters to their teeth, pieces of hull flying in all directions.

One by one the hazelnuts vanished until their bulging cheeks made the squirrels look like cartoons of old men with toothaches. Then they'd dash away to bury their harvest. Sometimes they stopped, sat straight up, and seemed to be thinking about where to go and what to do next. But usually there was no obvious system in their frantic work. They just ran a little way, dug a hole, thrust the nuts in, and carelessly covered them up. We watched, certain the squirrels would never remember where they had stored their winter food.

Along the edges of the woods, where the ground was damp, the yellow touch-me-not flowers faded. I spent hours touching the swollen seed pods. They snapped open, the pod sections curling back like springs, throwing the seeds everywhere. I could hear them pelting down in the dry leaves far away. I liked to bring the pods to the house, cradling them gently. I'd tell Mother to hold out her hand and close her eyes. Her face always squinted up when she did that. She never knew if it was going to be a baby toad, a double-yoked egg, a bright-colored beetle, or what. Very carefully I'd roll the touch-me-not pod into her palm and tell her to close her hand on it. She'd jump when it exploded, then open her hand and look with a delighted smile at the curling pod sections and black seeds.

Fall was quicksilver, filled with changing moods and feelings. There were days when it was bitter cold in the sharp northwest wind, yet marvelously sunny and warm in the protection of a rock ledge or along the side of a building. There were days full of windless smoky warmth, the sky deep blue and cloudless, the sunshine brilliant. On such a day we ran wildly through the fallen leaves, leaping into the air, trying to fly away into the endless blue like the soaring red-tailed hawks. And the next day would be cold and melancholy, the sky leaden, the low-hanging clouds with a look of snow in them, the cold wind finding us no matter where we tried to hide.

There were dark days when the trees made their own sunshine. We would stand in a grove of soft maples or poplars, rain coming down softly from the gray sky, the red and gold leaves giving everything around us a sunshine glow that blinded our eyes.

One of the sure signs of fall was the restlessness of the itinerant hired men who helped with the harvest. They got out their road maps, worked more on their cars, began glancing at the sky whenever a cold wind blew. At the supper table they talked less, slowly withdrawing from us so that they hardly said good-bye when they drove away. We rarely knew where they were going. Now and then a postcard arrived months later from a warmer place, a hello and good-bye message that was filled with misspellings. I felt about those nomads as Mother felt about the birds. I envied them, wondered where they were, wondered if I would ever see them again.

First frost came. The flies warned us, clustering in the late afternoon on the screen door to the warm kitchen. We covered the last of the summer flowers with old sheets, the garden filled with white ghosts as the moon came up. Next morning we woke to a frost-whited lawn and to a job I hated above all things. I had to knock hundreds of numbed flies from the screen door, sweep the black heap into a dustpan, and throw them into the hot kitchen stove.

"They're just flies," someone would say, watching my screwed-up face.

"We're burning them alive," I'd say.

There was a job that Father and Lyle hated as much as I hated the flies. Each fall the two heating stoves had to be carried from the woodshed and set up in the dining room and living room. The stoves were heavy, covered with sharp edges, and hard to get a hold on. If they were set down to rest, the legs sank into the ground. With faces and hands already black with soot, Father and Lyle would come staggering out of the woodshed and stumble over the walk, the stove tilting dangerously because Father was taller. They groaned their way up onto the porch, one of us holding the screen door open. I don't think they ever made it through that door without one of them skinning a knuckle. Mother sympathized enough to allow them all the "goddamns" they needed.

The dining-room stove always came first.

They worried their heavy load in close to the wall near the chimney, trying to lift and look up at the same time. The opening into the chimney was almost to the ceiling, covered in summer by a brass plate with a painting on it.

"Little more to the right."

The stove shifted.

"No, dammit! To the right!"

"I did move to the right."

"You did not. You moved to the left."

"Well, I moved to my right."

"Dammit, you should know by this time that when I say right, I mean *my* right."

The stove moved and teetered under the chimney.

"There, put it down."

"Say, why the hell's it crooked?"

"Because it's on my foot, that's why."

"Oh."

The stove shifted.

"All right. Let's get these pipes up."

Several short lengths of pipe had to be joined to reach from the top of the stove to the chimney opening. The pipes clattered and rolled around the floor.

"By God, there's nothing in this world ornery as a piece of stovepipe. When they're just right, they bend like paper. When you want to bend them, they're like cast iron."

They banged and pushed at the pipes, trying to fit them together. Soot flew around the room, crunching under their feet as they moved.

"Who the hell was supposed to clean these pipes?"

No one answered.

"Dammit, we got two pieces with dampers."

"One must be for the living room."

"Well, who the hell mixed these pipes up?" Crash, as the pipe was thrown down. More soot.

No one answered.

Finally the pipes were all in place, including the elbow at the top. They had to move the stove a little. The pipes would come crashing down.

"I thought you were holding those damn things."

"I thought you were."

"Well, I wasn't."

"I can see that."

Again the pipe was built up. If they were lucky, they remembered to put the little brass collar around the elbow the first time.

"Wait a minute. The pipe's too short."

"I just don't understand how a damn set of pipes can fit fine in the spring and be an inch too short in the fall."

Here Mother's face would appear around the edge of the kitchen door, ready to duck. "You forgot to put the things under the legs again."

"Oh, hell."

"All right. I'll lift her. You put them under."

The pipes, of course, would fall down again.

Finally both stoves were in place, the pipes reasonably straight, the dampers more or less in the right position. Father and Lyle would stomp out, leaving the soot for Mother to clean up, and one of us to install the stove doors and footwarmers. Sometimes Father paused long enough in the kitchen to suggest we leave the stove up next summer. Our wise mother didn't argue, but next spring the stoves would get carried off to the woodshed, leaving a reverse trail of soot, barked knuckles, and "goddamns."

We boys usually listened to all this from the safety of the porch. Our stomachs were sore for days afterward from the way we tried to hold in our laughter. One by one, as we got older, we had a turn at helping with the stoves. Then we understood what all the uproar was about. I don't know about my brothers, but to this day I can't walk by a piece of stovepipe without feeling it's going to leap out and get me some way.

The whole episode was referred to as "the day we put the stoves in." It took a place in the fall calendar roughly equivalent to such phrases as "the time we had four feet of snow for Thanksgiving" or "the day Bob Miller's pickup truck ran through the outhouse. With his wife in it."

Yet, on the evening of the day we put the stoves in, the dining room was warm and cozy, all the irritation gone, a pleasant smell of fresh stove blacking and woodsmoke in the room. Lyle would be sitting where he sat every evening until spring, his stocking feet propped up on the nickel-plated footwarmers. He always toasted himself up good before he made his wild dash upstairs to the room he called "the icebox."

The two heating stoves and the kitchen range—we called it the cookstove—all burned wood. It was my job to carry a supply each afternoon from the old woodshed, which had a musky smell from the time Laurance had trapped skunks and hung the skins there to cure. The wood was oak, cut the previous winter so it would be dry. I piled great armloads on the porch, out of the rain and snow. There were heavy chunks for the heaters, always a few very big ones for bedtime so the fires would last all night. Wood for the cookstove was about sixteen inches long and split into sticks two or three inches through. Whenever Mother asked me to split her a couple armloads of extra-fine wood, I knew she was planning something special for supper. Maybe a cake that needed a very hot oven. Maybe even waffles, the smoke-blackened waffle iron over an open stove lid, flames licking up around it, firelight gleaming on Mother's perspiring face.

※

As the young pigs fattened, stockbuyers came by in their big cars and pickup trucks, made tentative offers, and said they'd be back. It was a tough time for Father. There were no set prices. A buyer tried to get stock at a low price, and farmers tried to sell for as much as they could. Father watched the pigs and kept track of the market in the newspaper. The pigs went on eating corn, every pound meaning more money if prices held up. But if too many pigs hit the Chicago market, the price would go down and we'd have fed ours extra corn for nothing.

When Father thought the time and pigs were right, he called several buyers and asked what they'd pay. One buyer was a charming, handsome man who, Lyle said, had a golden voice and a rubber checkbook. Whenever we sold to him, Father asked for the money in cash. Yet Father liked the man. It was my introduction to the idea that you could like someone you didn't trust.

Trucks took the squealing pigs away, Father going along to make sure we got honest weight at the stockyard scales. The stockyards were smelly, fly-filled places, a hangout for the storytellers. Once when I went with Father, someone was telling about the time an old man, who drank vanilla for the alcohol in it, went to the store and asked for a dollar's worth of rope.

"What for?" the storekeeper asked.

"Going to hang myself."

The storekeeper held up a sample of rope. "Figure this is about the right size?"

The man nodded.

The storekeeper went to a side room, cut off about twenty feet of rope, and brought it back.

The man went down to the stockyard, put a loop around his neck, tied one end to a crossbeam, and jumped off a post. The rope broke. The storekeeper had cut it almost through in several places. The old man went running back to the store, a piece of two-by-four in his hand, so mad he forgot all about hanging himself.

Something in the crisp air of fall got all the storytellers remembering things and talking as if it might be the last chance they'd ever get. At the stores, blacksmith shops, filling stations, barber shops, and depots they all gathered to swap yarns—the old men, the crippled-up men, the young men who had decided not to work anymore. Other men might stop by and tell a story or two before leaving, but they didn't make a profession out of it.

I remember once going to Petersburg with Father to buy enough flour to last us until spring. There were two stores in Petersburg then. Now they're gone and the town's not much more than a wide space in the road. One store was run by a man named Glew. It was called "Sticky's." The other was run by a tall, very thin man. People called that one "Bony" Steinbach's.

On this particular day all the storytellers were gathered on the steps at Sticky Glew's. The other store had a porch, and they gathered there on rainy days. The steps were covered with wood shavings. It was the first time I'd had a chance to see how whittling went along with storytelling. Half the men there had jackknives going on pieces of pine. I watched, fascinated, wondering what works of art might appear. The knives worked steadily, the pieces of pine changing from thick to thin, blunt to sharp. Finally, a piece of wood would be gone, all whittled up. Was it the paper-thin shavings that were the works of art?

All this time the talk went on, as though the whittling helped the men remember.

"Say, how about that time the old stump dodger went off the track up there at the crossing? Stove tipped over in the caboose, started a fire. This dressed-up-fit-to-kill lady from Chicago started screaming. Went running off across the bottom and got stuck in the slough. We had to pull her out of there with a horse. My God, she was madder than a wet hen."

"You know we ain't had a good train wreck for years. 'Bout time we shoveled a little sand across the tracks again."

A car coasted by. The driver waved.

"There goes Clarence Zintz somewhere. Reminds me. I been thinking about them horse thieves. Used to steal horses here, sell 'em in Grant County. Steal horses there and sell 'em here. Clarence claims they had themselves a cave over along the Wisconsin River. He figures they left a pile of money in there."

"Why would they do that?"

"Well, they got caught one night, crossing the river. Every last one of them was hung."

"What does Clarence know about it?"

I could see that tobacco, like the whittling, was part of the story-telling. A man would pause, leaving everyone hanging while he took aim and spat. Pipe-smokers did the same thing while they got their pipes going again.

"Why, one of Clarence's relatives was in that gang. He was hung right along with the others. I figure Clarence goes over there and looks for that cave now and again."

A car pulled up in front of the store, radiator steaming. It was George Holliday, the mailman.

"Little behind schedule, aren't you, George?"

"'Course I am." He pointed into the back of the car. It was piled high with Sears and Montgomery catalogues. "Those damn mail-order books. I swear I'm going to throw 'em in the river some fall."

George sat down on the steps. "Say, you heard about this guy up in Star Valley? House is up on the ridge. Gets his mail down on the valley road. Well, he got tired running up and down that hill for his mail. Rigged his mailbox up on a rope-and-pulley gadget. Lets the box down every morning. Waits till the mail comes, then just cranks her back up the hill without even getting out of his chair."

Father came out of the store. He put his hand on my shoulder. "There's an ice cream cone all paid for in there."

Father saw George. "Mail all delivered?"

"Nope."

"How come?"

"Car overheated." He winked. "Postal inspector can't argue with that. Damn car boils over when it's forty below zero. Reminds me of the time out West. We was coming across the mountains. Car boiled all the water away. Well, we had some cases of beer in the back . . ."

I went inside for my ice-cream cone, working awhile on a decision between strawberry, vanilla, and chocolate. I settled for strawberry, and Mr. Glew began building up a good cone. The store smelled of chocolate, smoked meat, kerosene, and new clothes. Red-coated soldiers charged across a counter display of Putnam dyes. A dozen glass-topped boxes had a rich variety of chocolate and marshmallow-covered cookies, a penny apiece.

I got my cone. Father and I went across the street to Bony Steinbach's, which may have been the first self-service store in the country. Mr. Steinbach, who moved and talked equally slowly, liked to sit up by the cash register and tell people where to find whatever they needed.

Father asked for a price on a barrel of flour. The storekeeper did some figuring on a brown paper bag, named a price, and Father nodded. Then Mr. Steinbach tried to sell Father some unbreakable lamp chimneys. He dropped one on the floor to demonstrate. It broke.

"Must have been cracked."

He dropped another one. It broke.

"Well, I guess they're all cracked." His face moved into his slow and easy smile. "They didn't break when the damned salesman dropped them. How about a good buy on fifty pounds of sugar?"

That time of the year you could drive on up the river to Bell Center and find what sounded like the same bunch of men.

"Remember that time somebody told old man Palmer this guy was fooling around with his daughter. Palmer talked kind of funny. What he said was, 'I will hit that man so hard it will make a hole in him. Then I will pull his head through that hole and tie a knot in it.'"

Sometimes it was all questions. What ever became of Buckshot Moon? Where's Two-Bit Johnston now? What happened to Russian John? Was there somebody named Crow used to live in Crow Hollow?

There were a half dozen or so last names that always brought a snort of disapproval. I guess those people were our minorities. A kid born with one of those names didn't have a chance unless he found some way to get out of that country. He had to be twice as smart as other people before anyone would pay attention to him. I remember one boy who walked ten miles a day, round trip, to high school. He worked his way through college and became a school superintendent, but when some people remember what his last name is, they still don't really believe he could have done all that.

Each group of storytellers had its walking encyclopedia. He knew what President William McKinley's middle name was, how deep the ground froze in 1917, whether it was Clyde Winters' first or second wife who just about killed him with a piece of firewood.

"No, it wasn't nineteen twenty-one at all. It was nineteen twenty-three, same year two of our cows had twin calves the same night. We never did figure out which calves went with which cow."

Go on to Seneca to the filling station and the talk was the same.

"By God, things have changed some, all right. My father could remember when the stagecoach came through here couple times a day. Whenever he got hungry, he started talking about the food at Langdon's Inn where the stage stopped. There was venison, prairie chicken, wild turkey, brook trout, grouse. He claimed there even used to be elk in this country."

"'Course there was. They say old Will Sterling used to tell about coming up the Kickapoo by canoe back in the eighteen thirties with his wife and two kids. Said there was a big Indian village down in Haney Valley, bear and elk thick along the river. Hell, that was close to a hundred years ago. I guess there might even have been a buffalo left then."

"By God, what happened? All the game. Springs that used to run all summer, dry year or wet. What happened?"

Some days, when the sky was dark with low-hanging clouds, the voices of doom took over.

"Bad winter coming. You watch the squirrels."

"There'll be people freeze to death before spring."

"Gonna be a lot of sickness. You'll see old Doc Farrell's sleigh going by every time you look out the window."

At the Seneca blacksmith shop the white-haired blacksmith always seemed to have a hammer in one hand and a bottle in the other.

"By God, Jack, even half drunk you're the best blacksmith for a hundred miles around. Wasn't for liquor you could make a million dollars."

The smith tipped up the bottle. "Who wants to be a millionaire when you can feel like one for fifty cents?"

They got to arguing at the blacksmith shop one day, when Father was waiting for a plowshare to be sharpened, about whether or not there had been a boy down toward Prairie du Chien who had lived with the Indians.

"Sure there was. Name was Charley Ross, they think. He's buried in that little graveyard down at Wyalusing. Little place. Not hardly enough land to whip a dog on. Boy was found out on an island in the Mississippi. Said he'd been living with the Indians for five years. Man name of Bidwell found him."

"No, it wasn't. It was John Hartford. He was Leita Slayton's grandfather."

The argument went on and on. Finally one of the men went across the street to the store and telephoned Leita Slayton. He came back smiling. "Like I said, it was John Hartford found him. Leita says an old Indian woman used to come to the Hartford house and ask for a drink of water. Seemed like she was trying to get a look at the boy. Boy died in an epidemic three years later. The Indian woman never came back after that."

When cold weather came, the storytellers seemed to disappear, though you could still find a few of them hugging close to a pot-bellied stove in a store.

"They haven't gone anyplace," Lyle told me. "They're just sitting at home thinking up a new batch of stories for next year."

One late fall day when the leaves were blowing and the birds flying south, a closed-in wagon came slowly along the road from the west, pulled by an old gray horse that wobbled back and forth between the shafts. The wagon had windows on the sides, with little curtains. The wheel rim and hubs were bright red, the spokes bright yellow. On the side there was a painting of a valley, with a bright blue lake and white-covered mountains far above.

The driver was a woman, sitting on a little seat that was protected by the curving roof. She wore a long purple skirt, a purple scarf on her head, and a white blouse with ribbons and lace.

The wagon stopped in front of the house, where the bare limbs of the elm tree hung out over the road.

"Come quick. It's Gypsies," Mother called. Only Lee and I were close. We were already watching from back by the woodshed. All our lives we'd heard tales of how the Gypsies stole children.

The woman turned and said something into the wagon. A younger woman appeared. They were both dark-skinned and very slim. They jumped down from the high seat and ran into the yard, long skirts flying. Mother eyed their low-cut blouses uncertainly. I guess she didn't realize how well we'd been introduced to such mysteries by the brassiere and petticoat pictures in the mail-order catalogues.

The women made a little bow to Mother.

"You have nails?" the older one asked, voice deep, the accent strange to us.

Mother nodded to Lee and me. We ran to the milk house to bring nails, but found the two women right behind us. They came inside, their hands darting in and out of the brown paper bags we held out, taking different sizes and dropping them into their skirts. When we pulled the bags away, they looked around the milk house at the neat collection of tools hanging on the walls. They ran over to inspect the bright red gasoline engine that ran the pumpjack. I could smell woodsmoke and a spice that was not quite cinnamon. They moved to the washing machine, lifted the lid, and stared inside, looking puzzled.

They didn't speak. I wondered what they thought of our settled, organized world. I tried to picture them doing the farm work day after day on our isolated ridge, where a week might go by when the only other person we talked to was the mailman.

The younger woman made a little sound. She nudged the other woman and pointed. On the workbench was a toy boat we had made for playing in the watering tank. Lee picked up the boat and held it out. The younger woman took it with a quick smile and it vanished into her skirt.

They ran out of the milk house. Mother was waiting beside the porch with a big loaf of homemade bread. They smiled at her, gave their funny little bow again, and ran to the wagon, gold earrings and bracelets dancing. The wagon rocked as they climbed to the seat. A smoke-blackened copper pot banged where it hung on the side of the wagon. For the first time I noticed the tiny stovepipe sticking up from the roof, a pointed weather cap on top of it.

The younger woman disappeared inside. The other woman broke off a piece of bread and handed it back. The curtains moved at the window. A face looked out. It was a child. I wanted to run and look inside that wagon more than I had ever wanted anything in my life.

We waved. The face at the window disappeared.

"Wait," Mother called. "Get some apples. And a few eggs," she said to Lee and me.

We ran to the orchard and picked up fallen apples, the big Wolf Rivers and the crisp little Sweet Apples. I went on to the chicken house and took six eggs from the nests. We ran back to the wagon and handed the eggs and apples up to the woman. She nodded with each handful. The big smile flashed again. She reached out, touched both of us lightly on top of the head, and said something we couldn't understand.

The horse got into motion, dry grass from the roadbank sticking out of its mouth. The wagon moved down the hill, steel wheel rims ringing on the rocks. I kept watching the window. The child did not appear again.

"Where are they going?"

Mother smiled. "To where it's warmer. They follow the seasons north and south."

"Like the birds?"

"Yes."

"Where do they live?"

"The wagon. It's the only home they have."

It was the first time I had ever seen Gypsies. I was disappointed. Where were the dark mustachioed men? Where were the fortune-teller and the tambourines? Where were the violins and the dancing?

"I thought there was always music."

Mother put an arm around Lee and an arm around me. "Maybe there will be music tonight, when they stop to camp."

That helped. I could picture them with a campfire going, maybe down in the valley where the road crossed Halls Branch Creek. The horse would be eating corn from Young's field. There would be music and maybe even dancing after they had cooked in the copper pot and eaten the food we'd given them.

The sun was getting low. The afternoon was cool, the colors deepening. We watched the wagon until it disappeared over the last hill to the east. Mother sighed and went back into the house. We had baking powder biscuits instead of bread with supper that night.

29 Ghosts

I didn't believe in ghosts, but fall seemed filled with reminders of the past. As the leaves fell from the sumac, hazel brush, and wild grape vines, the foundations of forgotten buildings came back into view. Arrowheads turned up in the furrows during the fall plowing. A fox barking from the woodpile reminded us of the wolves that had once howled from Lost Valley. In the woods a large mourning dove might fly up ahead of me with a whirring of wings and a flash of gray-blue and dull red. My heart would race as I ran after the bird, trying to see where it had landed, always hoping I had found a last passenger pigeon.

I could not believe they were gone.

The men at the stores and filling stations still talked about them, the stories filled with magical phrases:

"Darkened the sky."

"A sound like distant thunder."

"Flock in Pennsylvania with two billion birds in it."

"Fire once with a shotgun and bring down fifty, sixty birds."

"A good net would get five thousand a day."

"Whole trainloads shipped out of Prairie du Chien for the Chicago market."

"Took four days for that flock to fly over."

"Nesting area up in the sand counties was twenty-seven miles long, three, four miles wide."

"Fellow said they figured the nest area was narrow like that so the ones in the middle didn't have to fly so far for feed."

"Barrels of them stored away in salt in the basement."

"Hunters had to keep changing gun barrels."

"When they was feeding on acorns it sounded like all the popcorn in the world popping at once."

"Flocks was already getting smaller by the time Wisconsin was a state back in eighteen forty-eight."

"Trouble was nobody wanted to stop. I guess there wasn't many ways to get your hands on cash money in those days."

"Sure hard to believe they're gone."

"I keep figuring there's bound to be a few left some wild place. Maybe down in Rush Creek or along Copper Creek. They say there's still beaver up in there."

I found a bird book with a picture of the passenger pigeon. They were sixteen inches long, it said, and could fly sixty miles an hour. "Range: formerly Eastern North America, north to Hudson Bay; now exceedingly rare, less so in the upper Mississippi Valley than elsewhere."

I ran triumphantly to Mother. "There! We're in the upper Mississippi Valley, aren't we? I bet I find one yet!"

Mother took the book and looked at the copyright. She shook her head and pulled me close against her. "I'm sorry. The book was written in nineteen three. I think there were still a few passenger pigeons then."

There were reports now and then that someone had seen one. It always turned out to be a mourning dove. I went on searching anyway, in all the hidden corners and thick woods of the farm, listening for that sound of distant thunder I had not heard, looking for that certain flash of color I had never seen. Mother watched me in those fall days. I knew I was worrying her, but I couldn't stop.

"How could they all be gone?"

"People hunted them too much. Do you know what gregarious means?"

"I think so. When things like to be in bunches?"

She nodded. "Your grandfather says the passenger pigeons were very gregarious. There had to be a certain number or they wouldn't go on reproducing. Some naturalists believe that number may have been in the tens of thousands or even a million."

"You mean when there was still a million of them somebody might have shot just one bird and it was like he'd killed them all?"

"Something like that."

"Did the other birds know what was going to happen?"

"I don't think so. I hope not."

Mother sighed and looked at me for a long time. I waited, knowing she was deciding something. She brought out a magazine. I hadn't seen it before, even though it was several years old. There was an article in it about the passenger pigeons. Mother read it to me, and it was filled with phrases, like the stories of the old men, that caught and hung on the mind.

"By nineteen hundred only fifteen were known for certain to exist. All of those were in captivity."

"As though outraged by what had happened, the birds often refused to mate."

"By nineteen nine there was only a single pair left. They were at the Cincinnati Zoo. They mated. The eggs didn't hatch."

"Then the male died."

"The female was named Martha. On September first, nineteen fourteen, at one o'clock in the afternoon, Martha died. She was the last known passenger pigeon anywhere in the world."

Mother closed the magazine. She was crying.

"Nineteen fourteen," I said. "Did it have something to do with the war?"

"No. At least not the way you mean."

"I wasn't born yet, was I?"

"No."

I still searched for a last passenger pigeon. It was a habit that followed me and came back in the restless days of fall. I don't think I gave up completely until I was much older. One fall while on a picnic at Wyalusing State Park I found a plaque on the high bluff, commemorating the last Wisconsin passenger pigeon ever seen in the wild. The ending words were, "extinct through the avarice and thoughtlessness of man."

I ran away, along the long row of Indian mounds that lined the ridge, the acorns crunching under my feet. I ran into the woods and stayed there until my friends began to call and look for me.

30 One-Room Community

The beginning of school was a mark of fall that had nothing to do with weather. I remember a certain morning. We woke to the excitement of change, ran out into the misty sunrise, rushed through breakfast and chores, then ran down through the woods toward the one-room schoolhouse in Halls Branch Valley, three-quarters of a mile away. Only our running kept the growing coolness away from us as we traded the red sunlight of the ridge for the shadowed places where sunrise had not yet come. We didn't even stop at the spring for a cold drink or at the sandbank where our bottle cars were stored. Feet and pants legs wet from the dew-soaked grass, we ran down into the main valley, then up along the creek. On the road, close to the far hillside, there were other children, too far away to be recognized, except for one, a hunchback boy who was twice as big as the others. We yelled and waved. They began to run. We raced ahead of them, up through the meadow, dodging the bull thistles and the bright clumps of blue vervain we called horse nettle.

Hearing the yells of children coming down from farms on the far ridge, we climbed the high fence, rolled across, and dropped down into the schoolyard. We were first, even ahead of the teacher. We waited, the chill of the shadowed valley reaching us now that we had stopped running. Other children came. We joked a little and pushed each other, but mostly we stood in little groups looking at the schoolhouse, already feeling confined to life imprisonment. It was at that moment—as we exchanged the hard work and freedom of summer for the captivity of school—that fall began.

Teacher came, striding in her no-nonsense way along the road from the farm where she rented a room and took her meals. She gave us a half-smile and unlocked the schoolhouse. A few girls and younger boys followed her in. The rest of us stayed outside until a window slid up and a hand reached out, ringing the familiar brass bell. We straggled in, suddenly stiff and uncomfortable in our new clothes, feet pinched and hot in shoes. The door closed behind us. The sunshine and green of the outside world were light-years away.

Teacher stood at the front of the room, looking very young and very stern, tapping a ruler on her palm.

"Just sit anywhere. I'll assign seats later."

We raced and jostled for a place in the rear, then crowded into the hard seats with their carved tops, pencil grooves, and empty holes for glass inkwells. The noise ended. Then laughter began: Tom Withers, the big hunchback boy, had jammed himself into one of the smaller seats, his long legs sticking far out into the aisle. Teacher tried to help him move to a larger seat, but he was stuck. The desk creaked and lifted as he struggled. His long hair swung across his face. The laughter grew louder. With Teacher pulling, Tom escaped and slumped into another seat. His face was bright red above his blue chambray shirt.

Teacher marched to the front of the room, heels clicking. Her face was white. She leveled a finger at us. The laughter stopped.

"I'm ashamed of you!" she said, her voice shaking. "All of you! Now you listen: we don't laugh at another person's difficulties!"

We squirmed in our seats. A chorus of voices said, "Yes, Teacher."

She picked up her attendance book, her eyes going from face to face. The old schoolhouse clock ticked away above the blackboard, slow, slow, slow. The room smelled of new clothes and soap. Teacher looked at her list, then back at us. She read off a name. "Anyone know where he is?"

"Moved away," someone volunteered.

She crossed off his name. A boy we had played baseball with, argued with and wrestled with, four months before, was gone forever.

The school day moved ahead. Textbooks were handed out; seats assigned, younger grades always along the window side; classes began. Being in "class" usually meant going to the front of the room to recite, read, answer questions, write, or do problems on the blackboards. Sometimes "class" meant staying in our seats to take tests, do arithmetic problems, or draw a picture. There were eight grades in that one room and each grade had three or four classes a day. Classes were small because there were only twenty-one of us.

The one-room system only worked when everything was happening at once. On that first day we had trouble. A boy with new overalls walked to the blackboard, stiff pants legs scraping against each other.

"Somebody sawing wood?" a voice asked.

There was laughter. The boy worked at the board, the back of his neck brick red.

We shared in the triumphs and agonized at the mistakes of those in class at the front of the room. A verbal answer started heads nodding in approval or shaking in disapproval.

"You have your own work to do," Teacher kept reminding us.

Once, when a question went unanswered, a hand shot up in the back of the room. "I know! I know!"

"You're not in this class," Teacher said.

"Oh."

The hand jerked down. There was laughter, then sudden silence. But it didn't matter. Teacher was smiling.

"All right," she said. "Just for today, why don't you answer anyway."

We boiled out of the room for morning recess and set up our baseball diamond in the meadow, using dried cow-manure pats for some of the bases. At lunch hour we started playing ball and discovered, too late, that a cow had come along and put down a fresh marker for second base.

Two first-graders had lost their lunch buckets. Teacher made the rounds and asked for contributions of food. A third-grader went back too far chasing a long fly ball. He raced off a six-foot-high bank, ran halfway across the creek in mid-air, then dropped out of sight with a great splash. We first galloped downstream to retrieve the floating ball, then went back and rescued the boy.

A girl got her finger stuck in the cap of her new fountain pen. Tom Withers ran away at afternoon recess. Teacher watched him go and didn't call him back.

By the end of that first day, our one-room community was beginning to work. Teacher, her young face looking much less official now that strands were escaping from her severe hairdo, was more willing to risk a smile.

"No homework tonight," she said.

Suddenly the room was a yelling, seething mass, with twenty-one of us trying to get out the door at the same time. My brothers and I ran up the hill above the school, checked the apples in the deserted orchard, looked over the hickory-nut crop, and ran on home, remembering to tell Father about a fence that needed fixing and that squirrels were getting the corn in the field next to the woods.

"How was school today?" Mother asked as we drank milk and ate slices of fresh bread with honey.

"It was all right."

"Anything unusual happen?"

"No."

Mother smiled. She had taught in a one-room schoolhouse herself and knew what the first day was like.

Next morning, school began as if it had been going on for months. We didn't know it at the time, but we just may have been participants in the best educational system ever devised. In that richly varied one-room community there was no artificial separation of children into good and bad, smart and dumb, young and old. We were all in it together. Subjects and years weren't tied into neat bundles. They were overlapped, so that there was only one subject: education. I made my way, year by year, up through the grades, but that was only on the record book. I was in all the school years each year. I watched the younger children at the blackboard. I listened to them recite. Each time, it was a review of information already studied. Each time, I brought something new to it from my own widening world. I watched and listened when older children were in class. It was an introduction to the demands school would make on me next year, or the year after that.

The process was so natural to me that I took it all for granted. It was like life on the farm, with everything happening at once, each thing related to everything else. I had trouble later in high school and college. I was bewildered by the separation of subjects into isolated units, as though chemistry lived on some separate planet that didn't even share the same orbit with history. There was no such separation in our one-room community.

There were no secrets, either. Teacher would call the roll. "Where's George?" she'd ask a brother or sister.

"He had to stay home and help."

"Doing what?"

"Tobacco harvest." (Or silo-filling, shredding, woodcutting, driving cattle to the stockyard, fencing . . .)

Teacher would think about it, understanding the demands of a farm. "All right. He should come tomorrow. I'll give you his assignments."

"Where's Alice?"

"She's sick."

"Anything contagious?"

"Ma doesn't think so."

"All right. Tell Alice we hope she's better by tomorrow."

"Where's Paul?"

"He cut his toe, splitting wood."

"Is he all right?"

"I think so. His sock was all red. Mother said to say he'll come tomorrow. He couldn't walk good today."

There was a boy named Anthony, three years younger than I, with a pale face that seemed all eyes. He was sick a lot and the question "Where's Anthony?" was one we heard very often. Anthony had brothers in school, but for some reason he attached himself to me. We called him "Nuisance," but he didn't mind. He grinned at us, happy to be noticed. It was the first chance I'd ever had to be an older brother to anyone, except maybe a kitten, and I looked out for him.

Teacher asked about Anthony one day.

"He swallowed a nickel," his brother said.

There was laughter.

"Wasn't his nickel, either."

"Is he all right?"

"Doctor Farrell came. He thinks so."

Anthony came back to school a few days later.

"What happened to the nickel?" Teacher asked.

Anthony blushed and answered in his clear, choirboy voice, "I laid it."

Part of the richness of that one-room school was in the variety of children. Everyone was from a farm, but each family represented a separate world. There were different ways of speaking, different clothes, different religions, beliefs, and superstitions. Some children always had all the pencils and paper they needed. For some, the loss of a penny pencil sent them away in tears at the end of the day to a home where there were no more pencils and maybe no more pennies either. Some children came with nothing. Teacher quietly supplied them, probably paying for the things herself.

"If you know the farm, you know the child," people said sometimes at school meetings. "What are the fences like? Are the taxes paid up? Do they rotate their crops? Do they haul out the manure?"

"Don't expect too much of that one," a new teacher might be told about a first-grader.

And the teachers—the good ones, stern and caring—would fight such talk. "A child is new! Are you going to brand a first-grader because the manure is not hauled out?"

Teachers worked with us in a way that said each of us was important. They moved us up the grades, from the window side of the room to the chimney side of the room, as the years passed. Some children stayed, some dropped out. Some escaped from their limiting backgrounds. Some grew up and probably didn't haul out the manure on their own farms either.

Some teachers never came back for a second year of the chaos. There was one, before my time, who was never quite the same after the day an eighth-grader threw a shotgun shell into the heating stove. The shell exploded. Stovepipes came crashing down. The stove door flew off. The teacher, the storytellers claimed later, jumped ten feet in the air, made a dent in the ceiling, and came down running.

Father was on the school board, and one of his jobs was to look over applications from teachers. He came home from a board meeting one evening still laughing about a letter of "nonrecommendation" that had come from another school district.

"The letter said she doesn't know much about anatomy, especially ears," Father told us. "It seems this boy had some dried beans in his pocket at school. He got one stuck in his ear."

"A bean?" Mother interrupted. "Why in the world would a child put a bean in his ear?"

Father looked disgusted. "You were a teacher. You have four boys. You want a reason?"

"I withdraw the question," Mother said.

"Anyway," Father continued, "you know what that teacher did about that bean? She decided to wash it out. So she poured water in the other ear."

"Poor thing," Mother said, laughing all the same.

There are three teachers that I especially remember. One was a man. I recall him as part of a year when it seemed that all we did was play baseball. I don't know what the girls did. The teacher played with us, of course. If we were careful to let him go on batting, he forgot what time it was. Some of those lunch-hour ballgames went on until midafternoon. That year, we even played baseball after the ground was frozen solid. When we missed a high fly or a pop-up, the ball bounced back up almost out of sight.

That man only taught one year at Halls Branch. I guess we talked too much at home.

The other two teachers were women, both Irish, both appreciated much more now than they were at the time. Their names were Irene O'Neil and Bridget Collins. The eyes of either could sweep a room and I would be sure she was looking mainly at me. They cajoled, demanded, counseled, and coaxed us into being better than we were, working harder than we wanted to, learning more than we cared to know. They had a driving energy. You had only to see them walk across a room to know that. Most of all, they could organize that roomful of diversity into a functioning unit. Just how they did that, I still don't know.

They could do anything. Get out a splinter. Stop a nosebleed. Tape up a cut leg that would bring an ambulance screaming to a school today. They checked heads for lice, pulled certain children aside and suggested that a bath, at least once a month, might be a good idea. They kept the furnace going and lighted up the smelly kerosene stove each noon so we could heat the jars of soup or stew we carried from home. They tugged overshoes off the smaller children and pushed them back on again at the end of the day. They had to worry about whether to let school out early if a storm came or threatened to come. When the snowdrifts were deep or the temperature down below zero, they had to decide which younger children needed an older one to walk them home. They had to worry about what to do on a stormy morning if a child did not appear. There was no telephone at the school or at the nearest farm.

Some of the work was delegated to the older children and that, too, was part of our education. I read spelling words to younger children, listened to their ABC's, and checked them on their multiplication tables. Older children helped me in turn.

Those two women shaped our lives, and we took it for granted that they were in complete command. They merge now into one. When I think back, I don't think of names or of two of them. I just think "Teacher."

One of the things Teacher taught us was that outrage is something you should have and should show. Teacher showed us that when we laughed at Tom Withers. She showed it on a day when I was so lost in a book I didn't know my sixth-grade arithmetic class had gone to the front of the room. I heard Teacher speak my name. She was right at my elbow. I realized she had spoken several times. I jumped to my feet, dropping the book, and hurried to the front. The others laughed. Teacher straightened up with the fallen book. Her face was white.

"Quiet!" she yelled.

She marched to the front of the room. I had never seen her look so angry before. "Don't ever let me hear you do that again!" she thundered. "Don't ever let me hear you laugh at somebody because they are that interested in a book!"

Everyone was looking at me. I was embarrassed and hung my head.

Teacher smiled suddenly. "What was so interesting?"

"The monarch butterfly," I said.

"Tell us."

I tried to repeat what I had found, still not quite believing it myself. All my life I had seen the big orange monarchs perched on the summer flowers. They especially liked milkweed. In the fall they vanished along with all the other butterflies. I had thought they were killed by frost. The book said they did not die. They flew south, like the birds, migrating all the way from Wisconsin to the Gulf of Mexico, a thousand miles away. They laid their eggs there. Those eggs became new monarchs, and in spring they flew north again. The thought of those beautiful and fragile butterflies, migrating like bright-colored flowers, was more vivid than any fairy tale.

I stopped speaking. Teacher opened the book, read a moment, and nodded. "That's what it says. And I think it is an accurate book."

She walked back to my desk and put the book down. Then sixth-grade arithmetic began.

31 Tom Withers

As the shortening days of fall settled into a routine at school, all of us except Tom Withers surrendered to our confinement. Tom went on squirming uneasily in his seat, his long legs always far out in the aisle to trip anyone who walked by. He remained tuned to the outdoors. If a cloud went across the sun, he sat up straight and craned his neck to see what was happening. He knew when the wind shifted, when the creek was rising, when the temperature had changed. In winter he knew when the snow was softening and would announce to the room, "Good day for snowman."

We knew by watching Tom when a weather change was coming. He was more restless than usual and kept going to the window to look at the sky.

"What's the matter, Tom?" Teacher would ask.

"Storm."

"Today?"

If he nodded, Teacher too would begin to check the sky to see if school should let out early.

Once, when the call of migrating geese came to us, Tom ran to an open window and began climbing out.

"Tom," Teacher called.

He stopped halfway through the window. His mouth moved but no words came out.

"You may use the door."

He gave her the widest smile we had ever seen and ran outside. We heard the fence creak. A few minutes later a rumbling sound came from the hillside above the school. We all ran to the windows. A great rock came rolling down the hill. It went all the way across the meadow and splashed into the creek.

Teacher sighed and shook her head.

There was one fall when it seemed we spent half our recesses arguing about religion. Carefully skirting around the words Jesus and God, we debated endlessly, the Protestants bringing the authority of last Sunday's church school, the Catholics quoting from their Saturday catechism sessions. Once we argued for days about whether someone had or had not inscribed the Lord's Prayer on the head of a pin.

Tom Withers sat on the ground and listened to us, never speaking. Then one day he stood up, held his hands in the air, and started to say something.

We waited.

Tom lowered his hands. "You meet me. After school." He pointed to a hillside.

"Why?"

He wouldn't answer.

After school, five of us started home the usual way so Teacher wouldn't notice anything. Then we doubled back and gathered in the thick woods on the hillside far above the schoolhouse. We waited. Teacher left, walking down the valley. We turned to Tom.

He climbed onto a rock, raised his arms above his head, and looked straight up. The valley below was silent. Not even the singing of the creek reached us. A little blue smoke still came from the schoolhouse chimney.

A sound began in Tom's throat. He stretched his arms higher. His mouth opened and the sound roared out: "THEY AIN'T NO GOD!"

"GOD, GOD, GOD," went the echo.

"STRIKE ME DOWN DEAD IF THEY'S A GOD!" Tom yelled.

The echoes rolled back and forth across the valley. "GOD, GOD, GOD." A door slammed at the farmhouse next to the school. Mr. Watson came out, hooking his suspenders up over the shoulders of his long underwear. He looked round, scratched his head, and went back inside.

Tom still stood on the rock, arms raised.

We waited. Then a little whirlwind came along the hillside, rattling the dead oak leaves, seeming to attack one tree at a time. It took hold of the tree where we stood, thrashed with it, filling the woods with sound. Then it moved on.

Tom lowered his arms. He looked at us, baring his teeth in a smile, jumped from the rock, and ran along the hillside out of sight.

We waited a little longer and then, without a word to one another, went our different ways. We didn't talk much about religion at school after that.

There was a large white pine tree near the schoolhouse. A lone mourning dove perched in the lower branches day after day and sent its sad call out over the valley. Each time, Tom squirmed in his seat and covered his ears with his hands.

"What's the matter, Tom?" Teacher asked.

"Sad. So sad."

Once he ran to the window and screamed. The calls stopped. There was a whistle of wings. After that, Teacher left the windows closed on that side of the building. At recess and lunch hour, Tom drove the dove away by pounding on the tree trunk with a piece of furnace wood.

The dove always came back. One morning when the calls began, Tom exploded out of his desk, papers and books flying. He ran outside, Teacher right behind him. We crowded to the windows. Tom had a slingshot made from a forked stick and strips of rubber inner tube. He was shooting rocks at the mourning dove. Teacher reached out for the slingshot. He pulled it back and shot again. She stepped in front of him and started talking. It was in that strange way that I first heard the Indian legend about the mourning dove.

Once, in a valley like this one, Teacher said, there was an Indian village. In it lived an Indian princess. She was very beautiful, and also very vain. She made friends with all the Indian braves, but as soon as a brave told her he loved her, she laughed at him and sent him away.

Each year the princess grew more beautiful. Each year the braves came from many tribes to court her. It was always the same. She smiled and led them on, then sent them away, broken-hearted, unable to forget her.

One of the braves she rejected had magical powers. He waited until winter came. Then he made a handsome snowman and dressed it in the finest of clothes. He breathed life into the snowman and sent him to the princess's village. The brave hunted with the tribe. He courted the princess. No one had ever been so handsome or so brave. There was only one thing that puzzled the Indians. The stranger would not sit with them at the campfire.

As spring came, the princess fell in love for the first time. The weather warmed. The brave felt himself beginning to melt and ran away through the woods. The princess followed, calling his name. She found a moccasin, a legging, a jacket. One by one, she found all his handsome clothes strewn along the path. The trail ended. There was nothing but melting snow. The brave was gone.

The princess went on searching through the woods, calling and calling, wandering far from her village. Finally, the man who had breathed life into the snowman took pity on her. He turned her into a mourning dove. Ever since, the mourning dove calls endlessly, still searching for the lost brave.

Teacher stopped talking. Tom looked up at the pine tree. The dove began calling again. Teacher reached out and took the slingshot from Tom's hand and led him back into the schoolhouse. He didn't seem to mind the calling of the mourning dove after that.

When spring came and the world turned green again, Tom could not stay inside. Often he didn't come to school at all. Sometimes he appeared at recess, played with us, then ran away when the bell rang. He came one day when I was in the little thicket along the creek trying to make a willow whistle. I couldn't get the tube of bark loose from the willow stem. I knew Tom had crept up from the creek and was standing behind me. I waited for him to push me or try to take my pocketknife. Instead, he reached out, took hold of the willow stick, and pulled. I let go. He took the knife in his other hand and cut a v-shaped notch in the part I was trying to loosen. Holding the stick against his leg, he turned it around and around and tapped it with the back of the knife. Then he twisted the bark. It loosened and he worked it off, all in one piece. He hollowed out the stem to make the air chamber and flattened one edge where the air would go in. Then he slid the tube of bark back over the stick.

"Blow," he said, handing it to me.

I blew. The sound cut the air, so high and clear that I could imagine other children looking up and smiling.

"Blow a lot," Tom said. "A willow whistle is a one-day whistle."

I didn't understand.

"Dries out," he said. "Bark cracks."

He bared his teeth in his rare smile and handed back the pocket-knife. He ducked back into the willows and ran down the creek, crouching low, his feet sending up splashes of water.

My whistle lasted several days. Then it dried out and cracked as Tom had said it would.

32 Corn

Long after the oats were safe in the granary and the last cutting of hay was stored away in stacks or in the barn, the corn still stood in the fields, needing the sunshine of early fall to help it ripen and dry. We lived with corn longer than with any other crop. Six months might pass between the time we planted the seeds and the time the ears were harvested and stored away in the corncrib.

All during that long growing season, the corn talked to us in the wind. The bright green leaves whispered softly against each other in early summer. By August the full-grown plants swayed and spoke with new authority as the wind carried pollen from the tall tassels to the soft silk of the tiny ears. And in fall the drying corn rattled loud and harsh, hiding all other sounds. Even the ringing of the big dinner bell could not reach us in the cornfield on a windy day.

Many things could go wrong with the corn during the months that seed, water, soil, and sunshine worked their magic. Some farmers were superstitious. Expecting too much was a dangerous challenging of fate. A man on the other side of Seneca never did allow himself to believe there would be a crop. "No, sir," he'd predict, shaking his head so continually that we wondered why it didn't come off. "Not going to be any corn this year. You just wait and see. No, sir. No corn."

A story went the rounds each fall about a county agricultural agent and a pessimistic farmer. The agent saw the farmer's corn in July when it was knee-high and bright green. "Looks like a great crop," he said.

"Lot can happen yet," the farmer said. "Grasshoppers, drouth, too much rain, hail."

In September the county agent returned. The cornstalks were tall and straight, the ears long and full.

"Well now, it's not in the corncrib yet," the farmer said. "Wind could knock it down. Ears could rot on the ground. Early frost could get it."

Finally the county agent came by and found the farmer's crib bulging with corn. Now, he figured, that man's just got to say something positive.

"You know," the farmer said, "a crop that big worries me. Sure must take a lot out of the soil."

Corn harvest began with filling the silo, the tall tower of concrete, forty feet high and fourteen feet across, that stood against the barn. While the corn was still green the tall stalks were cut and hauled to a machine called a silo filler. A moving apron carried the corn into the knives. A howling fan sent the chopped up stalks and ears rattling up a tall pipe to the top of the silo. The mixture fermented and became silage, a smelly, succulent winter feed for the cattle.

Silo-filling time had all the hard work and complicated exchanging of help of threshing time, but because of school we boys were less a part of it. At recess and lunch hour we heard the howl of silo fillers and tried to figure out where the sound was coming from. Day after day we came home from school to find the farm strangely quiet.

"Your father and Lyle are silo filling at _____," Mother would say, adding a name. It might be Oppreicht, Sutton, Meagher, Paulson, Ertel, Lomas, Shreck, Slade—any of a dozen families.

Darkness came early in the shortening days. We ate alone, started the milking, and might be half finished before we heard the lonely sound of far-off steel wheels ringing on the gravel of the road. Then we knew Father and Lyle were coming home with the wagons they had used all day to haul corn to the silo filler. When the sound of the wheels got close, one of us ran to open the barnyard gate and help unhitch the horses, working together a few minutes in the close darkness before going back to finish the milking.

In late August and September each cold night had a threat of frost in it. Father watched the growing corn and worried with it. It was an important day when he came in from the cornfields with a big smile and said, "I don't think frost can hurt it now."

Silo filling took only a few acres of corn. The real harvest came after the frost and the winds of fall had dried all the rest of the corn to a rattling brown. Again Father roamed the field. He would strip back the husk. If the ear squeaked when he twisted it, the corn was ready. If the ear was swollen and unyielding, the corn was still too wet.

Cornhusking meant peeling back the husk, snapping off the ear, and throwing it into a wagon box. Lyle was our champion cornhusker. He moved through the field, hands flying, picking two rows at a time, the horses pulling the wagon along at a pace matched to his. The ears came out of Lyle's hands and went bang, bang, bang against the high board on the opposite side of the wagon box. When the box was full, he trotted the horses back to the farmyard, shoveled the load of corn into the crib, then trotted back to the field.

In the early days there were many different kinds of corn—big white ears of Silver King, bright yellow ears of Golden Glow, and the many-colored ears we called Calico and Indian corn. Hybrid corn took the place of all those, eventually. It gave us a better yield and the stalks stood up better in the wind, but a rich variety of colors was gone from the cornfields. Gone, too, was the surprise of finding a throwback, a bright red ear among the yellow or white.

"Each time you find a red ear, someone owes you a kiss," Mother told us.

When she was a child there were still husking bees. The corn was brought in, stalks and all, to the barn, and a whole neighborhood gathered to husk out the ears, dance, and drink apple cider. Older people still talked about the husking bees. In fact, the fall was filled with talk of corn. Because it was the last crop of the season, it seemed the most important of all. A field of corn ready to harvest was the perfect picture of autumn and the gifts of the land. At school one day Teacher was reading to us about the first Thanksgiving. "Just imagine," the book said, "how the Indian cornfields looked to those hungry Pilgrims."

Teacher stopped reading and looked at us with a sad smile. "On the other hand," she said, "just imagine how the hungry Pilgrims looked to the Indians who owned those cornfields."

We knew from her face that she had said something important, but we didn't know what it meant.

Cornhusking went on into the middle of fall, with all of us helping on Saturdays. Sometimes we worked with snow falling. The cold wind went through our clothes and dragged the sharp, dry leaves across our faces. Our hands were numb with cold, our wrists sometimes so lame by evening that we couldn't unbutton our jackets. Still, there was an almost savage pleasure in the corn harvest that was not there with any other crop. We were racing against the coming cold and snow. We could hear each ear go banging into the wagon. We could see the rich harvest of the land slowly going higher in the slatted corncrib.

Each time I unloaded a wagon, I was reminded of how we had played in the corncrib when we were younger, pretending it was a prison. Hanging on the slats, peering out at our captor, we would try to look pathetic as we pleaded for release. We never got into trouble with the game the way Johnny Anderson, a neighbor boy, did. I went to his house to see him once and as I came into the yard his mother started screaming. She was locked in the corncrib. Johnny was on the outside, crying. He was afraid to unlock the door.

"You let her out," he told me. "But first let me get a head start." Johnny ran for the woods.

I let her out. Without a word to me, she went running after Johnny. Both of them disappeared into the woods. I went home.

Johnny told me later that he got away. He didn't come home until after dark. By then, he said, she was worried enough about him that she wasn't mad anymore.

There was something else I remembered each year at corn harvest. One day when Father was fixing fence way out at the far northwest corner of the farm, I took him a bucket of lemonade. As I walked along the dusty road, I saw an old Ford touring car hidden in the brush of Denny Meagher's woods, across the road from our cornfield. I told Father about the car when I gave him the lemonade. He thought about it for a minute, then propped up his shovel and posthole digger against a tree. "You show me."

We walked along the line fence and crossed the road into Meagher's woods. Father wouldn't let me talk. We moved carefully through the bright red of the sumacs. I showed him the car. He went up to it, reached in, and found some empty burlap bags—gunny sacks, we called them. He looked across the road at our cornfield. It was early corn, already turning brown and rattling in the wind. There was yellow showing at the ends of some of the ears.

Father crossed the road. I started after him. I was pretty sure whose car it was—the new neighbor, the one people said had killed his own brother.

Father saw me following and shooed me back. He smiled. "It's all right. There won't be any trouble. It takes two to make trouble."

He moved into the cornfield, walking very quietly. I followed anyway. In a minute he found the man pulling off ears of corn, stuffing them into a bag. Father pulled an ear off a stalk, walked up, and tossed it into the bag. The man jumped, and started to run. Father stepped in front of him. The man stood there and Father went on snapping ears of corn and tossing them into the bag.

"You should have told me you needed corn. We've got some of last year's in the crib you could borrow. That'd be better. Some of this isn't ripe yet."

The man didn't say a word. Father slowly filled the bag. "That enough for now?"

The man nodded.

"Let me carry it for you." Father swung the bag to his shoulder and carried it to the car. The man followed.

"There," Father said. "I'll drop off a couple more bags tomorrow. Let me know if you need more. No hurry about paying it back. You'll be shredding this fall, I suppose."

The man nodded.

"Why not figure to wait until then," Father said. He put his hand on my shoulder. "Well, son. Let's get back to that fence."

The man took a step toward us. Father stuck out his hand. The man nodded again and took the hand.

Long before shredding time that fall, the man drove into our barnyard and unloaded half a dozen sacks of corn into the crib.

I couldn't forget that day. The next summer Junior and I were cutting thistles out of the oats that were growing where the cornfield had been. For a moment it was fall again. The wind was blowing. The corn was rattling. Father was throwing ears of corn, one by one, into the gunny sack.

I looked up and found Junior smiling at me. "You're hearing something," he said.

The sounds of fall stopped. The oats were moving a little in the warm wind of summer. Father had made me promise never to tell anyone. "I was remembering the cornfield that was here last fall," I said.

"All right," Junior said, with that skeptical and accepting smile that is always the clearest picture I have of him. He began cutting thistles again. It was lonelier in the field the rest of that day.

33 The Cat with a Right-Angle Tail

One year, during a frantic day of fall harvest, the cat got his tail caught in the screen door. It wasn't anybody's fault. The cat had been running in and out with us as we carried things from the garden. One trip, he just didn't quite make it before the wind pushed the door shut. He was only caught for a minute, but when we opened the door his tail had a right angle in it.

The cat didn't even howl. He licked the bent place for a few minutes, then jumped into Mother's lap.

"Look at that," she said. "I think he wants to show us he doesn't blame anybody."

That cat must have had a name before this happened. He'd been around for several years, but the only name I can remember came later. It was Stubby.

Stubby was a very special cat. He was a calico—yellow, white, and brown—plus a couple of other in-between colors, and he was a male. Some people wouldn't believe that. They kept turning him upside down to check up on him, saying it was impossible for a cat with all those colors to be a male. Lloyd Holliday, who carried the mail sometimes for his father, was on our side. "Not impossible at all," he said. "Just unlikely." Lloyd claimed that once in about every fifty-four thousand cats you might get a male calico.

Stubby was special in another way. He alone of all the cats had the status of house cat. He could come and go as he wanted, except at bedtime. Then he was supposed to go outside for the night. The funny thing was, none of us could remember any decision about Stubby becoming a house cat.

"Oh, there was a decision, all right," Father said. "It was just that we didn't make it."

Putting Stubby out at bedtime was Father's job. He would close his book at the dining room table and fold up his glasses. When his glasses case snapped shut, we all stopped whatever we were doing.

Stubby had his ritual too. He would stretch out on the floor and sleepily lick a paw, never taking his eyes off Father. Father would get up, stretch, and start to yawn. Then he'd leap. Stubby would leap in the opposite direction and the chase was on.

We all kept out of the way and tried not to take sides. Mother grabbed chairs as they toppled and muttered about the carryings-on of a grown man. Sometimes she forgot herself and cheered a little when the cat pulled a shrewd maneuver.

Once honestly cornered, Stubby sat down and began licking his paw again, as though the whole business was far beneath him. Even in the way he let Father carry him to the door there was something that said, "I could still raise plenty of hell if I wanted to."

One night the chase brought down the stovepipe and scattered soot all over the room. Mother looked at the mess. "You know, life might be simpler if we just let the cat stay in at night."

Father laughed. "Not sure we dare do that. If we give in, we'll wake up some morning and find that cat running the farm."

"And next thing after that," Lyle added, "the cat will be putting us out at night."

So the ritual went on, livening up our long evenings better than a three-ring circus. There was one variation. In winter, Father had figured out a way to just about drive the cat crazy. Stubby liked to spend his evenings by the heating stove. Father would snap shut his glasses case as usual, stand up, and walk toward the stove, with Stubby ready to jump. Father would open the stove door, take down the poker, the cat half leaving the floor with every move. Finally, Father would bang the stove door closed and grab for him. It never worked. Stubby was always a jump ahead and the same old chase began.

The day the mailman first saw the cat's right-angle tail, folks on the rest of the route got their mail a little late. "Haven't been so rattled up by anything since the time I ran over the two-headed rattlesnake," George said. "Hell's bells, how'm I going to convince anybody you folks not only got a male calico cat, but one with a right angle in his tail? What happened, anyway?"

"Well, sir," Lyle said, "we been puzzling about that. Near as we can figure he must have swallowed that carpenter's square we're missing."

George nodded. "Could be. Tell you what. I'll try explaining it that way to people and see if they believe me."

The cat's having a right angle in his tail didn't change the bedtime ritual. It went on just like before until one cold night when the thought of getting into bed in an unheated room made everybody want to stay in the warm dining room. The cat was by the stove, lying on his stomach, eyes closed, paws folded under his chin. The front part of his tail was resting on the floor. The rear part was sticking straight up. Every now and then the end of the tail twitched over against the stove's footrail with a light bang.

"You hear that?" Lyle said.

Father looked up over his glasses. "Hear what?"

The tail banged again. "That," Lyle said.

We all turned to look at the cat. His eyes were still closed. He was quiet except that every few seconds there would be that bang as the tail hit the rail.

"That part of his tail's going to drop off," Lyle said. "Had a cat get his tail hurt like that when I was a kid. Tail dried up. One day it just dropped off."

The cat opened one eye and looked up. The tail banged twice.

"Humph," Father said and went back to his book.

I looked at Lyle closely. I had never thought about him being a child once and maybe carrying a new kitten around the way I did, turning it over and puzzling out if it was a he or a she.

An hour or so later, Father started trying to herd everyone off so he could fix up the fire and go to bed. He closed his glasses case. Stubby opened his eyes and stretched. The tail banged against the rail. Father made his leap. He missed. The cat made two trips around the table, just ahead of Father's outstretched hands. Then he made a dash to get under the couch. Father grabbed, missed, and got hold of the upright part of the tail.

The cat went straight ahead.

Father went over backward, the end of the tail in his hand.

Lyle looked at Father's open mouth. "By golly, you could drive a hayrack in there without ever touching."

Stubby poked his head out from under the couch. He yawned, walked past Father to the door, and meowed to be let out.

The next night, Stubby was back in his usual place, stub tail twitching now and then. When Father closed his book and took off his glasses, Stubby got up and stretched. He walked to the door and meowed, pretending it was all his own idea. Father opened the door. Stubby walked casually out into the cold night.

Father came back to the table and sat down. He seemed disappointed. Finally he looked up at us and grinned. "Well, who won?"

It was hard to say. We had lost our bedtime entertainment. Stubby had lost part of his tail, but he wasn't what you'd call crushed. From then on he didn't fight with Father, he just tolerated him.

Even the mailman, who always had an answer for everything, wasn't quite sure. "All I know is it made a lot better story before," George grumbled. "I liked him better with a tail."

"So did I," said Father.

34 The Killing Frost

Sometimes fall forgot it was supposed to be getting us ready for winter. I remember a year when Mother's flowers were still blooming bravely in November. There had been a few inches of wet snow in early October, but no frost. The sun came out, the snow melted, and "squaw winter" was over. Indian summer came with its smoky warmth and bright blue skies.

The storytellers spent half their days arguing about how many years it had been since cold weather came so late.

"Don't think we ever went frost-free later than mid-October."

"Not talking about some light frost. That don't hurt nothing. Talking about a killing frost. Seems like it was nineteen six we didn't get killing frost till the tenth of November."

"You talking about on the ridge or in the valley?"

"Dammit to hell! I'm talking about both."

One morning near the middle of November I ran to school through the start of another perfect Indian-summer day. Bright-colored leaves hung almost motionless on the maple trees. A little white fog was lifting out of the main valley into the blue sky. I tossed milkweed seeds up. They floated in the air on their silken parachutes, then settled slowly back to the ground, waiting for the wind. It was the kind of day that started us talking about skipping school. We would find some hidden spot on a hillside, sprawl out in the sun-warmed leaves, and let the day go by around us. But no hurry, we thought. Indian summer's going to last forever.

By ten o'clock that morning Tom Withers was at the windows every few minutes looking at the sky. Teacher joined him after a while. She pushed up the window. Cool air came in and we could hear the wind in the trees along the hillside.

"Cold coming," Tom said.

"Will it be a killing frost?"

He nodded. The honking of wild geese came to us. Tom leaned far out the window, trying to see them. Teacher looked at him and smiled. "You can go, Tom."

He started running for the door.

"Tom, wait."

He stopped.

"No rock-rolling."

The wind rattled our papers as he rushed out the door.

By morning recess there were low-hanging gray clouds moving across the sky. A big flock of grackles gathered in the willows along the creek. They circled and scolded, then all rose at once and flew off down the valley. Woolly bear caterpillars crawled along the foundations of the schoolhouse, trying to get in. Across the fence, Earl Watson was digging potatoes, wearing a winter cap with the earflaps down.

Teacher kept checking the thermometer outside the door. By noon it was down to thirty-six degrees. Sparrows were fluttering at the windows, looking for shelter from the wind.

"Get your coats on," Teacher said. "There'll be a hard freeze by morning. You'll be needed at home. Take your lunches. You can eat as you go. Remember, I'm letting you out to go home. Not to play baseball, visit each other, or go looking for walnuts."

"Yes, Teacher."

I ran up the hillside. Hundreds of robins were feeding in the edge of the woods next to the old orchard, so busy they didn't even see me. A lone bluebird sat on a limb singing "Summer's over." I finished my lunch, filled the pail with fallen apples, and ran for home, the wind lifting my hair, cold against my back.

I found the cows huddled in a little ravine, backs arched, tails to the wind. They followed me up the lane, running so fast that milk squirted out as their udders swung from side to side.

I climbed the gate. Father was shutting off the windmill. It was turning very fast, the tail whipping back and forth in the gusts.

"Let the cows in," Father yelled. "I'll give them some hay."

The cows crowded through the gate and headed for the manger, where they were protected by the tall windbreak.

I ran on to the house. The wind was carrying the smoke off in a straight line from the kitchen chimney. Flies flew up in a swarm when I opened the screen door. The kitchen was warm and steamy, filled with the smell of cooking tomatoes. Mother pushed her hair back from her face and gave me a quick smile. "You're home early."

"Teacher said we'd be needed."

"Bless her."

"What needs to be done?"

"Everything. Your Father says the ground will be frozen by morning. Everything has to come in from the garden. I've only done the tomatoes."

I began by pulling up the carrots, beets, turnips, and long, white-rooted vegetable oysters. Some of the carrots were so long and so wound around each other I had to use a five-tined manure fork to get them up. An old white hen joined me, the same one that liked to follow the corn-cultivator in the summer. She scratched in the new-turned ground and ate worms until a gust caught her and sent her running and cackling toward the chicken house, her feathers fanned out by the wind.

There was a dull rumbling as Lyle came by with a wagonload of potatoes, horses trotting, potatoes jumping and rumbling in the bottom of the wagon box. There was another sound that was something like that. When a summer storm was coming, with its far-off beginning of thunder, Father used to say, "Potato wagon coming."

Lyle waved to me and said something. The wind carried his words off in the opposite direction. He may have counted on that. It was the kind of day he liked to say, when he thought no one would hear him, "By God, it's colder than a left-handed tit on a cast-iron witch."

I picked the last of the green beans and lettuce. The lettuce leaves were too big and would be bitter, but they were the last we would have for seven months.

Junior and Lee came home from high school. Laurance was working for my Uncle Lou that fall. Lee hurried out to help with the potatoes. Junior took the car and went to get sand from along the road. We would need it for storing the root vegetables.

I picked up hundreds of ground cherries, bright yellow and round as marbles in their paper-lantern husks. Later, we would take them across the field to a neighbor's, where a blind old lady would sit in her rocking chair and husk them for us, her hands seeing the good ones and bad ones, sorting them with never a mistake.

Leaves were blowing along the ground and the bare limbs of the big maple rattled in the wind. There was ice on the drinking cup at the well. Once when I went inside to warm my hands Mother handed me two dish towels. "Let's chase the flies out."

We propped the outside door open and started in the dining room, waving a cloth in each hand, driving the flies toward the door. They tried to turn back when they felt the cold, but we herded most of them out.

The kitchen was piled high with carrots, turnips, and beets still needing their tops cut off. The pressure cooker, filled with cans of string beans, was puffing and clicking like a steam engine.

I kept checking with Mother for instructions. Each time I saw her she seemed to have something different cradled in her apron—empty canning jars from the cellar, tomatoes, string beans, lettuce, some flowers still in bloom, a clump of dill weed.

"Want me to dig the horseradish?"

"No. We have plenty from last year. But get the rhubarb."

"All of it?"

"Only the biggest and reddest stalks."

"What about the cabbage?"

"Pull the heads up and pile them next to the woodshed. We'll let them freeze. The men will cover them with sawdust tomorrow."

"What about the squash?"

"Only the hard ones."

Some of the squash vines were twenty feet long. I trailed them off into the grass and weeds, finding squash on some, bright yellow blossoms on others. I also found burdock burrs and Spanish bayonets that hung on to my clothes and stuck through into the skin. The big Hubbard squash were dark green with a deep orange spot where they lay against the ground. As I was carrying a bag of them in, one got away and clattered down the cellar steps ahead of me. It didn't even crack.

Mother came to the door once to look up at a long, wavering line of wild geese. They were flying with the wind, so high we could hardly hear their honking. "I hope they didn't wait too long," Mother said.

I knew what she was seeing in her mind. The migrating ducks and geese would come down somewhere for the night. Sometimes a quick freeze caught them in the sloughs along the rivers and froze them into the ice. They died there or were eaten alive by foxes and mink.

We kept passing each other at work, too busy to talk. Lyle and Junior were carrying baskets of potatoes into the cellar, dumping them into the big bin that ran all along one side. Father was putting tar paper around the foundation of the house and piling sawdust against it to keep out the wind. On days like that, Father walked fast, leaning forward more than usual, carrying half the world on his back.

Finally, the garden was done, except for the flowers. I went on to the orchard and helped Lee with the apples. The wind was still knocking them down, the big Wolf Rivers, some of them six inches across, making loud thuds as they landed. Mother liked to joke about those giant apples. "Bring me a Wolf River," she'd say, "I want to make a pie."

Lee climbed the trees and knocked apples down, not always one at a time. I stood below, trying to catch them. There were Wealthys and Sweet Apples on the ground with the Wolf Rivers. Some had fallen earlier. They were split open and had been "working" in the warm sun. Even with the cold wind stinging our noses, there was the sharp smell of cider in the orchard.

Bees clung to some of the apples. They had made one too many trips to collect the oozing juice and were too cold to fly back to the hive. We sorted apples as we picked them up, finding that the bees weren't too cold to sting. The good apples went to the cellar. The damaged ones went to the crowded kitchen to be canned for apple-sauce or to become the rich dark brown of Mother's apple butter, better on a slice of fresh white bread than any other food in the world.

Full darkness came. The wind began to fall and the cold was bitter, with a little snow spitting down. I lighted a lantern and Mother and I went out to dig the flower bulbs. The little gladiolus bulbs were like small pointed brown onions. Some of the clumps of dahlia tubers were as big as a gallon bucket. We knocked the dirt off and piled them into boxes. Mother sighed as we finished, realizing that we had forgotten, as we had forgotten each year as long as I could remember, to mark which clump of roots went with which color flower.

Mother sent me to tell Father it would be better to do the milking before supper. No food was started, unless we wanted to open a newly sealed jar of green beans. I found Father on his back under the Model T Ford, draining the water out of the radiator. I left the lantern with him and went back to the kitchen.

Mother got supper, cutting the potatoes up small so they'd cook fast. I sat half asleep behind the close warmth of her stove, cutting tops off beets, carrots, and turnips so I could bury the roots in the boxes of sand in the cellar.

That night, with the chores done and a fire roaring in the dining room stove, the house was warm and steamy, filled with good earthy smells from the orchard and garden. Except for some late corn still drying in the fields, harvest was over. We had lived another growing season in partnership with the land. Now the land's gifts were safely stored in the cellar, barns, granary, corncrib, and haystacks. Suddenly it didn't matter that the bright days of Indian summer were over and that the ground would be frozen by morning.

Part Five

WINTER

35 Short Days and Yellow Lamplight

In the long-night, short-day season of the year, the stars were bright when we went out into the cold morning stillness to do the milking. If there was a moon, we could check for a white pillar of smoke from a neighbor's chimney and see if anyone else was up.

The day was still dark when we came back to the house for breakfast, stomping loud on the porch to knock snow off our overshoes. Warned by our lanterns coming up through the yard, Mother was waiting with steaming dishes of eggs and oatmeal. Our coats went on the hooks behind the kitchen door, so thick and heavy it would hardly open again. We gathered at the dining room table and it was then that our day began.

We exchanged information—most important of all, did we need to come right home from school or could we spend an extra half hour sledding along the way? When the weather was bad, and I was still very young, there was the awful discussion about making sure someone saw that I was all right. My brothers would tease me about that, saying things like "Because your little legs are so short." Then it would all turn to laughter.

Warm, well fed, and feeling united into a family again after the separateness of the night, we went our various ways.

Daylight had only half come when we started for school. If the snow was good, we rode on our sleds, going over fences covered by drifts, through open gates, down the steep old hill road, past the spring all the way to the end of our land before we stopped. We each followed the same track, heaviest persons first because they went faster. Wind tears froze on our scarfs. Steel sled runners rattled on the frozen snow. Sometimes there was a wild yell. A sled would turn over. We'd crash into each other and a lunch bucket might go sliding on ahead, out of sight. The worst spills of all came when our sleds rode on top of the icy crust. Suddenly the runners would break through. The sled would stop. We'd go right on sliding along the crust, gathering speed, grabbing out for trees, brush, or stumps to stop ourselves. Knees and elbows torn from our clothes, faces bleeding, we went on to school. Once, a lunch bucket didn't turn up again until spring.

Full daylight came and was almost gone again when school let out. Then we had to make an agonizing decision. Were we going to drag our sleds all the way home just for that one morning ride? Of course we had to have them at school for recesses and lunch hour.

We hated one hopelessly extravagant boy who had two sleds, one for home, one for school. We talked about the advantages of that until someone, in an older-brother voice, would say, "You're forgetting something again."

"What?"

"No matter how many sleds you got, you still got to pull them back up the hill."

"Well, at least we'd only have to pull them up one hill. Not all the way from school."

"Hey! Maybe we could build a big sled. We could all ride down together."

"Yeah, and leave it at the bottom!"

"Yeah, and *all* pull it up at night."

"And maybe a bridge across the ditch, and over that fence, at the bottom. We could go all the way down to the creek without stopping!"

We got organized enough to get through several days of arguments about bobsleds versus toboggans. We chopped down one tree, felling it across the ditch for the start of a bridge. We began building a bobsled, using rough-sawn white oak, heavy as lead, hard as cast iron. We got two front runners made, found we could hardly lift them, and that was that.

At least the fallen tree was a sort of bridge for running across the ditch. We didn't always make it. Mother called that bridge "the thermos-bottle smasher."

We went on pulling our sleds back and forth, still envying that other boy, still forgetting in our envy that he didn't always have a sled magically waiting for him at the top of each hill.

On our way home from school, we'd rest a minute at the edge of the woods, then dash across the open pasture and up the lane, the cold wind tearing at us. We warmed up in the kitchen, eating bread with honey or apple butter while mother checked us over for the telltale white spots of frostbite. If our feet were wet from snow going over the tops of our overshoes, or maybe from breaking through an air pocket on a forbidden frozen pond, Mother opened the oven door and let us sit, drinking hot cocoa, with our feet in the oven until all the numbness and stinging of chilblains had become one vast toasted warmth. Then we went out to do our chores.

When Father and Lyle were off at another farm helping shred corn or saw wood, the cows might still be outside in the barnyard. They would bawl their complaints about that when they saw us coming and crowd to the barn doors. We put silage into the mangers, threw down more hay, spread fresh straw bedding, and opened the doors. The cows crowded in. Each of the older ones had a favorite stanchion and would fight off any younger cow that dared to trespass. We went along in front of them, getting licked by some, butted by others as we closed the stanchions that held them in.

Because I was youngest, I had the "miscellaneous" chores. I fed the chickens, carried warm drinking water to them, and made sure they had enough crushed clamshells for their gizzards. I got the eggs, some of them frozen and split open in the coldest weather. I carried wood from the woodshed, splitting some of the bigger blocks, warned by Mother every winter day for as long as I could remember not to stand under the telephone lead-in wire when I swung the ax.

I carried extra water and filled the reservoir on the kitchen stove, always spilling a little so I could see the drops go dancing and spitting across the hot surface. I chopped frozen cabbage out of the sawdust at the west end of the woodshed. I asked Mother if she wanted anything from the cellar, my appetite showing sometimes. "Do you want me to bring you a jar of red raspberries?"

She would smile. "Now isn't that funny? I was about to ask if you thought raspberries would be a good idea for dessert."

"With cream?"

"Yes, with cream."

Before going inside, I filled the one-gallon kerosene can from the big barrel near the dinner bell. Then I got out all the lamps and lanterns, filled them, cleaned the chimneys with wadded newspaper, and trimmed the wicks so they would burn evenly, with no high spots to smoke up the chimneys.

I checked the wicks, one by one, taking matches out of the tin box Father had used to bring lily of the valley bulbs from his mother's garden in Norway. The lilies still grew each summer under the elm tree next to the road.

Matches were a halfway forbidden thing. We didn't fill our pockets from the box when anyone was looking, and Mother didn't say anything when she found them in our pockets on wash day. It was different with matches for the lamps and lanterns. I could take them out of the tin box and let the lid bang shut with Mother right there in the kitchen.

If a wick didn't burn straight, I trimmed and tested it again. The big Rayo lamp had a tubular wick, and the flame burned in a bright orange-yellow circle. I worked longest on that lamp, making sure it was exactly right. It would burn all evening at the dining room table.

The wicks played tricks on me. Someone would turn a lamp higher or lower and suddenly the wick was crooked, one edge burning too high and blackening the chimney.

"Your lamp is smoking," someone would say to me. I'd light a spare and go to work on the uneven wick.

When the before-supper chores were done and the others were coming up through the barnyard, I helped Mother carry in the steaming dishes, usually remembering to wash the kerosene off my hands.

Then we gathered at the dining room table and the day was pieced together.

"Who was out of school?"

"How much wood left in the woodshed?"

"Will they get through shredding at the Zintzes' tomorrow?"

"There was a big flock of quail in the barnyard."

"Some kids want to meet and go sledding on Saturday. Can we go?"

The meal was over quickly because there was still the milking to be done. I lighted the lanterns for the others, but usually stayed inside to help Mother with the dishes. The house was drafty from the door being opened and closed. The dining room was empty, the big lamp turned down low. From the kitchen table at the east window, I could see my lanterns make their flickering trip to the barns.

When the dishes were finished and the coffee ground for the morning, I'd get my coat and go out to help with the milking. That dark trip from lamp-lighted house to lantern-lighted barn was like a journey through a deserted land. Snow would sing under my feet with a sound that said the temperature was close to zero. There always seemed to be a great horned owl hooting. I walked under the distant stars, feeling as alone as I imagined I might feel on an ice floe, drifting in the Arctic Ocean.

The barn was warm, filled with the sound of cows chewing and milk squirting into pails. Junior was always teetered back on his three-legged milkstool, head against a cow's flank, singing quietly, hands pulling on the cow's teats in rhythm with the song.

Every now and then a cat would sit down beside one of us and meow to have milk squirted at it. We always obliged, with at least some of the wavering stream going into the cat's open mouth.

When milking was almost finished, two of us carried the full ten-gallon cans across the big snowdrift to the milk house and started running it through the separator. One of us turned the crank at exactly the right speed while the other poured the whole milk into the separator tank. The milk flowed down through a spout and into a whirling cylinder filled with disks. The cream came out in a small, yellow stream from the top spout, the white, foamy skim milk from the large lower spout. The warm milk steamed in the lantern light of the unheated milk house.

The others brought the last of the milk from the barn. We poured skim milk into buckets for the weaned calves. They butted the pails, thinking they were still sucking from their mothers. If a calf was just learning to drink from a bucket, we would put one hand down into the warm milk and let the calf suck our fingers.

The rest of the skim milk was carried down the hill to the hog house and dumped into the cast-iron tub of the feed cooker. That finished the chores. We went to the house, taking the cream with us to keep it from freezing.

We came in out of the dark cold of winter and gathered again in the dining room, crowding close to the stove for a few minutes before the lamp pulled us into a circle around the dining room table.

We got out our homework. Father would be reading or planning next year's fields, figuring what seeds and how much fertilizer and lime we needed, his stubby pencil moving slowly and firmly on his ruled tablet. Mother would be mending clothes, often reading at the same time. When we asked how she could do that, she said, "I read something that has a lot of thinking between the sentences." Usually it was the Bible or a book of poetry.

Sometimes one of us would start chuckling over what we were reading. The others couldn't stand it.

"What's so funny?"

We would read aloud. Soon the whole room was filled with laughter. That could start a discussion that ranged over every continent in the world. At school next day a written report on Chicago might, for some unexplainable reason, turn out to have a kangaroo in it.

Several times each winter we got out the old brown leather suitcase full of pictures. Soon the tabletop was covered and we'd be asking "Who's this? Who's that?" Mother and Father would pick up the pictures and try to tell us or go off into a long discussion about who married whom, and what happened to the third eldest daughter from the second marriage.

Sometimes the unrecognized people were us at a younger age. There was one of Laurance when he still had light blond hair. And Lee, so dressed up we couldn't possibly know him. He was holding Stubby at a time when the cat still had a tail. That picture always started a long discussion, but we never did remember Stubby's original name.

There was a picture of Junior, maybe four years old. He seemed to be jumping up and down, his mouth hanging open in a way that reminded us of Father's face the night the cat's tail came off.

"He was seeing his first train," Mother said. "In Gays Mills."

There was a picture of me, crying. "That's funny. I don't see any lump on your head," Lyle would say. He was always finding some way to bring up the time I was building a wooden box and swung the claw hammer back too far. "Yes, sir," Lyle would say, studying the picture, "I'll bet that's the time, all right. You was crying like a lost calf. Your Mother asked what happened. You said you hit the corner of your head with the hammer."

Each time we went through the pictures, I tried to fit together the pieces of Father's life. There were pictures of him as a boy in Norway, as a young man in Wisconsin, as a lumberjack, as one of a group of unshaven fishermen, all of them looking like Western badmen from a Wanted poster. There were pictures of Father all dressed up, wearing a bowler hat, pretty girls with long dresses hanging on his arm.

"Who's that?" I would ask, pointing to one of the girls.

"I don't remember."

I would look from a picture of Father to Father himself. Sometimes he'd smile as if he knew what I was trying to do. And each time I would decide the pictures were not my father. They were younger men. My father was sitting at the dining room table sharpening his pencil, shaving by shaving, with his old bone-handled pocketknife.

As though to say "enough of the past," Father would begin picking up the pictures.

⁓

When Mother decided to use the evening for baking, the smell of new bread filled the house. One by one, we would slip out until the dining room was deserted and we were all gathered around the kitchen stove, eating slices of hot bread.

If it wasn't bread, it had to be some other kind of food. We were always starving by the middle of the evening. We'd shell little ears of popcorn, and the popping sound and smell of hot butter in the kitchen would bring faces peeking around from the dining room. We'd go to the cellar for apples, or make fudge, first cracking hickory nuts, the dry shells flying around the room like bullets. Sometimes we even tried making taffy, pulling the long loops until the candy was almost white, getting it stuck on ourselves and, once, all over the dog.

For some reason food made us think about playing cards, and the two ideas didn't mix, or, rather, mixed all too well. When the cards got too sticky to shuffle, we went to something else. Laurance lost in a pile of bee magazines. Junior always fixing something—a clock, a part off the car—so that we got used to springs flying at us and screws rolling around the table. Lee might be studying the taxidermy course that was going to make him a fortune. He had already mounted one scrawny squirrel. Lyle said it reminded him of the year there weren't any acorns.

Nothing very exciting or unusual happened on winter evenings like those. The seven of us just gathered in a close and quiet warmth, feeling secure and immensely pleased with ourselves when we said good night and went off to our cold beds.

Such evenings were more fragile than we knew.

Once Father brought home a new lamp for the dining room table, an Aladdin with a cone-shaped mantle. The light it gave was white, like the light from a bare electric bulb in a store. The new lamp gave more light, opening up the corners of the dining room, letting us scatter away from the little circle we'd always formed around the old Rayo.

I remember Mother standing in the doorway to the kitchen one night, frowning in at us. "I'm not sure I like that new lamp."

Father was at his usual place at the table. "Why not? Burns less kerosene."

"Look where everyone is."

We were scattered. There was even enough light to read by on the far side of the stove.

"We're all here," Father said.

"Not like we used to be."

Father looked at the empty chairs around the table. "Want to go back to the old lamp?"

"I don't think it's the lamp. I think it's us. Does a new lamp have to change where we sit at night?"

Father's eyes found us, one by one. Then he made a little motion with his head. We came out of our corners and slid into our old places at the table, smiling at each other, a little embarrassed to be hearing this talk.

Mother sat down with us and nodded. "That's better."

36 The Year the Corn Shredder Stayed All Winter

Lyle claimed the old men in Petersburg could start swapping stories some morning, changing things as they went along, and go on for three days before they realized they were all telling each other the same story.

"It's got to the point," Lyle said, "where they wouldn't recognize the truth if they found it in their own hip pockets."

There was something I didn't understand about the storytelling. Those men would spend all one day getting the facts exactly right about the time the big log raft got hung up in the Devil's Elbow down by Steuben. Then they'd talk all the next day, dead serious, about how the Kickapoo River ran upstream for two days after a politician made a speech in Wauzeka.

I asked Lyle how the men decided which stories were fact stories and which weren't.

Lyle thought about it for a while. "All I can think of is, some things are just too important to be left up to the facts."

I guess that's how it was with the story of a man named Nubbin and the year his corn shredder stayed at our place all winter. Every time I heard somebody tell about that, the hammer Nubbin was always swinging got a little bigger, the snow got deeper around the corn shocks, the ending got more disastrous.

It all began because we were short of hay one year and Father decided we needed some corn fodder for cattle feed. Instead of husking all the corn in the field, we cut some, gathered it into big corn shocks to dry, and waited for the shredder to work its way along the ridge. We waited quite a while. The tractor, corn shredder, and Nubbin, the owner, were all getting old. Things kept going wrong on each job and it was early December before the rig came chugging and smoking up to our barnyard gate.

I'd been hearing about Nubbin. I expected a giant, but he was short, about the size of Lyle, had a bright red nose, big bushy eyebrows, and a scraggly beard. The story was that he was superstitious— never shaved on a week that had a Friday in it.

"Hey there, boy!" he yelled at me. "Open up that gate for me. Going to shred your corn, then stay in the house the rest of the winter."

He let loose with a stream of tobacco spit that left a little brown crater in the snow. I opened the gate. The tractor shuddered, then began to creep up through the barnyard. The shredder, which looked a little like a small threshing machine, jerked along behind. It was an old one, made of wood, with red paint peeling from the boards. A spoke was missing from one rear wheel, and the rim was flattened. Each time the wheel made a full turn, the whole shredder rattled and shook.

Nubbin parked the rig out back of the barn and started setting up for the next day, stopping every few minutes for a nip from a brown bottle he kept in the tractor's toolbox. He got the pipe up that went from the shredder into the haymow and rigged the wooden trough with a chain in it that carried the ears of corn out of the shredder.

Next morning a half dozen neighbors came with wide racks on their bobsleds. They went out in the field, shoveled and pried the shocks out of the snow, and started hauling them in. Nubbin had the tractor going. It was wheezing and coughing, between explosions. Lyle pulled a wagon under the corn trough, and the men started putting the snow-covered corn stalks through. They rattled and banged around inside and the chopped-up fodder began going up the pipe. A few ears of yellow corn showed up in the trough. The tractor started coughing harder than ever and began running on only one cylinder. Then it stopped.

A single ear of corn had dropped into the wagon box. Father brought it over to Nubbin. "It's husked nice and clean, all right. But we were hoping to get more than one ear."

Nubbin waved him away, took the brown bottle out, and had a nip. He put that bottle back and took out another one, just like it, and poured something into two little petcocks on the tractor engine. He cranked for a while, his face getting redder and redder. Pretty soon fire shot out of the exhaust and the tractor started up, running on both cylinders.

Two loads of corn went through. Then a face appeared in the opening to the haymow. "Hey, Nubbin!"

"What?"

"It's snowing in here."

"Well, what do you expect, rain? Don't you know it's winter?"

Several more loads made it. Then the big belt, running from the tractor to the shredder, broke. The end flipped out, hit Nubbin on the head, and wrapped around him like a boa constrictor. When the men got him unwrapped and back on his feet, his face was bright red again. He still had hold of that big hammer he was always carrying. He let out a yell, reared way back, and threw. The shredder hadn't quite stopped running. The hammer clanged into the spokes of a pulley, and everything stopped with a crash. Links from one of the drive chains flew around like bird shot.

Nubbin scratched his head, jerked the hammer out of the pulley, and looked at it.

"It's no use, Nubbin," somebody yelled. "There's just no way you can throw a hammer at itself."

"Maybe not, but I can sure as hell have a drink." He got out his bottle. Everyone else went home, and Nubbin began pounding the shredder back together again.

Things never did seem to work after that. Day after day the neighbors came and hitched their horses onto the loads of corn they'd left the day before. Nubbin raced back and forth from tractor to shredder to bottle, trying to keep everything going. As things fell apart, he fastened them back together with wire, rope, and his mysteriously never-ending supply of nuts and bolts of every size. Most days, eight or ten loads of corn would go through, with mechanical trouble and Nubbin's temper getting worse together. The ending was always the same. Something serious would go wrong. Nubbin would throw his hammer, and shredding was over for the day.

The shredder became part of our lives. No one could remember when it hadn't been there. Day after day my brothers and I were told to come right home from school to help with chores "in case they work late trying to finish up today."

At school I would listen for the popping, wheezing noise of the tractor, sometimes going to stand near a window so I could hear better.

"Is it going?" a friend would whisper.

"No."

He'd shake his head, feeling sorry for me.

One day when I stood by the window listening, Teacher reached the end of her patience. "For Heaven's sake, open the window and tell us if it's running or not!"

I did that, with everyone watching me and waiting. There was no sound. I shook my head. My audience groaned.

"Now then," Teacher said, "close the window and let's get back to work. And tell that shredder man I hope he finishes up so we can get on with school."

Winter storms came and went, burying the shocks and loads of corn. Nubbin's bushy eyebrows always seemed to be filled with snow.

When he came in to eat, it would melt and run down his face. "Only time he ever gets water on it," one of the men said.

The crew was there for at least one meal a day for half the winter. Lyle was telling people we'd run out of potatoes, butchered two extra hogs, and bought a barrel of cabbage.

A neighbor's horses started coming over every time they got loose. "Fool horses been there so much, they think it's home."

Whenever Nubbin had things pounded back together, we'd ring up the crew and try again. The men shoveled snow off the corn, and a mixture of corn fodder, ice, and snow went rattling up into the barn. Some of the ears in the crib had stalks three feet long hanging on, and Lyle said the shredder wasn't even waking up the mice that had bedded down inside the husks.

As if we didn't have enough trouble already, the men got restless and started playing tricks. Once while Nubbin was still eating, a couple of men took off the main drive belt, put a twist in it, and put it back on. Nubbin came out, got the tractor started, and put it in gear. The shredder started groaning and creaking. The men were trying to feed cornstalks in and the machine was pushing the stalks right out again. Ears of corn began going back inside the shredder, kernels flying in all directions. Nubbin stood there with his mouth open, his face getting red. He yelled and let go with his hammer. It went right through the wooden side of the shredder and started clanging around in there. Nubbin stopped the tractor and fished around for his hammer. While he was doing that, the two men took the belt off and put it back on without the twist.

Nubbin still didn't know what had started everything running backward. A man came up with one of the stalks that had gone through earlier. An ear was still hanging on it. "Hey, Nubbin, look at this! Your shredder took one of those ears that went back in and put it onto a cornstalk again."

They say that was the closest Nubbin ever came to throwing his hammer at a person.

Another time the men switched Nubbin's bottles around. The tractor did fine on the wrong bottle, but Nubbin turned green for about three hours.

Pretty soon there were snowball fights going half the time. Somebody made a snowman that was just Nubbin's size. When Nubbin came out from eating, there was the snowman with his stocking cap on its head and his big hammer stuck under its arm.

"First time anybody ever saw a snowman getting beat to death with a hammer," was the way it was told later.

Lyle came to the house one cold day for a bucket of hot water to put in the radiator of the stalled tractor. "What's the matter this time?" Mother asked.

"Belt slipped off the exhaust pipe," Lyle said on his way out.

A little later somebody phoned to see how the shredding was going. "They've broken down again," Mother said. "The belt slipped off the exhaust pipe."

Half a dozen people heard that on the party line. Mother never did live it down.

Just when everything was working fine, for a change, a stray snowball hit Nubbin on the back of the head. He may have thought the big belt had tried to get him again. He roared, threw his hammer; and the pieces flew.

Father decided he'd had enough. "All that horseplay's going to get somebody hurt." From then on, any time the shredder wasn't working, the men husked corn by hand and just ran the stalks through.

It was sometime in February when the last load of corn was done. Nubbin shut off the tractor, drained the radiator, and headed for town. The only things he took with him were his brown bottle and his hammer.

"Hey, Nubbin, you sure that's the right bottle?"

Nubbin stopped, pulled the cork, sniffed, and took a long drink. "You're damn right it is!"

With Nubbin gone the men stood around looking at each other as if they'd just found out it was still winter.

"You mean," a man said, "I've got to start doing my own work, cutting wood and all that?"

"We could get her running backwards again. When all the ears was put back on, we could start over."

"Can't do that," Father said. "We're all out of anything to eat."

"Well, too bad. You know, I been cussing Nubbin and his damn shredder for better'n three months. You know something else? Come tomorrow morning I'm going to be working all by myself, feeling like somebody forgot to invite me to the party."

In early March, Nubbin came back with his bottle, hammer, and another tractor. He hitched onto the old tractor and shredder and towed them away along the ridge to the east.

"I'm glad we're rid of him," Father said.

When it came time to get the machinery ready for the spring work, it turned out we weren't quite through with Nubbin. Lyle hitched onto the big gangplow and said, "Gid-y-ep." The tongue dropped off, the double trees came loose, and the horses kept on going. For a few seconds Lyle was left sitting there on the seat with his mouth hanging open. The slack ran out of the lines before he had a chance to let go, and he went flying after the horses.

We didn't realize we were on the verge of a discovery until Father got weak from laughing and sat down on the mower. The seat skittered out from under him and dumped him on the ground. Meanwhile, Lyle was trying to get up by holding on to the corn planter. A wheel fell off.

The source of Nubbin's never-ending supply of nuts and bolts was no longer a mystery. Every time we moved a piece of machinery, it collapsed. There was hardly a nut, bolt, or cotter pin left on the place. For a while a lot of new words floated around the machine shed.

Nubbin, of course, had the good sense never to show up again on Seldom Seen ridge, but the story of the time the shredder stayed all winter got better every year. Before long Nubbin's hammer was so heavy he couldn't lift it anymore. Then the storytellers had to start making Nubbin bigger and that meant there had to be an explanation for why a man who weighed two hundred and eighty pounds and could swing a fifty-pound hammer with one hand was called a name like Nubbin.

"One of these days," Lyle said, "we're going to have to start that story running backwards, like the shredder."

37 Season Within a Season

Even when I was very young, Christmas was a time of memory. It stretched back across the years, filled with all the kaleido-scopic rememberings of other Christmases, always moving us close together in a special time of loving and being loved. It reached back even beyond my own birth. I could see earlier Christmases in the way Mother hung a favorite, faded ornament on the tree, in the way Father's face softened when he began to sing a Christmas carol in Norwegian. Always one of my brothers would say, "Remember the time the dog knocked the tree down?" I couldn't remember, but I could see it. It became so much a part of Christmas that one year I beat everyone else and said it myself. No one realized that I only remembered through their remembering.

There was a tinseled star at the top of the tree, always speaking of ancient times and three wise men, reminding me of Father traveling across the wide sea, guided home by stars, lighthouses, and, now, by Mother's lamp burning in the kitchen window.

Christmas was, and is, lights and colors, warmth and laughter, remembered voices and all the sad and happy sounds of childhood. It is the feel of heavy brown wrapping paper, the tune of a music box with a bright yellow knob, the smell of pine pitch and of an orange being peeled. It is the first flash of the incredibly red dump truck I got when I was seven years old, the buttery smell of sugar cookies, the feel of the finely worked wool of a new turtleneck sweater that no older brother had ever worn. It is the silvery tinkling sound of a candy wrapper as I unveiled a mysterious chocolate, then put the smoothed-out foil into an encyclopedia along with the faded flowers and bright candy wrappers from other years.

Christmas was a season within a season, filled with mystery and wonder. How could it be such a part of us, yet still seem to come from outside ourselves? How could it be new each year, yet always be the same Christmas, the way it is with an old and familiar tree that is always there, yet always has new growth?

I don't know the answers. I only know that each year we reached out to find Christmas and make it happen, and each year Christmas reached out and found us instead. It found us even in that strange winter we always spoke of as "the time we didn't have a Christmas tree."

The season began as usual. The last day of school came, and that was the first day of Christmas for us. Teacher, as always on that day, had a frantic look. We could not stay in our seats or keep from whispering.

"Let's meet! Let's go sledding!"

"When?"

"Tomorrow! Day after tomorrow! Next week!"

"Let's each say we're going to stay at the other's house. We'll dig a snow cave. We'll sled all night."

"If there's a wet snow, let's all come back to school. Let's start a big snowball. Let's roll it down the hill until it's big as the schoolhouse."

"Yeah, and maybe knock the schoolhouse down!"

We squirmed in our seats, and we weren't even there. We were racing up and down the hills on our sleds, defying gravity, snow flying up to pelt us, giving us faces so white that only our eyes showed through, and the adults fainted and screamed when they saw us, thinking we were ghosts.

All Teacher could think of was the school program that night. We were her performers, and we couldn't even remember our own names.

"Quiet. Get back to your seats. Stop that whispering."

We stayed an extra half hour to practice the singing. Teacher couldn't seem to get us all to use the same words. For "Jingle Bells" was it "Bells on bob tail ring," or was it "Bells on bob-tailed Ned" (or "Nag" or "Nob")?

"You've got me so confused I don't remember myself," Teacher said. "Let's agree it's Ned."

We tried another song. "No! No! It's 'We Three Kings of Orient Are,' not 'We Three Kings of Oriental.' And when you're singing 'Silent Night,' remember that it's 'round yon virgin,' not 'round, young virgin.' Can you all remember that?"

"Yes," we cried, the feel of our sled ropes already in our hands. We would have said yes if she'd asked if we each had thirty-nine heads.

A first-grade girl had to stay after school for more work with Teacher. She had decided to recite the Lord's Prayer and she kept saying, "Our Father Who are in Heaven, Halloween be Thy name."

We ran for home, pulling our sleds, still making plans.

"Let's build a ski jump!"

"Let's pour water all over the hillside west of the house and slide on the frozen crust."

We had used water once to make an icy crust on the big snowdrift between the house and barn. Father and Lyle didn't know about that. They started across the drift carrying a ten-gallon can full of milk. It was a good crust all right. After Father and Lyle fell down, they stayed on top and slid all the way down to the chicken house. When the milk can caught up with them, it still had enough in it to slosh them good. Father suggested we not do that anymore. He also suggested we spend the next day shoveling a path through the big snowdrift.

But a whole hillside of ice would be different! We'd go flying down toward the fence, skim under the lower strand of barbed wire, teeter on the edge of the ditch, and go all the way to the woods!

Junior wasn't there to ask things like how would we get the water out there and what if we hit a bump just as we went under the barbed wire. He was at home with a cough. When we came crashing into the kitchen, Father and Mother were talking about whether or not Junior should go to the school program that night. Junior was looking from one to the other as they talked, his face pale, eyes very big. He smiled when they decided it would be all right.

We did the chores before supper. Lyle finished the last half of his hot coffee in one noisy gulp and hurried out to get the horses and the big bobsled ready. With the yellow light of a lantern to show us the way, we went out to the sled. Lyle had filled the two-foot-high sled box with straw and put all our old blankets on top. Mother had heated several of her irons on top of the kitchen stove and brought them along, wrapped in old towels, in case anyone's feet got cold.

We blew out the lantern and climbed in, pulling blankets around us. Lyle was up front. He flipped the lines, said, "Gid-y-ep," and we glided out along the ridge to the west, the wind reaching for us, the tug chains ringing like bells behind the trotting horses.

Our eyes adjusted to the darkness. A faint blue light seemed to hang just over the surface of the snow. We could see the graceful roll of the drifts along the road, the smooth outline of snow-covered fields, the faint shadow of the next ridge to the north and beyond that the lights of Mount Sterling.

Father was wearing his old horsehair coat and had promised Mother he would leave it in the sled. Mother's hands were tucked deep into her big fur muff, holding it up to protect her face from the wind. Junior was huddled almost out of sight in Father's big sheepskin coat. The sled runners rattled sometimes when we hit crusted snow.

"Look! "Mother said, pointing.

There were glittering little pinpoints of light shining in a field where the wind had swept away the snow and uncovered patches of smooth ice.

"What are they?"

"The reflection of the stars," said Father.

We lay down on our backs, protected from the wind, sinking deep into the straw with its smell of summer, and we looked up at the distant stars.

"How many do you think there are?"

"A billion, I bet."

"A trillion."

"Eighty-nine thousand quadrillion."

"So many you could spend the rest of your life counting them and still not count them all."

"Is it always the same stars?"

"Of course it is."

"I mean if you tried to count them, would they all just stay there and be the same ones?"

"Hey, maybe there's stars that just visit us, maybe once every thousand years."

"Comets do that, not stars."

"Well, why shouldn't a star be able to do that if a comet can?"

"Shush," said Mother. "Just enjoy them."

We went on into the shelter of the woods. The wind was almost gone, the breath of the horses quick and white as they walked up the steep hill beyond the deep ravine. We topped the hill and turned down into the narrow school road, sled runners gliding silently through the undisturbed snow, bare limbs of trees so thick above us they almost shut out the stars. An owl hooted. Something quick and small, a rabbit maybe, scurried away from the road and vanished in the woods.

"There's the light," Lyle said as we came down into the little hollow that led to the schoolhouse. The runners of other sleds were rattling on the icy road beyond the creek. Horses were whinnying. Yellow lights bobbed up and down in the meadow east of the schoolhouse where people were coming on foot, carrying kerosene lanterns. We found a place between two other teams, tied up to the top rail of the fence, and Father and Lyle covered the horses with blankets.

The schoolhouse was warm, filled with the light and smell of a half dozen kerosene lamps. One was flickering. Mother smiled at me. "It needs you to trim the wick."

The big wreath we had made from pine limbs and bittersweet berries was hanging under the clock. The blackboard had hundreds of little dabs of chalk on it.

"I told you it wouldn't look like snow," Junior said when he saw the blackboard. His voice was a hoarse whisper. He stayed with Mother in a front seat, his hands tucked inside her muff. Soon the room was crowded, some people dressed "in their best bib and tucker," as Mother would say, some in work clothes that carried a barn smell through the warm room. There was a burst of laughter when a long-legged man tried to squeeze into the desk he'd used when he was in the eighth grade.

"Look," he said pointing at the desk top, "there's my initials."

Several high-school boys stood at the back of the room, whispering and laughing. A girl near them got up, marched to the front, and crowded into another seat, her face as red as the ribbon in her hair.

Teacher welcomed everyone. Mostly she talked about how hard we had worked. I think she was asking people not to laugh at our mistakes.

We all trooped out of the cloakroom for our first number, jostled into position, and sang "Jingle Bells," almost everyone remembering to say "Bells on bob-tailed Ned."

The next number was "Scenes from an Early Wisconsin Christmas." The piano began. An Indian crept out, an arrow ready in his half-drawn bow. When his head feather slipped, he grabbed for it and the arrow went up in the air and came down on the piano keyboard, playing one sharp pinging note. The woman at the piano, I think her name was Elsie, slid over to the other end of the bench. It tipped and dumped her off. She reached up and went right on playing while she was getting up from the floor.

Tom Withers came in, crawling on all fours, playing a hungry bear. The Indian was supposed to shoot him, but he couldn't find his arrow. Tom ran in circles, one of them carrying him too close to the Christmas tree. His head went through a loop in a string of popcorn. Tom kept on going. The tree tipped and came down on top of him. He roared, as a bear or as himself we never knew, and galloped off with the string of popcorn following.

The audience did its best. People were able to control their laughter until a boy came out for the first lines of our scene.

"Christmas in early Wisconsin," he said, "was not an easy time."

"By God, you can say that again," boomed a voice from the back. "What with bears in the house and all."

The room filled with laughter. Men were pounding their legs and wiping tears out of their eyes. The women stopped first and began shushing everyone until it was quiet again.

A third-grader marched out to do her piece about Christmas fairies. After four sentences or so, she forgot her lines and switched over and did "The Village Blacksmith" instead. The audience applauded anyway and she walked off, head high, looking very pleased.

A boy did part of "Snowbound." I don't think he understood the opening lines because he always put a question mark after them. "The sun that cold December day, it sank from sight before it set?"

A girl began reciting "The First Snowfall." Halfway through, her little brother wandered up front and stood looking up at her. She went on speaking, shooing him away with her hands, but he stayed right beside her. She stopped for a minute, sighed, then took his hand and went on with the poem, the little boy beaming at her. There was a line in that poem about someone kissing a child, then lines something like "And she kissing back could not know that the kiss was meant for her sister, lying deep under the falling snow."

The girl took the little boy back to his seat and walked to the cloakroom. The audience was very quiet, except that one old lady in a white shawl was crying. Then the applause came, longer for that girl than for any other part of the program.

We all lined up and started singing "Joy to the World," but were interrupted by the sound of horses fighting. Half the men ran outside, and we waited, frozen in the middle of a line, until everyone came back. The piano started again at the beginning. We went on from where we were. At the end, an angel was supposed to walk across in front of us. One of her wings fell off. She tripped on it and said, in a clear whisper, "Darn! I told her it wouldn't stay on."

Everything else went all right unless you counted a key sticking on the piano and a man prying it up with his jackknife.

At the end, we all jostled into line again and sang "Silent Night." I don't think we said the virgin was round. The old lady started crying again. Teacher walked out in front of us and said, "Everybody sing!"

The whole schoolhouse rumbled and vibrated as all the voices joined in.

We waited for the applause to end, bowed, and started to walk off, but there was a cold blast of air from the door and Santa Claus bounced in with a big bag on his shoulder. He went ho-ho-ing around the room, stopping every few steps to pull up his slipping belly, asking who had been good all year in a voice suspiciously like that of one of our closest neighbors, Amel Oppreicht. He came up to the front, reached into his bag, and handed each of us a little brown paper sack full of hard candy, peanuts, and a big sticky popcorn ball that stuck in the top of the sack like a bottle stopper.

Santa went all around the room with little sacks for the younger children and for Junior, pretending each time that his bag was empty. Then he bounced back out the door. We could hear him yelling out in the schoolyard. "Gid-y-ep, Dancer! Gid-y-ep, Prancer!"

We crowded to the windows. He was riding off in a sled. Bells were ringing, and he yelled, "Merry Christmas to all, and to all a good night!"

The sled, the voice, and the bells faded slowly into the night.

The piano started up again. Everyone crowded around to sing carols, and the smell of the kerosene stove filled the room as women began making coffee and hot cocoa. Soon it was ready, great steaming pots of both, along with about a hundred different kinds of cookies that were shaped like stars, trees, and bells, most of them covered with bright-colored sugar.

Warm, and so full of cocoa we could hear it sloshing when we wiggled our stomachs, we started home. Lanterns were going in all directions, the night filled with young and old voices.

"Merry Christmas!"

"Good night. Merry Christmas."

"See you in two weeks."

"Don't forget we're going to roll a big snowball."

We went up the road, Denny Meagher and his sister, Margaret, close behind us in their sled. We said good night and Merry Christmas to them, then turned out along Seldom Seen ridge by ourselves. The moon had come up. The trees made sharp black shadows on the snow. Mother began singing "O, Little Town of Bethlehem," her voice high and clear, getting lost out against the bright stars. Father's deep voice joined her, his Norwegian accent more noticeable when he was singing. We all sang, except Junior, as the horses trotted toward home.

We got out in front of the house and Lyle took the horses on to the barn. Junior was coughing, looking very white when Father carried him inside.

"Open the davenport," Mother said to Lee and me.

The davenport was in the living room. We opened it and Father put Junior down, then carried coals from the dining room stove for a fire. Sticky from the popcorn balls and still working on the hard candy and peanuts, we went off to bed with two weeks of vacation ahead and plans enough to fill a year.

Junior was still sick next day and the day after that. The door to the living room stayed closed except when we tiptoed in to put more wood in the stove.

Dr. Farrell came from Seneca, bundled up in a big coat and a fur cap, riding in a little sleigh that we called a cutter. We ran out to take his horse.

"I'll give her some water and oats," Lyle said.

"You will, will you?" Dr. Farrell roared. He had a voice, Lyle liked to say, that was like a cream can full of walnuts rolling down a steep hill. The doctor headed for the house with his bag, then yelled over his shoulder, "By God, it's a help all right, having the horse taken care of."

We watched from the dining room doorway while he warmed his stethoscope over the stove and listened to Junior's throat and chest. He left the thermometer in for a long time " 'Cause it's cold as a damned icicle to start with!" When he read the thermometer, he came out into the dining room, closing the door behind him. Father and Mother were waiting.

"Scarlet fever," Dr. Farrell said.

"What does that mean?"

"Means he's going to be a mighty sick boy. Keep the other children out of that room. Be better if only one of you goes in there." He went on talking to Mother while we got his horse and hitched it to the cutter.

Junior kept getting worse, his fever so high we could hear him mumbling and talking in his sleep even with the door closed. Once he said in a loud, angry voice, "I said I wanted skis!"

It was a strange Christmas season. We didn't do any of the things we'd planned. Mother hardly had time to talk to us, except to tell us what needed to be done. Dr. Farrell came every day. Then, maybe four or five days before Christmas, Mother told us there wouldn't be a Christmas tree.

"We'll do something about it later, maybe. There just isn't enough time now. Anyway, the doctor says we have to keep the house quiet." She was almost crying when she went into the other room and closed the door.

"You help her all you can," Father said. "Don't wait to be asked."

"Is Junior going to get well?"

He looked at us for a long time. I used to wonder when he did that if he was thinking in Norwegian and had to change it back to English.

"We don't know," he said.

I don't remember how Laurance felt about what was happening, but Lee and I began to feel cheated. In the safe isolation of the big dark closet at the head of the stairs, we dared to come right out and tell each other there wasn't any Santa Claus. I'm sure we already knew it wasn't Santa who brought our presents, but he had gone on being a part of Christmas for a long time and we still believed in Christmas, all right. But what kind of a Santa Claus, even if he was just a "spirit," would let Junior get this sick at Christmastime?

We still ran to meet the mailman every day, hoping for packages, especially packages with revealing rattles or holes in them. One day George Holliday handed us one that didn't need a hole. He winked and laughed. "Here you are. What comes in a package four inches wide, five feet long, and curves up at one end?"

"Junior's new skis," we said.

"How is he?"

"Still sick."

"Well, when he gets his skis, he'll be better."

"He won't be getting them. We don't even have a Christmas tree."

"Well, hell's bells," George said. "No wonder he's sick."

We took the skis to the house and gave them to Mother. She put them away. "He might not even know if I gave them to him."

Lee and I spent more and more time in the dark closet, trying to get Christmas to happen. All our other Christmases began to form in our minds as we talked. We always cut two or three branches from the white pines in the yard and tied them together to make a nice full tree. We hung all the ornaments, some of the tin ones old and dented. We put up the star and threaded popcorn and cranberries onto strings and draped them around the tree. There was a little package that unfolded and magically became a big red paper bell to hang over the dining room table, so low we had to be careful not to put the lamp under it. On Christmas Eve we always turned the lamp down low and lighted the candles on the tree, Father watching from the kitchen door with a bucket of water in his hand. We would look at the burning candles and eat the little round candies with pictures in the center that were a promise of what was to come in the morning.

Christmas Day always began with the presents, but there was much more. Father would put out his sheaf of grain for the birds. There were navel oranges and bright red apples that made our own seem pale and small, and always a letter from Norway with a strange stamp, the envelope lined in brightly colored tissue paper. We'd all sit down and Father would tell us what the letter said, giving us a once-a-year glimpse of a grandmother and aunts and uncles who were only pictures in the old leather suitcase.

Soon, the smells of Christmas dinner would spread through the house, so strong and good we forgot our presents and gathered, starving, in the kitchen to hurry Mother along. Father said a blessing in Norwegian and we ate until we couldn't hold another bite, then ran around the table four times and ate some more.

After dinner Mother would bring out the package of books. Each year, just before Christmas, she sent off a letter to the State Lending Library, asking them to send us about thirty books for three adults and four boys. She gave our ages and a few words about each of us. She'd never let us read what she said, though sometimes she'd include our suggested additions, things like "Please don't send *Black Beauty* again this year." Then someone in the library in far-off Madison would read the letter and would, we liked to think, sit down, close their eyes, see us, and decide what books to send.

Only then, with everyone gathered in the warm house, with presents, books to read, and all the good things to eat, would Christmas have really come.

Lee and I could go back over all that in the closet, but this time it didn't happen. We ran into the dining room on Christmas morning and it was just like any other day, except that Mother looked sad and hollow-eyed and Father was walking restlessly around the room. Dr. Farrell came right after breakfast. We heard him say something about "today being a critical day."

When the doctor left, Mother brought out a present for each of us. They weren't wrapped with the usual bows and ribbons. I guess Father must have done them. Lee and I got the double-barreled popguns we'd been wanting. Wondering how we could have missed a package that slim and long, we tore them out of the boxes, cocked them, and started to pull the double triggers. Father grabbed us.

"Better go outdoors with those."

We went out and tried target practice for a while, using twigs, corks, and pieces of ice for bullets. It began to snow, big wet flakes. We rolled giant snowballs, leaving paths of bare brown lawn behind us, and made a snowman, then used our new popguns to shoot marbles into his front for buttons.

It didn't feel like Christmas, even with the snow falling. We sat down with our backs against the snowman and waited for something to happen.

What happened was that a man we'd never seen before came walking along the road from the west. He was wearing a stocking cap and had a stick over his shoulder with a little bundle on the end. Sometimes tramps came by with a bundle like that, heading for the railroad along the Kickapoo River. The man saw us sitting there against the snowman and waved to us.

"Merry Christmas!" he called in a big voice.

We waved back, and he went on walking down the road with the snow falling around him.

We started talking about Junior and Christmas again. The first thing we decided was that Junior should get his skis. But we had to do more than that.

"We could say Santa Claus came by with them."

That wasn't going to be good enough for skeptical Junior.

"What if somebody did come by? And saw us sitting here?"

"Yeah, somebody like an old man with a stocking cap and a bundle on his back."

"What if he asked how come we weren't happy and playing?"

"Yeah, and we said because our brother's sick."

"And maybe he'd be like Mr. Holliday. He'd say, 'No wonder he's sick. What you need to do is take him his present.'"

"And tell him he's going to be all right."

"Do you think he'd believe that?"

"Maybe the old man better have a beard."

"Yes, a red beard."

Dr. Farrell stopped by again and we followed him into the house. He came back out of the other room and said, "He's no better."

"Can we see him?" Lee asked.

Mother shook her head.

"We want to give him his skis."

Mother looked at Dr. Farrell. He sighed. "Oh, it can't hurt anything. But don't go up close. Stay away from the bed."

Mother got the skis. We unwrapped them and took them in, closing the door behind us. Junior was lying on his back, two pillows under his head. His eyes were open but he didn't look at us. He was making a funny noise when he breathed, and his freckles stood out very plain. He didn't even seem like Junior.

We held up the skis so he could see them. We started telling him about the old man.

Pretty soon Junior looked at us. When he started shaking his head a little bit, it was Junior all right.

"Tramp," he whispered.

"No, it wasn't! He had a long beard."

"A red one!"

Junior stopped shaking his head and seemed to be thinking about that. We shoved the skis onto the bed and pushed them up beside him. He took a deep breath and closed his eyes.

We tiptoed out.

"Did you give him the skis?"

"Yes. And he went to sleep."

Mother started for the other room. Dr. Farrell stopped her. He went in and closed the door. When he came out he looked surprised. "That's right. He is asleep. I think he's breathing better."

Mother hugged us. For the first time it seemed like Christmas.

Four or five days later, when Dr. Farrell came by, he said Junior could get up the next day. Mother smiled and said she thought maybe she'd go to bed when he got up. She looked at us. "I'm sorry about the tree."

"Hummp!" said Dr. Farrell. "Seems to me Christmas came anyway!"

38 Blizzard

If we ever got through a year without a howling blizzard or two, I don't remember it that way. A blizzard was the very heart of winter. They could come from early November to late April. Once there was one on Armistice Day, November 11, and duck hunters were trapped out in the Mississippi River bottoms. Some of them froze to death a mile away from heat and warm food.

We four boys liked blizzards. They challenged us, made us feel like intrepid trappers or mounted policemen following a dogsled somewhere in the great barrens north of Hudson's Bay. There was only one thing we asked—no blizzard just before Christmas. Our surprises came by mail, and we wanted the roads to be open.

It seems to me the worst winter storms came in February, when there was no warmth left in the land to temper the cold wind. I can't be sure. I find that all the blizzards of those years have gathered into a feeling of one great classic storm that came roaring out of the northwest to test us and see if we could survive. The storm cut us off from all other companionship. We were alone with the elements on our exposed hilltop.

The blizzard tried to sneak up on us. It started with a wind-driven, freezing rain and a sky so gray and cold that only a fool would ever expect to see warm sunshine again. Ice coated the ground in a smooth, treacherous layer. We strapped little steel-toothed ice creepers onto our overshoes before we went out, then walked flat-footed to make sure the teeth were gouging into the ice. The only tracks we left were the tiny holes of the teeth. Mother watched us from a window, worrying that we'd fall and put similar little holes in ourselves.

The trees were covered with ice, branches cracking against each other. Long dripping icicles hung from the eaves of the buildings. The clouds were low, going very fast, and had a greenish look.

Suddenly nothing was dripping. The ice under our feet was no longer wet. The rain changed to tiny round bullets that stung our faces and rattled on the buildings. The windmill groaned around with its load of ice as the wind changed and came blasting straight out of the northwest. The pelting sleet changed to snow. It didn't seem to be falling at all, just flying horizontally past us in the wind. Even though the flakes were small, it was soon snowing so hard we could no longer see from the house to the barn. An angry blaze of sunset showed briefly in the west. A sundog's bright red streak stuck straight up from the horizon. Loose snow began covering the smooth ice, making it slipperier than ever, but at least the snow was a cushion when we fell.

Father rounded us up. "Blizzard coming. Let's get our work done. Don't anybody go wandering off in this."

I gave the chickens warm water and extra feed. I carried a mountain of wood from the woodshed, piling it high on the porch and filling the space behind the kitchen stove. Sparrows were flying around the eaves, looking for shelter, some of them trying to get through the screen onto the porch. The bird feeder on the big maple tree was deserted.

Everyone else was working at the barns and hog house. The cows and horses came out, slipping on the ice as they headed down the hill to the tank. They nosed pieces of ice aside and drank, then ran back to the barn doors.

The wind was stronger between the house and woodshed when I went out for a last armload of wood. Ice was cracking off the trees and falling. In a few places the snow would build up to several inches and then the wind would search it out and blow it away.

The farm buildings were all that was left in the world. There were no woods to the west, no farm to the east, no other ridges to the north, no rolling fields stretching toward Lost Valley. It was getting darker. When the snow gusted around me, only the house and wood-shed stayed in sight.

I could hear someone calling. I went down past the windmill, walking wide around it because of the falling ice, and found Father at the chicken-house door, ear flaps down, his clothes covered with white. He cupped his hands and yelled into my ear. "Tell your Mother we'll go ahead and milk before supper. That way we won't have to come out again."

I nodded and ran for the house. At the porch I turned to look back. Father and the chicken house had vanished in the white. A cloud of steam came out of the kitchen when I opened the door and ducked in. The snow followed me and spit against the top of the hot stove. Mother already had a lamp on the kitchen table so it would shine out the window toward the barns. "It's like seeing a lighthouse through the storm," Father once told her. Always after that, she made sure the lamp was there on bad nights.

She brushed snow off my shoulders. "I'm glad you're not out there coming home from school in this."

I told her about supper. She nodded, thinking of the longer eve-ning ahead. "Better start a fire in the other room."

"The other room" was the living room, a snug room with a low ceiling in the thick-walled, log part of the house. Most evenings it stayed cold and dark. Using the short-handled fire shovel, I scooped live coals out of the dining room stove and carried them, smoking, sparks flying, to the living room stove. I put corncobs and small pieces of wood over the coals. Soon the fire was roaring and I opened the little metal register that let the heat go to the upstairs bedrooms.

Mother came in and sniffed the air. "Smells musty in here. Get a few more coals on the shovel."

I did that, and she sprinkled some ground coffee over the coals. There were little sparkles of light as the coffee caught fire. Smoke came up and the good smell of burnt coffee spread as she walked around the room with the shovel.

"There, that's better."

The others came tramping into the kitchen, snow following them, the wind a loud roar while the door was open.

"Whoosh," Father said, rubbing snow off his face. His eyebrows were white. He smiled at Mother. "You know, snow's so thick I was past the well before I could see your light."

Lyle stomped in and slammed the door. He was shivering and headed for the dining-room stove without even taking off his jacket. "It's the kind of night makes you wonder what you did with your summer's wages." Snow sizzled on the stove when he pulled off his coat.

There was a crash from the porch, then a rolling sound. "Ice falling," Father said.

We gathered for supper at the dining table, stove roaring inside, wind roaring outside. The windows rattled and the whole house shook a little in a strong gust.

Mother looked around the table as though counting us. "I'm glad you're all inside."

So were we.

After supper, Mother made a batch of chocolate fudge. When she took it off the stove, I took the pan outside, setting it down into the soft snow that was sifting onto the porch. I let it cool, then brought it back in for her to beat and pour into a pan. I made popcorn, two heaping bowls with melted butter poured over the top. Every head in the dining room turned when I walked in with the first bowl.

Mother followed with the second bowl and the fudge. "Let's go in the other room," she said.

It was warm in the living room. I lighted the pull-down kerosene lamp which had a big china shade with pale wild roses painted on it and glass prisms hanging down all around. Father came in and poked the fire. One by one everyone joined us, Lyle last of all, carrying a chair with him so he could sit close to the stove and toast his feet.

We started on the fudge and popcorn. Mother began to play the piano. In a minute Father went over and stood behind her, a hand on her shoulder. She switched to another song and he sang with her. We joined them, singing and eating at the same time.

"It'll sound better when the popcorn's gone," Mother said.

Between songs the sound of wind on the west side of the house was a solid roar.

Bedtime came early. We filled the heating stoves to the top of the doors with chunks of oak and closed the dampers so the stoves would burn all night. The lamps were blown out, leaving a kerosene smell in the air. We went off to our beds, where mountains of quilts and blankets pushed us down deep into the mattresses. The house began to relax for the night. Floor boards popped back. Walls and ceilings creaked and groaned as the house cooled. Outside, the roar of the wind went on, gusts slamming against the siding, rattling eavespouts and grumbling in the chimneys. Sometimes the wind fell for a moment and there was the cold and ghostly rustle of snow against the windows.

The stoves didn't always settle down when we did. A piece of wood might be too dry or a damper not closed far enough. We would hear flames roar up the chimney, stovepipes snapping as they expanded. Buried warm and deep in the covers, we each waited for someone else to get up and check. When I was the one to give in, I would find the cast-iron belly of the stove a red-hot glow in the dark, light coming out through the seams to dance and flicker on the ceiling. I would take care of the stove, then crowd close to toast myself, first one side, then the other, before racing back to bury myself under the covers.

The wind was the first thing we heard when we woke next morning. We had slept later than usual, but it was still pitch dark outside. Father called us. We waited until we heard the dining room stove roaring, then ran out there to get dressed, hoping Mother wouldn't notice we had slept in our long winter underwear instead of our flannel nightshirts.

Snow was a foot deep on the porch when we went out. Father disappeared toward the hog house, carrying a smoking, glowing bucket of live coals to get a fire started in the water-tank heater. The wind blew out our lanterns before we got halfway to the barn. The drift below the milk house was almost to the top of the gate. White frost lined the cracks of the barn door, and steam was coming out around the edges. The barn was warm, the cows mooing for feed and company.

We did all the chores so we wouldn't have to come out again until afternoon, then ran for the house, shielding our faces from the driving snow.

"Is it still snowing?" Mother asked.

"Can't tell," Father said, "if it's snowing or just blowing."

The blizzard went on. A day like that was a little like Christmas. We did only the chores that had to be done. The stove in the other room burned all day. We were isolated. The road was drifted full. The telephone didn't ring because the ice had broken the line somewhere. Even after daylight came, we still needed a lamp in the dining room. We played cards and got out all of our old games. Even when we were older, a long blizzard day made us young again. We found our wooden blocks and made cities, built crazy-looking machines with Tinkertoys, made long fences of dominoes. Touch one domino at one end and click-click-click the line collapsed, one by one, curving and circling, seeming to take forever.

"Hey! If we had enough dominoes we could build a line clear around the world. We would touch one end. They'd go clicking-clicking out of sight to the east. About ten years later they'd come clicking-clicking back from the west."

"Wouldn't work."

"Why not?"

"What you going to do about the oceans?"

"Oh."

"Hey! Maybe we could invent a new kind of dominoes. They'd float, standing straight up. Nothing in the world could tip them over until another domino clicked against them."

We argued. We experimented in the kitchen wash basin and might have made a million dollars if we hadn't gotten the floor all wet.

Something in the blizzard made us relentlessly hungry. An hour after breakfast we were cracking and eating hickory nuts, walnuts, and butternuts behind the kitchen stove, using one of Mother's heavy irons as an anvil. Lyle came padding out of the dining room in his stocking feet to watch us. He stepped on a sharp nutshell, then yelled and hopped on one foot like a chicken.

Mother always seemed to have extra books stored away for blizzards. She gave me *Bambi* on a day like that. When I reread it years later, I was surprised to find it wasn't always snowing in the book.

With the doors between rooms open and all three stoves going, the whole house was warm, though the temperature might vary twenty degrees from one corner to another. We roamed restlessly from room to room. When other books ran out, we gathered in the closet at the head of the stairs and hauled out the old encyclopedias. They were leather-bound and so old we expected them to say the world was flat. Each with a volume in his lap, we competed to see who could find the most fascinating facts, never daring to invent too much on our own because someone was sure to check.

"Hey!" Lee said once. "It says Wisconsin has the winter climate of northern Sweden or central Russia."

We looked at each other and were instantly changed. The wind was howling around us. We stood in our black bearskin caps and coats on the edge of the Bering Strait, trying to see the other side. We were caught on an ice floe. We were wrapped in quilted goosedown clothes and peering out into the storm from our igloos. Icebound explorers, we tramped onward toward the Pole, our guides turning back, our dogs frozen, food almost gone.

"Hey! When the blizzard's over let's build an igloo."

"Let's make a harness and see if Shep will pull a sled!"

"Mush!" we yelled.

"Mush, you fool dogs. There's a blizzard coming and Fort Henry's twenty miles away!"

"What's going on up there?" Mother called.

Up there? We were in the Arctic. One's mother couldn't call him in the Arctic. One's mother stayed patiently at home waiting for someone to bring word that he was dead or had triumphantly reached the Pole and would be home after a wild parade in Paris and then another in Zanzibar.

"Mush, dogs. Mush!"

"I said what's going on up there?"

"Nothing. We're just playing."

We closed the closet door and spoke in hoarse whispers. We were Royal Mounted Policemen, trailing our man up into the far reaches of the Arctic Circle, so far north it was dark all day. Somewhere up by the windswept North Pole we caught our man. Huddled over our campfire, with the wolves howling and circling around us, he told us, in a story so strange and pitiful it had to be true, that he'd only done what he did to save his sister from an evil man. We turned our backs and let him mush away, to start a new life somewhere on the northern shore of Hudson's Bay. We went back to turn ourselves in and resign from the Royal Mounted Police, disgraced and outcast forever.

Then, holed up at the edge of the pine barrens, we were bearded trappers, leaving giant snowshoe tracks in the ten-foot-deep snow as we covered our trapline. A devilish wolverine dogged our footsteps, setting off our traps by reaching under them, flipping them over, the steel jaws closing on the frozen snow. We hunted him only to come back and find he had crawled down the chimney of our cabin and torn the place to shreds. Food almost gone, no furs to take to the trading post, we finally tricked the wolverine. We set our traps upside down. The wolverine came to the first one, reached under to flip it over, and was caught. The trapline was saved. Then a Mounted Police-man, the Inspector himself, staggered in, lost and nearly dead. We saved him and took him six hundred miles back to the fort. Crowds cheered as we brought him in. The young sister of the man we had let escape was running toward us. . . .

The smell of food brought us back from the Arctic. We ate, and Father mushed us out into the blizzard to do the chores. The drift at the fence was up to the eaves of the chicken house. We shoveled snow away from the barn doors. The cattle came out, walking stiff-legged, then stopped to lick themselves. Gathering energy, they hobbled to the tank, where the heater was smoking and the water steaming in the cold. They were already bawling to get back inside before we had the gutters cleaned out and fresh bedding put down.

We finished the chores again. The thermometer on the milk house said ten below zero. The fine snow blew into our faces, taking our breath away so that we gasped and choked and felt as if we were drowning.

"I need some things from the cellar," Mother said to me when we were back inside. I lighted a lantern, went into the pantry, and closed the door. I moved things to one side, pried up the rusty lifting ring, and raised the creaking trap door. The smells of all the vegetables and fruits of summer came up out of the cool blackness. Lantern in hand, I felt my way down the steep, narrow steps. Sometimes there was the sound of small feet scurrying out of my way. I hung the lantern on a nail and turned the wick up high, even letting it smoke, so the dark corners would pull back away from me. It was like standing in the middle of a cave filled with lost treasure. I filled a pail with potatoes from the big bin. I dug into the boxes of cold sand and brought out firm beets and carrots that still had a smell of fresh earth. I carried all these up, stacked them on the pantry floor, and went down for more.

I got sauerkraut from the ten-gallon crock, jars of pickles, green beans, and tomatoes.

Sometimes I shouted through the pantry door to Mother. "I don't see any rhubarb. What about a jar of blackberries?"

It was true enough. How could I see rhubarb when I was on the top step looking at the pantry door?

"All right. Bring the blackberries."

I brought them up, along with a big Hubbard squash so hard it would have to be cracked open with an ax. With a bowl of apples in one hand and the lantern still smoking bravely in the other, I came up the steps with the darkness reaching for my feet. I slid the apples onto the pantry floor, put down the lantern, and leaped out of the stairway and closed the trap door all in one quick motion.

Safe again from whatever it is that lives and waits in dark places, I took my spoils out into the kitchen. Mother sorted through them, her face alive with pleasure.

"You're a magician," she said. "In the middle of a blizzard you bring summer up from the cellar."

The warming apples spread their smell. Soon a face appeared in the door. "Did I smell apples? Can I have one?"

The storm went on. Frost formed on all the windows, creeping along the glass, delicate, fast-growing white ferns. The crystals thickened and became lacy trees with leaves like giant, shining fish scales. Finally there was just thick white frost with holes scraped through in special places so we could look out at the blowing snow.

Night came, then morning again, and still the roaring wind and snow went on. The second full day of a blizzard was different. Father wandered restlessly, looking for something to do. Mother brought out any pots that needed soldering. That done, Father would bring in broken harnesses. If the storm came when the seed corn had already been tested, we all shelled corn, our hands raw from rubbing the hard kernels off the ears. The cobs were Father's morning kindling, though sometimes Mother rescued them and boiled them in water to make a thin, sweet corn syrup.

The roar of the wind had been around us so long we hardly heard it anymore. The sounds inside the house grew louder—the tap-tap of harness rivets, the meat saw biting into a quarter of frozen beef, the coffee grinder, someone laughing at something in a book, the creak-creak of Mother's ironing board, the slap of her hand on rising dough, the moist buey-ooey sound of mouth-made car exhausts, a pound-pound from the kitchen that said only one thing in the world, raw beef on a wooden cutting board being pounded to make it tender. And there was Junior running a ten-penny nail up and down the strings of his guitar, trying to make Hawaiian music.

"Sounds like wolves," said Lyle.

"Ghosts," said Lee.

"Sounds like somebody running a silly nail up and down guitar strings," said Laurance.

Father cleared his throat. "Sounds unnecessary."

Junior grinned and retreated. Soon the mournful sound of his harmonica came from the living room, playing "Red River Valley," "Beautiful Dreamer," "Wabash Cannonball," "Little Red Wing," and a song that no one else remembers, about a man who said he was going to the state prison at Waupun.

Once, on a day like that, I was alone in the kitchen with Father and Mother. The dog was there—all dogs were called Shep then—and he was restless, wanting to get outside and run but turned back by the cold wind every time we opened the door for him. He came over to Father, who was riveting a buckle back onto my overshoe, and put out a paw to shake hands. Father laughed and Shep began trying to play, claws slipping on the linoleum floor.

"Say," Father said, "remember when you were little? We used to get down on the floor, I and all four of you, with Shep and wrestle. Shep would growl at me when I squeezed one of you and made you yell."

I didn't remember. I had to say that.

Father looked at me, the laughter gone.

Mother came over and put her head on his shoulder. "I think it must have been the older ones."

Father went back to tapping at the copper rivet, not noticing that Shep was trying to shake hands again. Then Father reached out and touched my shoulder. "Son, I guess a man gets so busy trying to make a living he forgets to be a father."

I wasn't good at finding the right words to say to Father, but I had to say something that would change the look on his face.

"There were other things," Mother said.

"I remember once," I said, "we were way out in the middle of the Mississippi. The two of us, in a rowboat. I was a lot younger. I thought it might be the sea."

"Did we catch any fish?"

"I don't remember. I just remember you rowing me in the rowboat." Mother smiled at me.

"And you used to tell us about an old mill. In Norway. There was a light in a window."

Father nodded. "I remember. Your eyes always got bigger than cream-can lids. Would you like to hear that story?"

"Yes."

He told it all again. And he wasn't my father in the story at all. He was a young boy, no older than I, running, running in the summer of a land I had never seen.

Mother gave us both a hug and went back to her work at the kitchen table.

Lyle's head came poking around the edge of the door. "You know, it's a funny thing about that light. A person might expect it to fade some over the years. Seems to me it gets brighter every time."

Father grinned and shoved Shep toward Lyle. "Go bite that man for me and I'll give you a bone for supper."

The day ended. By the time we came in from chores the thermometer stood at twenty below. Lyle wrapped himself around the dining room stove and shivered. "By golly, by morning it's going to be colder than a left-handed ti—"

I waited, but he caught himself just in time.

"Colder than a left-handed . . . ah . . . monkey wrench in Alaska."

Mother looked up from the sock she was darning. "Why, that's an odd expression. I never heard that before."

"Neither did I," Lyle said. "Made it up on the spot."

For some reason, that started Lyle and Father talking about all the tales of men lost in blizzards, maybe freezing to death fifty feet from the house. Out on the plains men strung ropes between the house and barn. Someone who was lost would run into a fence and follow it, hoping it was going toward help, not away from it. If you were lucky you ran into the side of a building and felt your way along it, looking for a corner and a door.

"Heard about a fellow who did that," Lyle said. "He froze to death anyway."

"How come?"

"Well, he kept going along that building and along that building for what seemed like a month of Sundays. Never did find the end of that building. They found him out there next morning. Didn't know if he froze to death or wore himself out from walking."

"All right. What's the catch?"

"No catch at all. It was told to me as a true story. You see that building the fellow ran into was a round barn."

The wind was suddenly gustier. As it tried to come down the chimney, puffs of smoke came out around the stove doors. At supper, a new sound came from the living room. The wind began a certain humming howl around the eaves. It made us think of ghosts and tales of Russian children being thrown one by one from a sleigh to slow up the pursuing wolves. It was a deep, throbbing howl that happened maybe once or twice a winter when the wind was very strong and coming from exactly the right direction.

We all stopped eating and waited. Then the other sound began, a fainter, vibrating imitation of the first. I felt the hair rising on the back of my neck. It was Mother's piano, playing all by itself, the strings vibrating in tune with the howling wind.

Father smiled at Mother. "Maybe it's just asking you to come play it."

After supper she did that and we sang, our voices blocking out the wind.

I woke that night, knowing something had happened. I listened. The house was so utterly still I might have been the only person left in the world. I could feel ice against my face where my breath had frozen on the covers. Reaching one hand out into the grabbing cold, I scraped frost from the windowpane. Stars were shining. Then I knew what had awakened me. The wind was gone. The blizzard was over. I pulled my head down under the covers and went back to sleep.

The ice was a half inch thick on the kitchen water bucket when we got up next morning. The thermometer on the milk house said forty-two below zero. Snow squeaked under our overshoes, the telephone wire hummed in the cold, and the big drift reached almost to the top of the chicken-house roof. The sun came up, a blinding red ball, with a rainbow-colored sundog guarding it on each side. White smoke rose straight up from the neighbor's chimney, and other farms and other ridges were there around us again in every direction.

George Holliday came with the mail, riding on horseback, our first contact with the outside world. We handed him a half-gallon pail of hot coffee. He made the half-mile loop to the east, came back, and hung the empty pail on our mailbox. Late in the day, the roaring, clanking snowplow came by, throwing up snowbanks fifteen feet high along the road to the west.

Despite all the activity, there was a loneliness in such a day. I kept feeling I should be looking for something I had lost. I tried to talk to Mother about that. She nodded and put her arm around me. Together we stood and looked out the kitchen window. Lyle was hitching a team of horses to a sled. Father was at the door of the hog house. Laurance was shoveling snow at the barnyard gate. I knew that tomorrow we'd be going back to school, feeling superior to the valley children who never had a chance to stand against the storm.

Mother sighed. "I know what you mean. The blizzard brings us all together."

"Like Christmas."

"Yes, like Christmas. Now we're all busy, going our own ways again. I guess a blizzard spoils us a little. I guess we shouldn't expect it to be that way all the time."

"Could we have a fire in the other room again tonight?"

She smiled. "Yes. I'll make some fudge."

"I'll make popcorn."

39 Promise of Change

Winter is long in Wisconsin. There are days when the land is tinsel-bright in the sun. There are times when it lies cold and dismal with no sunshine for weeks at a time. The temperature can hang unendingly at a damp forty degrees in what Doc Farrell used to call "pneumonia weather." Or it can stay below zero for a week. Once it went down to fifty-four below and trees froze and exploded with a sound like cannons.

Winter is a busy time, a thousand chores to do over and over again, machinery to repair, all the livestock to be fed, the battle against cold and snow. Yet, for all the work, winter is mostly a time of waiting.

Waiting is easier on the land. We were surrounded by promises that winter would end, spring would come again, and the sleeping land would awake. Crows began to gather and strut, jet black against the white. A dandelion stayed green under the snow close to a building foundation. The sun climbed a little higher each day, bringing a tantalizing hint of all the warmth and smells of summer. The buds on the big maple tree were swelling, making the branches a red fringe against the sky. A titmouse tried a first uncertain little three-note song— "Spring? Spring? Spring?"

There was another unfailing promise. A day would come when I'd see Father walking out of the barn into the bright sunshine, jacket open, his hands loosening his top shirt button. Suddenly he would stop. He would look at the sun, then out over the snow-covered fields, and he would nod and smile as though some message of change had come to him and said "seedtime."

Father would start forward again, steps longer, head back, already walking toward the rich green of the coming spring and the waiting land.

An Ending, A Beginning

Mother died the winter I was sixteen. There was no warning. The winter, the same winter that always killed her fall flowers and sent her birds away, caused her death. She fell on the ice and broke her leg. Dr. Farrell came. He growled at her, put a cast on her leg, and told her to rest. Before his horse was out of sight, she was beginning to run the house from her bed. The door to the bedroom stayed open, and her voice carried through the house. Our voices carried back to her, so she felt a part of things.

Two weeks later she woke Father in the night, saying she felt faint. He called Dr. Farrell, but in a few minutes she was dead. The rest of us were still sleeping. Dr. Farrell said a piece of tissue had broken loose from the fracture and stopped her heart.

The weeks crept by. The hushed and whispering feel of death went away, but the house stayed quiet and empty. We would find ourselves wandering from room to room. A thousand times I started out to look for her, to tell her something, to ask her something. In the evening, at the dining room table, one of us would suddenly raise his head from whatever he was doing and look around, still surprised to find the empty chair at the end of the table nearest the kitchen.

We could not believe she was gone. Even with the constant flow of the seasons to tell us that life is filled with endings and beginnings, there had been no preparation for life on our hilltop world without Mother.

As the winter went on, there were two things I began to dread, the next blizzard and the coming of spring. The blizzard came a month later. I woke in the night, the heavy covers pushing me down, the air in the bedroom cold on my face. Snow was whispering against the walls. The windows were rattling. That odd, deep howling of the wind was coming from the eaves along the west side of the house.

I waited, shivering. The other sound began. The piano was humming, imitating the wind. I listened and waited for the hair to rise on the back of my neck. That didn't happen. It wasn't a lonely, ghostly sound at all. I stopped shivering, pulled the covers up tight around me, and went back to sleep, thinking of her playing and singing at the piano.

The days lengthened. The snow began to melt. Easter lilies bloomed, pale violet against the brown of last year's grass. The birds came back. The land warmed in the sun, as it had in other springs. The green came again. The silly McMahon tree bloomed on one side.

Nothing had been said about a garden. One Saturday morning at breakfast I asked Lyle to get the ground ready. Everyone stopped eating. We all looked at Father. He put his hands up to his face and didn't speak.

"All right," Lyle said. He smiled, the first one I'd seen from him in a long time. "But don't be surprised if you find a horse's head sticking in through a window. I might as well try to plow a postage stamp."

Father got up and started out. He came back and put his hand on my shoulder. "You want any help?"

I shook my head.

Lyle began on the garden, first a load of manure, then the walking plow. I dug through the pantry and found the cardboard box with all the packets of seeds. Mother had written little notes to herself on the envelopes which held seeds we had harvested ourselves. They all made sense but one. It said, "Try a half row, next to the larkspur. Not blue???"

I went out with the box of seeds, the string, and the garden tools just as Lyle was finishing. His face was all puckered up. "Goddammit, Ben," he said. "Goddammit to hell." He turned his face away and whacked the horses with the lines. They trotted toward the barnyard, the harrow bouncing and clattering behind them.

The garden was smoother than I'd ever seen it. The moist dark soil was already warming in the sun, sending up the fresh smell that said "seedtime." Without thought, I began to follow the pattern of other years. I stretched the string across the garden, lined up with the west window on one side and the wild plum tree on the other, leaving the north end for volunteer ground cherries and tomatoes. I made a row under the string, and began to drop the seeds and cover them with moist earth.

White petals were falling from the McMahon tree. A robin was building its nest again in exactly the same place in the juniper tree. A meadowlark sang from the top of the big maple tree.

I planted radishes, lettuce, turnips, beets, beans, working my way slowly toward the south end. I didn't know yet if I was going to plant any flowers.

The soil went on warming in the sun, beginning to have a lighter color on the very top as it dried out a little. The knees on my trousers were damp. The mysterious living seeds passed through my fingers, one by one. I marked the end of each row with a stick, sometimes putting an empty seed envelope over it so I would know what was there.

I planted the peas, two rows close together, then a space and two more rows, still not knowing why we did it that way.

Finally there was only the space at the south end where the flowers had always been. I looked at it, lying smooth and undisturbed, and knew I couldn't leave it that way. I got the dry and shriveled dahlia roots and gladiolus bulbs from the cellar. Even as I put them carefully into the ground, I couldn't quite believe that life was stored in there, waiting for a chance to come out.

I began on the annual flowers, first the larkspur. Had she liked it so much because of the word "lark" in the name? I had never thought about that. I planted the half row of mystery seeds next to the larkspur, then the zinnias, nasturtiums, and cosmos. Last of all, I sprinkled the tiny black seeds of moss rose and patted them into the ground with a board.

When it was all finished, I straightened up to uncrick my muscles, putting my head way back, looking up at all the different shades of blue. Then, like Lyle, I started crying. I climbed high into the white pine tree, up to my special whorl of limbs. Curled around the trunk the way I'd done when I was younger, with the branches of the big maple tree reaching out toward me, I let go and cried for the first time without trying to stop.

I had not entirely lost her after all. The seeds germinated. Neat rows of new green pushed up in the garden.

The land remembers.

Afterword

The original Viking edition of *The Land Remembers* was published in 1975. Approximately a half million copies have been printed.

The book has stirred odd reactions. The first day it was in New York bookstores a writer friend came to see me. She slammed *The Land Remembers* down for an autograph and said, "Who do you think you are? Don't you realize regional writers aren't supposed to be noticed until they're dead?"

Of course in prickly-language New York she was complimenting me. I had to respond appropriately. "Well, pardon me for still being alive," I said. We both smiled. We understood.

I received another language lesson last Christmas season when I phoned a New York media person. At the end of our conversation I said, "Have a nice holiday," and he said, "Thank you, but I have other plans."

If I had been a proper New Yorker I should have said, "You know what your problem is? You got an attitude!" That's called "Bed witting." It's when you think of witty things you should have said only after you go to bed. See how dangerous it is to turn a writer loose in front of a keyboard? Well, someone described a writer as a person upon whom nothing is wasted.

Other oddities have surfaced in the thousands of letters I've received from readers. One man seemed very proud to say he had found a terrible mistake, a sentence ending in a preposition. I wrote to him, reminding him of a Winston Churchill story. When someone criticized Sir Winston for a sentence ending in a preposition he said he thought a preposition was a perfectly good thing to end a sentence with and that this kind of criticism was something up with which he would not put.

Another reader wanted to argue about weather. Surely, he said, you intended your description of Wisconsin winter to be about North Dakota because no other state even begins to have winters like that.

I wrote and asked him to report on the "spit test" for cold. On a normal cold day in North Dakota did spit turn to ice before it hit the ground? He never answered.

Another wonderful oddity came from Christopher Lehmann Haupt, who reviewed *The Land Remembers* for *The New York Times*. No other review (and there were hundreds of them) so beautifully captured the heart of the book. He was puzzled by his reactions to my account of growing up on a Wisconsin farm. How, he asked, could he be feeling nostalgia for things that never happened to him? He answered that question. "It's not nostalgia for my own past that *The Land Remembers* made me feel; it's nostalgia for a world he makes me wish I'd known."

Those words perhaps had deeper meaning for me than the reviewer could know for they revealed my approach to writing. I avoid summary and let the details tell the story. I ask the reader to become a participant and to some degree make the story his or her own. That approach is verified I think by letter writers and those who come to see me. By now every chapter of the book has been chosen by someone as clearly the best.

Another surprise. I thought I had written a book about a unique childhood, yet letters and visitors from every state bring a common theme—"Yeah, it was like that for me." How strange it is to know I shared a childhood with people all over this nation.

Quite often when my phone rings it is a local person and they say, "Hey, I've got some pilgrims here looking for you. Should I send them over?" I always say yes, and the use of the word "pilgrim" seems very appropriate, because these pilgrims are looking for something. Perhaps more than anything else their quest is for solid values and a sense of community. Young parents are hoping to bring up their children and live their own lives in a way that is in harmony with the land.

Other visitors, often men, who come alone, don't want me to talk to them; they have a story they want to tell me, usually something from their own lives. Here I get a message of loneliness. They don't believe anyone else in their lives would listen or would understand even if they did listen. But they are sure I will listen. I find a cultural warning in all this. Stories, and the need to hear and tell them, are a powerful part of the human past. For many centuries, stories have been a way to pass culture from generation to generation.

Many years ago I did some media work on the Navajo reservation in the Four Corners area of the Southwest. One interview was with a man who, at that time, was the only Navajo lawyer in existence. "To be a people," he told me, "we must tell our stories. If we stop telling our stories we will stop being a people. You Whites have stopped telling your stories. Surely what I see on your video screens is not your authentic story."

Stories of course must have a place to live, so places become characters. We come to know and interact with them just as we do with human characters. Places put their mark on us. Hill-country people are different from prairie people, ridge people different from valley people. I said that once to a high school class, and a girl, hands on hips, demanded, "What's wrong with valley people?"

"Nothing," I said. "They're just different."

"Oh," she said and smiled.

Many readers keep asking "what happened after." My brother Sam Junior had died at age twenty-four, a result of his earlier scarlet fever. After college I went into officer training in Chicago in 1942. Brothers Lee and Laurance were already in the Navy. Lyle and my father were left alone on the farm and Father was lonely and discouraged when they took me to the train. "Lyle," he said as we waited, "I'll rent you the farm. No. I'll sell you the farm. No, I'll give you the farm." And Lyle said, "If you give me that farm, I'll sue you."

I spent fours years in the Navy during World War II, most of it in landing craft for the landings in Sicily, Salerno, and Anzio. I wandered after the war, too restless to stay in one place. I shipped out a few times on merchant ships. I lived and traveled in Mexico. Once when I was back in Wisconsin I remember talking with my father and saying I had no idea what I was looking for. He smiled and said, "Of course you do. You're looking for yourself." And suddenly I had a sense that my mother was there in the room, even though she was dead, and that she was smiling at me and I could almost hear her say, "So you were wounded after all."

There was a long moment of silence and I realized that Father was watching me closely, waiting in that patient way he had when he knew there is more that needs to be said. It was then I told him for the first time what had happened in Italy, how I had left my landing craft in a half-destroyed port south of Naples and gone to a U.S. Army clinic. There I was told I had jaundice, which explained my yellowing eyes and terrible feeling of melancholy, and was sent to the hospital. Two fellow officers took my place on my LCT and that same evening the LCT hit a floating mine. Everyone aboard, seventeen enlisted men and the two officers, was killed.

It was more than the death of nineteen men. It was the death of all innocence about war. Who I was and everything I had known and been was forever changed, even though I was only twenty-three. For a time there in the hospital I felt guilty for being alive when all the men from the ship were dead. Then as the jaundice loosened its hold on me the feeling of guilt changed to a feeling of obligation. I had a debt I must pay to those men by how I live my life. Life became a precious gift that had been given to me. I must not waste any moment of it and must live both for myself and for those who had died.

I did not realize it for some years, but out of those war events a writing career was being formed. The style and energy of my writing came from my need to represent people, give them a voice. My first major writing attempt was a war novel, which never found a publisher.

Then I moved farther back in time and wrote *The Land Remembers*, driven by the need to give a voice to those who lived their values in lives close to the land.

Father died in 1959, the day after his seventy-ninth birthday. A relative from Norway had visited him the day before. They talked to each other in Norwegian. The relative told me Father had reminded him of an old Norwegian saying: "Man predicts, but God decides."

My brother Laurance died several years ago, collapsed while pushing a stubborn old lawnmower. At a simple memorial gathering someone asked me if I thought we should sing a hymn. "No," I said. "But if anyone knows the words, we might sing 'I Did It My Way.'"

Lee lives in eastern Wisconsin, near Lake Winnebago. He has not lost his dry sense of humor. Several years ago at a picnic, friend Pauline brought a cake for dessert. When she was cutting it, she complained it was too dry and it should not be because it had apples in it. "What did you use," Lee asked. "Dried apples?"

Lee had another little trick. Visitors would sometimes ask about our family. Very earnestly, Lee would say, "Well, our father is Norwegian. Our mother is English and we children are half and haaf."

And now I suddenly remember another incident. It was haying time. I was teetering around up on the load of hay and Lee yelled, "Be careful up there!" There was real concern in his voice and he realized that wasn't true to his personality. "Yes, be careful up there. If you fall off and break your fool neck, we'll have to quit and have a funeral. Then we never will get this hay in the barn."

Lyle remained the storyteller in my life. Once, I happened to be in Wisconsin at the time of my birthday. Lyle decided we should celebrate with a beer. In the bar he said, "How old are you now anyway?" I told him I was twenty-eight. Lyle shook his head and said, "My God, Ben, it was only two weeks ago I was holding you on my lap."

As I remember Lyle, I realize that more must be said about rural hill-country humor. Lyle gave us hints when he said some things are too important to be left up to the truth. Rural storytelling is

exaggerated of course but there is something more important. A
story is alive. It will not stay put. It has a mind of its own and it is dif-
ficult to determine when the storyteller is shaping the story and
when the story is shaping the storyteller. Add to that the fact that
each listener is being shaped, too, and the chaos is complete. I guess
the good news is that a story can slowly change so much that a new
story is created.

It was not like that with the story of Soldiers Grove and the calves.
That was a true story and became a lasting symbol of the grim depression days of the thirties. A farmer loaded three calves in his horse-
drawn wagon and took the calves to the Soldiers Grove stockyard.
There, the stock buyer offered the farmer so little for the calves that
it made him mad. "To hell with you," he said. "I'll give them away
before I sell them for that." And he drove down to the store, tied up
his horse, and got a piece of cardboard. On it he printed "FREE
CALVES—TAKE AS MANY AS YOU WANT." And the man
went into the store, leaving the three calves in the wagon. When he
came back out, after an hour, there were now four calves in the wagon.

That story was told again and again. It became an important
message. There was a spunkiness about it that said no matter how
tough things are, we are going to make it.

The last time I saw Lyle he was staying with a farm family, helping
take care of the dairy cows. As we sat on the porch, talking and waving
the flies away, an immense set of construction equipment came by—a
semi with two bulldozers on the flatbed, then another loaded trailer
and finally a front end loader. All this on the narrow, crooked little
road. Lyle shook his head and said, "You know, he'll have to take that
rig clean over to the next county to turn it around."

As I write this new afterword, I am living on the land of our old
farm and I now sleep in the bedroom where I was born. I came back
here from the New York media world in 1986. I am not as sentimental
about living here as people expect me to be. They find it hard to believe

that, having been gone for more than forty years, I can say parts of me were here all the time, no matter where I have wandered. Memories kept returning me. Let me hear the squeaking wheel of a turning windmill anywhere and I can see my father looking up at our own, saying, "It's asking me to give it some oil." Then drops of cold water are condensing on the steel pipe that carried the water to the cistern where honeybees were drinking. Such scenes had a way of enlarging to reveal more and more—the farmhouse, the red painted barn, the orchard. Or let me see a certain shade of blue and I am with Mother and we are putting seeds into the newly worked soil of the garden. Mother straightens to ease her muscles, puts her head slowly back, and says, "Look at all those shades of blue," and I did that then, and each spring at garden-time, I do it still.

The big maple tree, which I always thought of as part of the family, was still here to greet me when I returned. My father's presence was also here and I found it was my turn to look up anxiously when strong southwest winds swayed the maple toward the house. I watched and worried for ten years after I came back. Then the roar of the wind woke me one night just in time to see the tree fall toward the house. Soon, I found myself writing this eulogy:

There has been a death in the family. A faithful friend and companion, age approximately 107, a part of so many lives and so many memories, surrendered to a tornado on July 15, 1997. The name was Big Maple. It stood in the front yard of the ridgetop farm called Seldom Seen.

Big Maple became known to a larger public in my book *The Land Remembers*. Hundreds of "pilgrims," who visited or wrote letters over the years, had recognized the tree as a central character in the book. Those who came by wanted to lay their hands on its bark, make physical connection with what had been only words on paper.

Since the tree's end, pilgrims touch the massive stump and try to decipher the undecipherable growth rings. Children instantly run to the stump, climb up on it, and stand tall there, like new growth.

Big Maple was planted, with the help of her father, by Josephine Mullaney in 1890. She was six years old and had been born in a one-room log cabin a quarter of a mile to the east. When she was one year old, her family moved into the then new two-story log house that is still part of my home. Josephine Mullaney told me all this when, at age eighty-five, she first read *The Land Remembers*. "Surely," she said, "there is something left of me on that ridge farm. The tree, and perhaps where the bird's-foot violets grew by the old log bridge."

Big Maple died quietly. Watching through the dining room window, I saw it fall, the wind roar so loud the tree seemed to come down without a sound. Relaxed, almost detached, as I had learned to be in war during moments of crisis, I found myself asking, "If a tree falls fifteen feet from me without making a sound, what does that mean?"

Big Maple was a responsible friend to the end. It put down two limbs like elbows, which took the force of the fall. Top branches snapped off and blew on over the house. Father, who once started to cut the tree, need not have worried as he did each time a storm swept our ridge. The total damage: a dent in the ridgecap, some cracked wooden shingles, and a split fascia board. Even the birdfeeder was spared, a limb going carefully on each side of it.

These are the facts of Big Maple's demise, but as with any friend, it is its life that is important.

I was born in 1920. The tree was already called Big Maple when I first remember it, and it was already an extension of the house, a warm-weather living room. There were few summer, late spring, or early fall evenings when all of us—Father, Mother, us four boys, and hired man Lyle—were not there under the tree. With fireflies floating close above the lawn and whippoorwills calling, the tree gathered us again into a family after a day that had scattered us to tasks all over the farm. Chores were finished, the cows taken to night pasture. A cooling breeze played in the leaves above us, seeming to ease the fatigue of the day.

Mother, often mending clothes or darning socks under the tree, was a reminder in those days that a woman's work seemed never done. She loved the tree. We all knew that. Partly, it was because the tree was home to orioles and a perching place for singing meadowlarks and those hoarse-voiced harbingers of spring, the rusty blackbirds. Most of all, I think, she loved the tree because it gave us a time and place of unity. The rest of us often worked together, with time for talk and even moments of play, but she was alone much of the day. Eventide brought her family back to her.

It was a time for reflection, for thinking thoughts and saying words to each other that often had little to do with work and the farm. The talk was mostly adult talk, a kind of lazy pursuing of ideas, beliefs, and stories.

I didn't know this then, but the front lawn under the sheltering Big Maple was surely my first schoolhouse, perhaps the best kind of education there is because I did not know I was being educated. My brothers and I might be running from tree to tree in the game we called Little Joe Otter, but we were also hearing the conversation between Father, Mother, and the hired man. The values were clear. The duty to neighbors and community were revealed. The importance of honesty and trust became the central point of some story about a local happening.

Neighbors sometimes joined those conversations, bringing us an odd diversity of lives, ideas, and fiercely held opinions. When they left us, we could hear their fading voices, the talk that had come alive under the tree still going on as their flickering kerosene lanterns guided them back to their own homeplace.

Yes, Big Maple is gone, but we do not lose what is true and important. Under the tree I found my clearest sense of the wholeness of that family I was part of—part of without question, good days or bad. Now, the members of my family, and Big Maple, too, are continuing characters in my life-story.

Big Maple was preceded in death by its planter, Josephine Mullaney, by Father, Mother, Lyle, and my brother Sam Junior. Father had been wrong when he said the tree would destroy the house. (He never trusted it as my mother did.) Lyle was wrong, too. He had said it would outlast us all. I, my brother Lee, and brother Laurance survive.

More importantly, the big maple survives, in story and memory, an important reminder that humans are not separated from all the other living parts and places and mysteries of what Aldo Leopold called THE LAND—all things on, over, and in the earth. When I first heard him say that in a University of Wisconsin classroom, it was a moment of great discovery. His definition of land included me, made a place for me in the immense mosaic of life.

Thus it is that I feel no strangeness in saying there has been a death in the family.*

When a book lives for thirty years, as *The Land Remembers* has, it begins to gather anecdotes, little stories within the larger story. One such incident involved a painting used for a cover on the Avon paperback edition of *The Land Remembers*. It was a late summer scene, with green leaves still on a large tree and green fields in the background. I liked the painting and tried to buy it from the artist. He would not sell it, he said, because the colors were changing. He did agree, however, to give me the painting. It hangs now in the old farmhouse and it is clearly a late fall scene. But the story persists. When the

---

*This eulogy appears in the anthology *A Place to Which We Belong*, published in 1998 by 1000 Friends of Wisconsin Land Use Institute.

twenty-fifth anniversary edition of the book was being planned, I showed the painting to the publisher and explained the color change. "Oh, that's OK," he said, "We'll just filter the greens back in."

"Now wait a minute," I said. "If that painting wants to change seasons, we should let it do that."

"All right," he said, "but dammit, you know what's going to happen? You're going to look at that painting some morning and find snow on that tree!"

Another little story found me one evening on New York's crowded Seventh Avenue Subway. A young woman sitting next to me suddenly laughed. I turned and discovered she was reading *The Land Remembers*. What does one do in such a situation? Surely in a crowded subway car in suspicious New York City you don't say to an attractive young woman, "Would you like my autograph?"

Just as surely it seemed unthinkable to ignore fate and say nothing. "Good book?" I asked.

"Yes," she said, still laughing. "A very good book."

The subway train came into my station and I got off, leaving it at that. But again that is not quite the end of the story. No, I did not see the young woman again as many people would like me to be able to say. I did include the incident in the afterword of an edition of the book and that brought a surprise. I received hundreds of letters from readers who did not want the little story to end. Several letters mentioned the phrase "ships that pass in the night."

All in all there is a feel of loneliness in many of the letters, a theme of "might have been." Yet, there is something else, a positive promise that we can and must keep reaching out to each other and make connections.

Finally, there is something that no one but me remembers about *The Land Remembers*. Some three thousand words of the manuscript I first sent to my literary agent were never published. Those words were a foreword that attempted in part to say the land that became my childhood farm had its own history, going back to a time when a two-legged creature called "man" had not yet arrived. "Too academic for a beginning," my agent said, and, wisely I think, deleted the foreword before sending the manuscript to a publisher. So here, as an afterword instead of a foreword, are those three thousand long-lost words.

Circle of Life

As the changing seasons carry me forward in time, a stubborn part of me keeps reaching back to preserve, unbroken, my linkage with the land. Partly I reach back to find myself at some age of innocence when the land was my whole world. Partly I try to recapture those taken-for-granted persons I called Father and Mother.

Especially in the years since I left the land have I tried to recapture my father, for he was the exotic one, the stranger in a strange land.

Years ago I tried to write his story. I could not do it. I found a baffling interconnection of my Father with the land itself. When I reached deeper, the interconnections included my Mother, my three brothers, myself, and others—all of us bound together, with the land, into an immense circle of life.

I realize now that in trying to write of Father I was trying to sculpt a giant upon the Earth. A giant he remains to me, but he was not upon the land. He was of it and in it, a partner with the land.

Now, in a time of new awareness, I try again. It becomes the story of a farm and its people—a microcosm—for the land cradles all life. The land outlives us all, forever remembering us and writing an epitaph for the good or evil we do to it.

Birth of the Land

The farm was 260 acres of ridge-top land in the rough hill country of southwestern Wisconsin. But the story of that farm begins long before the line fences were drawn on any map.

When the settlers began to come from the East to what is now Wisconsin, they called it "new land." The words reveal so well the arrogance and shortsightedness of man. We think of new land as land not yet conquered by us in our restless and destructive search across the planet Earth.

It was not new land. For millions of years before any man left his tracks in the hills, valleys, and plains of Wisconsin, that land, with its rich multitude of plants and animals, was a successful, on-going ecological process.

The land was not eagerly awaiting the coming of one more species. It didn't need man.

The birth of that land, like the birth of the planet, is beyond our comprehension. We can theorize about cosmic dust, planetary collisions, rivers of molten rock, land rising out of the sea to be worn down again by wind and water, but how real is all that compared to the feel of the morning sun on the face, the smell of the seasons changing, the sight of the new green springing from the soil? Why must we know how it was created and set into motion?

We can't comprehend the reality of the land because we are too new. We think in neat beginnings and endings and in our own minute life span. Yet, we are trying to understand a process in which a thousand years is like one raindrop or one tiny falling seed. Man is one species, a newcomer not yet settled into harmony with the land—not yet accepting the harsh truth that the land has its limits of tolerance. We are strangers in the only home we know and we may be no more important or more permanent than the Dodo bird.

Once, close to the cycles of life—the seasons, the mystery of the earth, sea, and sky—earlier man was on the edge of knowing that we belong to the all, rather than the all belonging to us. Now, we are different. We have lost our Eden. We are too mortal to understand the immortal land.

In any area, the land is sculpted as uniquely as a fingerprint by the forces that create, shape and change it. Even so, the land of southwestern Wisconsin is unusual. When the massive glaciers inched their way down from the north, the lobes of ice went around southwest Wisconsin and came together again farther south.

(When I once came out of a book with this information, Lyle said: "See what I mean. Even the ice had more sense than we do. It knew enough not to plow up these damn hills.")

The ice scraped and smoothed off the surface to the east, west, north and south, leaving a unique island of rough unglaciated land. That island, which would be called the "driftless area" one day, was only 180 miles north to south, 120 miles east to west. The ridges were high and narrow, the valleys steep-walled, winding and narrow, almost every one with a stream.

While the ice was still shaping the area around it, that driftless land was already reaching toward maturity, a settled stage. Most of it was heavily wooded with oaks and maples. Here and there on the hilltops and upper hillsides there were open meadows, a promise of the endless virgin prairie lying west of the Mississippi.

The land was rich with trees, shrubs, grasses, flowers. There were millions of insects. The soil was swarming with molds, bacterias, yeasts, viruses. Wildlife roamed free—deer, elk, red and gray fox, bear, mink, muskrat, moose, martin, fisher, otter, badger, wolves, skunk, raccoon, woodchuck, squirrels, rabbits, lynx . . . There were even buffalo, though never vast herds as on the western prairie. Beavers were building dams, changing the shape of the land, broadening the valleys. Streams were rich with fish. There were millions of birds, and the flocks of passenger pigeons darkened the skies.

The cycles were set in that maturing land. The seasons changed, sending the birds away when the days shortened, bringing them back again when days lengthened. New animals came, restless, seeking, to thrive, to die out or to move on. New seeds rode in on the wind, were carried by water and by the fur of animals. Fish eggs clung to the legs of birds and were taken from lake to pond to stream.

So it was, many, many years ago, thousands of forms of life, each different, each a tiny piece in the complex interdependent mosaic of the land.

Then a new species came, one of the most restless of all. No one can say just when, but perhaps as long ago as 20,000 years, sometime after the glaciers had retreated to the north. Man probably came first in small groups, some traveling through, searching for more new land, some staying as long as hunting was good and there were seeds to gather.

The first of the new species lived simply and close to the land, leaving few marks of his presence.

About 3,000 years ago a group came that left a clear record in the remembering land. The record is in their tools and weapons, which were made of copper. Where did they come from? Probably from the north, following the trail of "float" copper, chunks of the easily worked metal left on the surface by the retreating glaciers. The copper utensils of this metal age people in a stone age time seemed to be copies of Eskimo-like ivory utensils.

Perhaps it was the same copper people at a later time, or some new group, that would be called the Effigy Mound Builders. They left a record of themselves in their fantastic earth mounds, some seventy feet long, in the shape of birds and animals. It may have been these people who first planted seeds and stayed to harvest a crop, forming a more deliberate partnership with the land.

Other people followed. Turn up the earth along certain stream banks and their story is there—the indelible record of villages, cooking fires, shell heaps, burials, fields, tools, and weapons.

In the 1600s Indians to the east told French explorers of a great central river. The French pushed west, hoping the great river would be the link to the western sea. Jean Nicolet reached what is now Green Bay, Wisconsin, in 1643. In 1673 Father Jacques Marquette and Louis Jolliet came from Green Bay by canoe down a swift running river (the Fox), portaged to a larger river (the Wisconsin), and followed it to where it joined the great central river of the Indian tales. It was the Father of Waters, the Mississippi. Another new people had come to the hill land of the southwest. In terms of U.S. history it was early. It would be a hundred years before Daniel Boone laid out the Wilderness Road through the Cumberland Gap to Kentucky.

The French claimed the land of the upper Mississippi, but they left little of themselves there, other than in place names such as Prairie du Chien. They stood on the rich soil, looked at the Indian fields of corn, squash, and beans, and they saw only the riches of furs. The European beaver had been almost exterminated. The demands of Europe and the East for furs made the skins of the land's animals a new kind of living gold. The French turned the harvesting of fur from a need to an industry. They set up fur trading posts and the Indians began to do what they had not done before, began to plunder the land, without thought, not for their own use but for trade goods. They were doing what my father would one day decide was a perversion of the land. They were cash-cropping.

For a hundred years the French trappers and traders roamed the hill land, 500 miles beyond what was thought of as the western frontier. On the broad flood plain, near where the Mississippi and Wisconsin rivers joined, was a large Indian village. Each year, thousands of Indians gathered for a great fair. Furs traded there were being shipped to England, France, Russia, and China long before the American Revolution.

Prairie du Chien is not recorded as a permanent settlement until 1771 (Indians don't count in history books). The British came. The French flag came down and the British flag went up. Then the British flag came down and the Stars and Stripes went up.

The assembled bits and pieces of history do not tell the story of those days. History was recorded by the newcomers who saw the Indian as a dangerous but unequal enemy at worst, as a colorful nuisance at best.

For the Indian it was a time filled with a sense of doom. Paths were worn smooth to the fires of old men who could look into both the future and the past.

Old tales came alive. Far to the south—beyond the great hot desert where trees had spines instead of leaves—there had been a vast Indian tribe. Stone temples reached into the clouds. Great stone rainbows carried water from the mountains to a fabled city in the middle of a lake. Stone trails crossed the lake waters, and over the trails came the rich harvest of the land.

Then, the tale said, a new people came across the salt sea in canoes as big as villages, sailing on tall white wings. They came as the prophecy had said white gods would come. But if they were gods, they were not good gods. They plundered and killed. They burned the records of history. They were willing to do anything for the soft yellow metal they called gold, and were protected by an amulet in the shape of a cross.

Bands of the white god-men came to the north, then went away when they found no gold. They left behind a new four-legged animal, which could carry a man three times faster than the fleetest warrior could run. On the Plains, Indians rode the new animal into battle and in the chase for the buffalo.

This had happened long beyond the memory of any man. But a tribe could remember. The evening fire could remember and bring it back to a man's tongue.

Now there were new tales. It was said a great white serpent had crawled out of the eastern salt sea. The serpent had rested and slept through a hundred winters and a hundred summers. Now it had awakened and was crawling westward, swallowing the forests, leaving bare land behind. Each night the serpent coiled itself into a circle, spilling out white, men-like creatures. Each morning the creatures became part of the serpent again and it crawled slowly westward.

The wandering Indian traders, speaking in strange tongues, told tales in sign language and drew pictures in the dust. Some brought grizzly bear teeth and the black glass from the mountains beyond the plains where snow lay like winter on the summer peaks. They told of white trappers high in the sacred mountains, of beaver and buffalo vanishing, of men on the shores of the western salt sea who carried their power in their hands, between black covers.

Traders brought seashells from the place where the Great River joined the southern sea and they said the white men were there.

The metal working people to the south passed through on their way to mine copper to the north of the hill country, and they said the great white serpent had already crossed the eastern mountains.

It was a time of ghosts and prophecies. The smoke took strange shapes above the dying campfires. The wind spoke in a voice no one knew along the high cliffs above the river. There was new meaning in the thickness of the cornhusks, the frantic migration of the squirrel, a circle around the moon, nighthawks flying before the storm.

The tribes were moving westward. The Winnebago had left the fresh water sea, east of the hill country. The Kickapoo Indians went across the Great River. New people were coming to the hill country. They were not like the French, who wanted furs. Not like the British who wanted to trade. These were called Americans and they wanted the land itself.

More Indians retreated to the west. The Sauk, led by Chief Black-hawk, stayed and fought for that southwest corner of Wisconsin.

Blackhawk fought well. His reasons are carved into a sign for tourists along the Great River Road: "I loved the Rock River Country, my villages, my people, my cornfields. I fought for them."

It was a losing battle. By 1832, the Sauk Indians were homeless and Blackhawk was a prisoner.

With the Indians destroyed, the migration was on. The tales of that new land carried back east by fur traders, explorers, and military men had the stature of folklore. How else speak of the vast virgin timberland but by the kind of tales that would become part of the legend of Paul Bunyan? How else explain the richness of the land but with tales of how a man had to jump back when he dropped a seed in the soil else he'd be knocked down by the new growth?

The Yankees listened to the tales, dismissed nine tenths of it, and tore up roots and headed west. Some passed right on through Wisconsin, came to the endless prairie, then turned around and came back.

"Why, a man could lose his soul out there," a settler said. "That country swallows a man without even a belch. There's no surprises. It shows itself to you all at once. No privacy either. A neighbor ten miles away can look out in the morning and see if you're up and got a fire going yet."

The hill country was different. It was an intimate and personal land, full of surprises. It kept its secrets until you had topped a rise or rounded a bend in a crooked valley. One narrow ridge was a full world away from the next narrow ridge. Down below, in the valley, was another different world. The valleys had different trees and animals. Even the seasons were different, watercress staying green all winter in the valley streams.

The hill country didn't keep leading a man on toward a horizon that was never there. It had a feel of home about it. Hell, even the scientists were calling it the driftless area.

The Yankees took the rich valley land and the virgin meadows, called oak openings. They found a spring or dug a shallow well in the bottom, built a cabin, and put the axe and plow to work.

Later the Europeans came, mostly Irish and Norwegian. The good valley land was gone. They came to the high ridge tops. Water was a problem. There was rainwater or there was the daily job of hauling water up the hill from some spring or stream.

The ridges were so narrow and hillsides so steep there were soon stories about how a ridge farmer would drop a milk bucket and it would roll all the way down to his valley neighbor.

"Not me," a new arrival would say. "I was warned. I brought square milk buckets."

"Not me either," an ex-sailor said. "I got anchors on mine."

Crawford County was the heart of the hill country. The Wisconsin River formed a boundary on the southeast, the Mississippi on the west with hills rising 800 feet above the river. And the crooked Kickapoo River wound up through the middle of the county.

West of the Kickapoo, 500 feet above the river, the high ridge land ran from north to south. It formed the rugged backbone of Crawford County which the U.S. land survey had laid out into townships and sections in 1845. At least the plat books said it had been surveyed. The lines were not always straight. It wasn't easy to survey steep hillsides and narrow hollows filled with brush and timber. Later, there would be tales that the main requirement for a surveyor was that he drink at least a quart of whisky a day. But no one cared much. In 1845 it was empty country, many of the Indians gone, the settlers not yet come in.

Near the center of the rugged ridgeland, township nine was laid out, and far off in the East, in Washington, the government began to use land to pay off its debts to service men. Some of the township went to Private James P. Parten of the Virginia Militia in the War of 1812. Some went to John Williams, seaman of the U.S. naval ship *Spitfire*, for service in the war with Mexico.

There is no record that either man ever saw that land. Speculators in Ohio owned it by 1856. It changed hands several times, prices high at first, then dwindling, and still no owner had ever stood on that land.

In 1864, forty acres of ridgeland were put up at a tax auction at the Crawford County courthouse in Prairie du Chien, twenty-five miles away. Charles McPherson bought the forty acres for $2.95, the amount of the unpaid tax. McPherson was a short, cocky man, known to his friends as "Banty." He built a cabin on a hillside above the east-west trail and began to chop a farm out of the woods.

It was a lonely place and farming was hard. The oaks challenged the axe, and when they were cut down, the stubborn stumps had to be dug out like you were mining coal. Deer ate the corn. Rabbits and grouse mowed the garden. The winter blizzards blew through the chinks of the log cabin so hard that the snow came in one side and out the other without ever stopping inside.

The buffalo were gone. Even the few Indians who were left were part of a new time. The fear was still there, though, and it was a rare settler who would greet an old and toothless Indian with anything but a cocked and ready rifle.

By 1875 Banty McPherson and his wife, Laura, had enough of that lonely ridge.

Patrick Mullaney tried it next. By 1880 he and Julia Mullaney owned almost 200 acres. The rough hill land was still not in great demand. The Mullaneys bought 160 acres of their land at tax auctions for a total of $11.66.

When he came to town, Pat Mullaney used to tell of watching the Indians crossing his land, carrying packs of ore from the little lead mines they'd dug above Halls Branch Creek, to the north. They took the ore down the ravine to the Kickapoo River where they loaded it into canoes, then paddled down to the Wisconsin River, then to the Mississippi and on down to the smelters in Galena, Illinois.

Pat Mullaney worked that land for thirty-seven years. When he sold the land, in 1912, to Joseph Young, the records in the courthouse in Prairie du Chien show it as a farm of "220 acres, more or less." Forty-eight years had passed since Banty McPherson built his cabin and started a farm there in the very middle of the hill country.